What top leaders are saying about *The Science of Protection*

"I highly recommend *The Science of Protection*. This is a must read for any CEO, Executive or Entrepreneur. As a CEO of a multi-million-dollar company, this book literally not only resonated but has changed the game for me. I have had my own business for 30 plus years and still wake up some nights thinking it could all be gone tomorrow. Raamon, Sara and Paolo have laid it out for you in 6 simple steps. Follow them and it will change your life."

—Jimi Petulla, *CEO Recording, Radio, Film Connection Inc.*

"Even just reading the introduction of *The Science of Protection* I was reminded I need to take time out to protect myself from overwhelm and burnout. I highly recommend this book to any high performing leader and to take action on what your inner outlier quietly speaks to you when reading it. When the learnings are implemented, they not only have the potential to save your life but also allow you to design your life exactly how you would like it, for yourself, your family and business."

—Andrew McCombe, *CEO Outlier TV & Golf Getaway*

"Protection: A person or thing that prevents someone or something from suffering harm or injury. I was blessed to have met the authors 6 years ago at a turning point of my life, a life or death moment for me. The first protection insight I learned from them was that protection starts inside me. Once I knew how to protect myself from myself things got much better. I now have the tools to manifest the life I want. This is a MUST-READ protection manual for anyone who wants to learn the skills required to PROTECT what they value most and bring more fulfillment to all areas. I'm so happy everyone can now access this protection wisdom consolidated in the pages of this timely book. They are "protection shepherds."

—Peta Wilson, *Actress / Inventor Wellness Entrepreneur*

"High achievement leaders often work crazy hours, burning themselves out and losing passion for the work they once had. The authors experience and journey bring a unique dimension to their advice. They've created a well laid out system in their thought-provoking book, *The Science of Protection*. A must read for all leaders and professionals leading a small group or a large corporation."

—Bill Ellermeyer, *Ellermeyer Connect*

"There's a reason why two out of five CEOs fail within the first 18 months of their role. It's because the two that failed haven't read *The Science of Protection*. This uplifting book will blow the lid off your preconceptions about what it takes to succeed in a leadership role. You'll develop the capacity to handle every problem or challenge so you can see opportunities before they arise."

—Louise Bedford, *Co-Founder Trading Secrets Pty Ltd*

"Wow. I wasn't expecting this. Protection from the inside out. A brilliant concept and perfect for the uncontrollable nature of our external world, including our business environment in the present times. It's beautifully put together with the great blend of deep wisdom but also the hard data and real-life examples. If you're looking for a way to make a quantum leap in your business and for that of your team and taking yourself from the vagaries of today's business world, I highly recommend this book."

—Mark Bunn, *AFL Footballer, Health, Wellness & High Performance Speaker*

"These guys know their stuff. Poignant, engaging, and insightful."

—Chris Wise, *Founder / CEO Wise Profits*

"Protection is obviously a timely topic right now and leaders have to be at the forefront of what will create protected progress for everyone, mentally, emotionally, physically, financially and environmentally. After reading *The Science of Protection,* my view solidified on why leaders must give more attention to their inner development to support, enhance and most importantly protect their outer achievements. It's an essential read for any leader that is creating breakthrough results in the 21st century."

—Michael Heinrich, *Founder / CEO Garten*

THE SCIENCE OF PROTECTION

Making High Pressure, Impactful Leadership Decisions that Protect and Enhance You and Everyone

Raamon Newman & Paolo D'Angelo
with SARA BURKE

The Science of Protection

www.newmavericks.com
Printed in the United States of America
Book Design: Carla Green, Clarity Designworks

ISBN hardcover 978-1-7353458-4-0

ISBN ebook 978-1-7353458-1-9

This book is dedicated to every leader, around the world, who's seeking greater protection, coherence and fulfillment for themselves and their team, and a way of life that will uplift the collective whole. Here's to you!

Contents

Preface

The catalyst for this book has come from behind-the-scenes work with over 50 CEOs and executives of multi-million and billion revenue companies. Over the last two decades, we've witnessed and helped some great successes unfold, but we've also witnessed the processes of leaders being undermined or diminished due to unforeseen events. A great example of this is a CEO who had to quickly leave this role leading one of the biggest divisions of one of the biggest companies in the world because of the severe life or death effect it was having on his and his family's well-being. This need to give leaders a deeper level of knowledge so they can protect themselves as they strive to achieve is supported by a Booze Allen Hamilton Business Study that 2 out of 5 CEOs fail within the first 18 months of their role.

In the last 10 years, top CEOs and execs aged 30-60 of legacy companies like Samsung, Nintendo, Relativity, Fonterra, Deutsch Bank, Apple, Goldman Sachs, JPMorgan, Fox News, ESPN, Tata Motors, Uber, Theranos and WeWork have either lost or stepped down from their position due to health, performance, behavior and conflict issues. Fundamentally this comes down to not having the deeper knowledge required to protect themselves while striving to achieve and progress.

Enough is enough. There has never been a more appropriate time for us to stand up and speak the truths of having protection as you achieve and progress as a leader. This is why we wrote this book. There's a massive secret in the leadership industry and we are about to blow the lid off of it. See, the secret—the thing nobody told you—is that protection is an inside job. And if we're being totally transparent, leadership is too. What we've witnessed again and again are leaders suffering beneath the surface, while risking it all to stay on top. The game of achievement is detrimental without protection. We believe leaders should be achieving based on fulfillment, not suffering. When we say enough is enough, what we really mean is, enough with the suffering. Leaders need to be equipped with the knowledge of protection, to achieve based on fulfillment and understand exactly how you can protect yourself, your team and your achievements and become an enlightened leader, who naturally protects the world, without being an over-protective dictatorial leader, and inspires everyone to live their full potential.

Growth is a two-step process, yet most leaders skip the first step. The first step is an internal foundation for protected achievement and progress. The second step is an external unfoldment and expression for being protected while you're achieving and progressing.

These six steps of the Science of Protection provide an organic unfoldment of this two-step process so leaders can more fully and consistently get what they want, protect it, and keep it.

1. Purification
2. Coherence
3. Leadership State
4. Capacity
5. Spontaneous Right Action
6. Deserving Power

Developing and activating these six fundamental qualities results in a high degree of invincibility that cannot be corrupted, diminished, or lost due to incoherence or negativity inside or outside of a leader or their organization.

I've enjoyed my own unique ride through life. I grew up in one of the most beautiful countries in the world, New Zealand, where I loved playing rugby and competitively running. My rugby and running journey, over the course of a decade, allowed me to win national and regional titles, and then eventually burn out, physically, mentally, and emotionally.

Like most athletes competing at a high level, I've experienced a number of heart breaks in my life. I've had unintended accidents, injuries, setbacks, conflicts, mistakes, failed aspirations and relationships, that have made me question my intentions, abilities, and worthiness.

I'll never forget the day I realized I wasn't going to breakthrough from being a top three national ranked athlete to being an international elite athlete. The emptiness and loss of purpose was excruciating. The positive that came out of this negative, and the beautiful thing about failure, was the inspiration and drive to evolve myself in a deeper way. The titles and words we use to describe who we are often fade in life, and there has to be something at the foundation defining you in these moments.

After a year of bewilderment, searching for a deeper sense of self, wisdom, and purpose, I decided to head to the United States to pursue work and business experience. In New Zealand we call this the BIG OE (overseas experience). The deeper intention, I now realize in retrospect, was to develop within myself more capacity, coherence, stability and agility. On a much more subconscious level, I was seeking knowledge that would allow me to accomplish goals and achieve success without causing stress, overwhelm or burnout for myself.

What happened next was never on my radar. I became a full-time meditating monk. I literally retired into seclusion, at the age of 25, in the Blue Ridge Mountains of North Carolina. I spent my first year seeking a deeper sense of Self knowledge, inner fulfillment, and peace. I planned to stay for that year and then reintegrate back into society, but one-year turned into three, and then five, and before I knew it, ten years had gone by. How could a person spend ten years doing something they never considered doing? In many ways, this is how protection works. The more we develop ourselves, the more protection we have, the more secure our options become. I ended up as a meditating monk, not because I was seeking it out, but because I was seeking growth and fulfillment and this gave me access to options I didn't even know were options. Let's come back to this in a later chapter.

We were not the kind of monks who roamed around in robes, as I'm sure you're imagining, but every other detail was traditional and as close to silent monastic living as possible. 8-hours a day and seven days a week, over 300 men from all different ethnicities, countries, religions and races united and devoted to the joy of silence. Every single day, we set out inwardly with eyes closed exploring the unbounded silence within, a massive unseen world, where everything good we all seek exists- beyond the noise of the conscious and subconscious mind. When I arrived in the US, I was sometimes swimming, sometimes barely staying afloat amongst the waves in the ocean of life. Surface living leaves you at the mercy of the weather, the waves, and predators. When I left the mountains and monastic life, I had descended to the ocean floor where life was quiet, calm and clearer than it had ever been. Protection is this way. When we lack protection, we live on the surface, at the mercy of every wave, storm and fluctuation. When we have protection, all of the waves and storms still happen on the surface, but we are removed from the effects and viewing from a place of calm and understanding. We'll talk about this more later on.

In 1999, I met my business partner Paolo D'Angelo, who was also in this full-time meditation program. He had given up a former career in competitive bodybuilding and his businesses in security, entertainment promotion and nutrition, also at the age of 25, to pursue this inward life. Paolo, being the skilled entrepreneur he is, had come up with a way to financially support his full-time meditating endeavor. He would do his long meditation program, 8-hours a day, and then consult with business leaders every couple of weeks; to help them debunk their stresses, increase their energy, gain more clarity, and see more truth. He was using his silence and protection through his meditation to help other leaders overcome the obstacles they were facing in business. So we teamed up to amplify the power of this unique yet profound service. This silent protection program is the foundation of what you see today with our consulting business, New Mavericks, and in this book.

A decade long inner exploration for me, decade and a half for Paolo, laid a profound new foundation for life, business, and the knowledge we now share with leaders and top performers around the world. We provide a shortcut to gaining what we experienced through a combined total of over 70,000 hours (25 years combined) of full-time silent meditation without them having to do it all themselves.

When I returned to worldly life and landed in New York City the summer of 2007, it was my immediate impression that the world was getting a little out of control and a big transition was on the way. There were hints of a global financial meltdown about to go into full swing with the dynamism of the marketplace becoming very volatile, incoherent and disorderly. I felt like I could see the confused desperation everywhere I looked. Everyone was looking for deeper answers, but couldn't see where the answers were because of the fog created by uncertainty, stress, and destruction.

During this time, Paolo was also reemerging back into societal life, after spending 6-years in the Himalayas, having been selected for a more advanced and elite meditation program.

So we reconnected and rebooted what we'd started 8 years earlier, this time in a more professional, formal and full-time manner. Very quickly, we were introduced to leaders of multi-million- and billion-dollar revenue companies. Every single one of these leaders had great status, position, influence, and money; yet lacked the deeper support and protection to ensure they would keep and build on their accomplishments while also maintaining their health, happiness, relationships and reputation. *They had it all, except for protection. Every single one knew they could lose everything at a moment's notice, because they had watched it happen repeatedly to other top performers.*

We've now spent the last 10+ years full time bringing this deeper silence, coherence, knowledge, wisdom, and awareness of leaders of multi-million- and billion-dollar revenue companies on four continents. This is why we consistently carry a 95% success rate. The solution to virtually all problems is rooted in having the silent force of protection in and around you. This is achieved and integrated through six fundamental qualities that uphold The Science of Protection that we've outlined and elaborated on in this book.

Through all the good, and the less than desirable, we've realized that coherence and being coherent is the biggest key we have to leading a life that has more invincible success in health, wealth, happiness, relationships, and reputation. Greater coherence is the key element for leaders to have greater ability to get what they want, protect it, and keep it, especially as they're achieving more and more. Incoherent thinking, behavior and actions causes mistakes, problems, injuries and accidents while being more coherent protects these from happening as much, if at all, and opens up better opportunities.

We now know that coherence determines how quickly and efficiently our inner reality, what we want to see happen, becomes our outer reality of what actually happens. This knowledge, this foundation of high performance based on coherence is The Science of Protection that we've spent the past decade developing and refining.

Like every Science, there are formulas to make this science work. The Science of Protection in this book will help you begin to access the Universal force that is Protection.

Settle in, as we lay out what protection is, why it's important, and what happens to a leader's success when they do and don't have it. The real-world examples in this book will bring protection to life for you.

Introduction

This book answers the question: *How can leaders protect themselves, their team and their achievements and become more enlightened leaders?*

As leaders we are always striving to efficiently accomplish what we want, when we want, as much as we want for as long as we want. The path to this level of success is never a flat line or a straight shot. There will always be trials and tribulations along the way. The key is to learn to go beyond the stress these trials and tribulations create - a skill most leaders never acquire. In fact, putting out fires and being stressed has become a badge that leaders willingly, and sometimes proudly, wear.

Protection is a must so you more easily, quickly and accurately accomplish what you want, when you want, as much as you want, for as long as you want, with minimal stress and damage to yourself and others. A master archer will tell you that their mastery contains both an inner and an outer component. They must master the art and science of aiming and firing, but also their mental clarity and capacity to perform at a high level. Olympic athletes spend as much time visualizing results as they do practicing for those results, again due to an inner and outer component to success. Leadership requires this same approach, so why don't we talk about this more often? Why are we not approaching high level leadership like we do mastery within all other high level, competitive endeavors? There is an inner and outer component to all mastery. There is also an inner and outer component to having protection while you achieve and progress, which this book will fully elaborate on.

How the Science of Protection Came About

We highly respect and appreciate the work of all thought leaders who are devoted to upgrading the thinking of people so they can make better decisions and take better actions to get better outcomes in life. When it comes to thought leadership and motivational change-making, we acknowledge Tony Robbins as the best. His contribution has been and still is enormous when it comes to leading and motivating people to create a better future for themselves.

Paolo wanted to add value and build on what Tony has already said about achievement. So, one day, while exercising on his stationary bike, he started listening to Tony's talk on the Science of Achievement. In this moment, Paolo had a light bulb moment when he realized that while achievement is clearly important, at the same time the protection of that achievement is equally important. Without protection, we can achieve and still lose in some way and experience suffering and not the fulfillment we were expecting. The goal with adding in protection is to minimize and avert the loss as much as possible so we can fully enjoy and be fulfilled before, during and after the process of achievement.

Paolo further realized that protection is what allows people to achieve in the first place—you can't get anywhere fast if you're always tripping over things, or being tripped up by others, and losing the gains you've achieved. Those gains must be protected so you can keep your achievements, even during difficult circumstances. Ultimately, through having good protection, lasting achievement and fulfillment becomes effortless and sustainable.

We like to think of the Science of Protection as a discipline that is complementary to the Science of Achievement because it is about protecting the leader and their people as they achieve and progress. This is how the Science of Protection was born and out of this came six steps that every leader can integrate in their thinking and actions to have greater protection 24/7/365.

The Science of Protection

The science of protection entails activating six steps that help you, your thinking and actions align with what is most life and business protecting and enhancing so you protect yourself, your team and your achievements and become an enlightened leader who contributes to protecting and unifying the world and the people in it.

Everyone wants to get something in life, be it material, physical, mental, emotional or spiritual (thank you, Maslow's hierarchy of needs) and no one wants to deeply suffer and be hurt in the process or after they achieve. (Thank you, loss aversion bias).

We have to be able to protect ourselves and what we achieve otherwise what's the point of achieving if it amounts to a whole heap of suffering? If we can't do this then we're always in damage control licking our wounds and less able to fully give, help and protect others. Once you have the oxygen / protection you need you can help others get the oxygen / protection they need.

The more we evolve into being the most enlightened version of our self, living our fullest potential, being of greatest service to others, and a shining example to future generations, the more we're able to protect ourselves, what we achieve and the world around us. An enlightened leader means someone who has a 100% fully developed heart and mind. We may not fully realize this ideal in this life but the main thing is we're moving in this direction of becoming more fulfilled and complete as an enlightened leader, someone who:

» Sees, knows and acts from higher truths
» Treats the cause not the effect of problems
» Inclusive and accepting of diversity
» Does what is good and evolutionary for themselves, others and the environment
» Is able to give maximum in service of others

- » Is free from darkness, lack, fear and the six inner enemies (we'll discuss in the chapter on purification)
- » Causes no harm to others or the environment and only uplifts and protects these
- » Is established in the highest values of silence, consciousness, awareness, coherence, health, light, peace and love

The Science of Protection is not a philosophical idea; it's a science about the underlying universal protective intelligence that is inherent in us and nature. This universal protective intelligence actually allows us to take more and better risks, not less, because we're more in tune with what is evolutionary for ourselves and everyone. This is because inherent in doing what is evolutionary is protection.

The six steps we've defined in this book to align yourself with the universal intelligence of protection can be applied to enhancing you, and those you lead, health, wealth, business, leadership, happiness, relationships and reputation. It will help avert these from being disrupted, corrupted or diminished by internal and external enemies, stresses, vices and incoherence's, or at least minimized.

The Case for Protection: Why It's Needed Right Now

Too many top leaders fail or fall quickly and it's disheartening to watch. Look around; the number of top leaders dying relatively young, suffering, failing more than prevailing, even losing everything, causing massive loss to others, is proportionally high.

> **In 2016, it was estimated that 67% of well-formulated strategies failed due to poor execution. There are many explanations for this abysmal failure rate, but a 10-year longitudinal study on executive leadership conducted by my firm showed one clear reason. A full 61% of executives told us they were not prepared for the strategic challenges they faced upon being appointed to senior leadership roles.**
>
> **It's no surprise, then, that 50–60% of executives fail within the first 18 months of being promoted or hired.**
>
> *–Ron Carucci, HBR Article, November 2017*

> **Research from McKinsey and Company shows that 70% of all transformations fail.**
>
> *–Brent Gleeson, Forbes Article, July 2017*

> **In the last 20 years, 30% of Fortune 500 CEOs have lasted less than 3 years. Top executive failure rates are as high as 75% and rarely less than 30%.**
>
> **Chief executives now are lasting 7.6 years on a global average down from 9.5 years in 1995. The average tenure of SandP 500 CEOs is now around five years, a drop of 20% since 2013. Long-lasting iconic leaders are the exception rather than the rule.**
>
> *–Equilar Study, February 2018*

"Something's missing" in the life of leaders. Why do we keep doing the same thing over and over, living this same cycle of lack, achievement, and suffering? We're stuck, looking for solutions to these myriad problems, when instead we should be looking to the root of these problems, to understand the knowledge that is lacking in every arena requiring high performance. A lot of leadership development today addresses symptoms and not the root cause of this damage and failure. The truth bomb we can drop here is, achievement is not the goal, and fulfillment is the goal. If achievement causes suffering then it doesn't create fulfillment. If this is the case, we have to go back to how we're achieving. We have to go back to what we're thinking and how we're acting. Even more importantly we have to go back to the state of consciousness and awareness we're thinking and acting from. This is where the existence of the science of protection comes from.

Leaders today must be able to purify and protect from the stresses and vices (like greed, anger, lust, vanity, jealousy and false attachments) that corrupt, diminish and limit themselves and achievements. This is not a belief, this is fact. In this book alone, you will find example after example of leaders failing, self-destructing, or dying way too early- all in the name of business achievement. Enough is enough.

This new performance and progress paradigm contains the knowledge, understanding, and vocabulary necessary to allow leaders to align with the new, rapidly shifting definition of leadership and success. The approach to self-development that we've relied on for the last 15 years is no longer enough.-Leaders don't need the latest findings on neuroscience, emotional quotients, and the other outdated development approaches. They require Protection. The Science of Protection, creating more invincible performance and progress- based on the six fundamental qualities shared in this book, is the new standard in high performance, leadership, and business.

We are simply humble instruments for this knowledge and are grateful you are here. It is our purpose, as our world exponentially accelerates into the future, to show as many leaders as we can how to align with this knowledge.

Case Study: Real-Life Client Experience

One of our longest standing clients, going on 10-years now, seemed to have it all. He'd built a company that was bringing in multiple seven figures a year, to multiple-billions over a couple of decades, and had been acknowledged and awarded as the best CEO in his country.

On a more personal level, his mental, emotional and physical health were overall very sound; he had a devoted and loving wife, children maturing into upstanding fine adults and grandchildren on the way. His forecast for the future was fantastic and filled with promise.

Until the day everything changed.

A slight paralysis of the left-side of his body, along with slurred speech were the only warning signs before life took an unexpected and devastating turn. When he awoke from what felt to be a long and deep sleep, he learned he had suffered a stroke, after blood flow to a part of his brain was cut off. In that moment, it became incredibly clear that he was not as untouchable as he thought, that he was not in as good of a place as he thought, and most importantly, that he lacked protection. If something like this could happen so fast, with no warning signs, and with no way to react or respond, the obvious solution to this problem was prevention, which is really just another word for protection.

Why Aren't Leaders Going the Distance?

High-performance leadership comes with huge responsibility and stresses. Unfortunately, not everyone survives the rigors. Not everyone has the capacity to survive the battlefield of business and go the distance, as this list will show you:

- » While exercising during a family vacation, Survey Monkey's CEO Dave Goldberg died suddenly at the age of 47. Goldberg grew SurveyMonkey from 12 employees to 450 and to a $2 billion valuation. He was considered an irreplaceable talent.
- » Steve Jobs was able to save Apple after he came back as CEO in 1996, but ironically was not able to save himself and passed away at the age of 56 from pancreatic cancer.
- » Autumn Radtke, the 28-year-old CEO of Bitcoin exchange First Meta, jumped to her death in Singapore on 26 February 2014. On February 10th she posted a link to an essay entitled 'The Psychological Price of Entrepreneurship' and commented that everything had its price.
- » Steven LeVoie founder of Arrowstream was shot by one of his own top lieutenants, at the age 54 in 2014.
- » Arthur Goldberg, a fitness buff whose casino portfolio included Caesars and Bally's, died in 2000 aged 58 from bone marrow failure.
- » Michael Walsh, age 51 and CEO of Tenneco, succumbed to brain cancer.
- » McDonald's 60-year-old CEO, Jim Cantalupo, died of a heart attack in 2004. The board hastily replaced him with 43-year-old Charlie Bell, who died nine months later.
- » Wendy's CEO Gordon Teter died at age 56 in 1999; his predecessor, James Near, had died in 1996 at age 58.
- » Kate Spade built an iconic fashion brand only to commit suicide at age 56 after suffering severe bouts of depression for years.

This short list is a mere fractional representation of the reality leader's face, day in and day out. The question you need to ask yourself is this: what is my life worth? Or perhaps, what is this business worth? Is the value equivalent? If your answer is no, you need to seriously consider the price you are paying and what that return will look like when it arrives for you. Protection is necessary now, we know without a doubt. The real challenge will be for leaders to grasp, embrace, and align with this truth before it is too late.

This is the reason we are here now. Not to scare or fear monger, but to inspire leaders to see the truth. You can be protected as a high performer. It is necessary. You don't have to suffer. You can simultaneously seek high performance and security. You can use this science to protect yourself, your team and what you both achieve, to become an enlightened leader, who protects others and the environment you live in.

None of the high performing CEOs listed above made it to retirement age. They gave everything they had to grow and protect their company, and in some cases their community as well, but weren't able to protect themselves in the process. Businesses and business leaders fail every day, financially, in health, or otherwise. There are global superpowers and corporations we believe will be around forever, based on their sheer size and reputation. And then… when those larger-than-life entities fail, we follow with the same shocked reaction. Analysts talk for weeks, sometimes even months, about the root causes of these massive failures, and we all attempt to wrap our minds around how something like this has happened, again.

How many Kodak moments have you experienced in your lifetime?

The year 2000 was a record-breaking year for the photography industry. In fact, that year, Kodak was raking in multi-billion-dollar revenues, and by 2012, they were bankrupt. The photo giant lost big and it wasn't for a complete lack of effort. They were investing money in digital and disruptive expansion ideas, but they lacked the broad perspective to realize those disruptive ideas were the future, not just a fad. Kodak is one example of a huge successful corporation that fell into bankruptcy and failure due to a lack of protection.

How can something so large fail?

In 1993, Apple began shipping a device that they started development on in 1987. Their Newton handheld PDA was presented as 'the next big thing', and presumably that seemed realistic, given the influence Apple held in the technology market and with their consumers. However, after five long and difficult years of terrible sales, and even being made fun of in National comic strips, Steve Jobs called for the Newton to be put out of its misery.

How could such an innovative company lack enough clarity to develop a massive dud?

In the 1800's, Western Union was the most important communications company that existed. Their size and capabilities with the telegraph didn't leave much room for competition. By 1876, innovation and disruption were occurring on a mass scale, as Alexander Graham Bell filed his first patent for the telephone. During this time, Western Union had the opportunity presented to them to purchase this patent from Bell himself, for a minimal price of $100,000. At the time, the President of Western Union, William Orton, could not see the usefulness of Bell's device and they passed on what was the largest opportunity the company would ever see. In fact, Orton is even quoted as publicly questioning the device, "What use could this company make of an electrical toy?" So if "hindsight is 20-20" and "you don't know what you don't know"... how can you begin closing the gap between what you don't know and hindsight, so that you do know more, and your foresight is as powerful as your hindsight?

How can experienced leaders be so out of touch?

How did Elizabeth Holmes, a college dropout who founded the blood-testing company Theranos, get such successful leaders and investors as Rupert Murdoch, Tim Draper, Education Secretary Betsy DeVos, and the Walton family, founders of Wal-Mart, to invest in something that turned out to be such a "massive fraud"? These are savvy, intelligent and successful high-performance leaders, yet this has proven to not be enough to be protected from fraud. What are the deeper human idiosyncrasies that allowed them and their money to be misled, corrupted and lost?

How can a high performer do so well and then not do so well?

Robert Nardelli led Home Depot from $46B to $81B from 2000 to 2005. In 2006, the housing slowdown stalled sales and the stock price fell to near $40 per share — around the same price when he started. Investors began getting frustrated at his $200 million salary, feeling it wasn't aligned with his performance but Nardelli refused to take a salary cut.

Wall Street cheered his January 2007 departure because analysts believed investors were not confident in his leadership abilities. How can a leader go from having great success of helping a company grow over 75% in 5 years to not being perceived as having the leadership abilities necessary to lead the company?

How can such an innovative business lack a broad perspective?

Example after example demonstrates how large corporations, their leaders, or both, lack clarity, vision, and the capacity to excel forward consistently.

- According to collated research and a Harvard Business Review report, the failure rate for mergers and acquisitions sits between **70-90%.**[1]
- An article on aei.org by Mark J. Perry revealed the following changes in the Fortune 500.

Change in Fortune 500 Firms			
Period	**Surviving Firms**	**New Firms**	**New Firms per Year**
1955 - 1994	153 (30.6%)	347 (69.4%)	8.5
1995 to 2016	188 (37.6%)	312 (62.4%)	14.2

- A July 19th article on HBR.org stated, since 2000, **52%** of the companies in the Fortune 500 have either gone bankrupt, been acquired, ceased to exist, or dropped off the list.
- According to a Booze Allen Hamilton Business Study, **2 out of every 5** CEOs fail, demonstrate a disappointing performance, within the first 18-months of taking their position.

How do leaders gain more clarity?

While plenty of self-help advice insists that clarity can be gained by developing habits, or by expanding your intellectual abilities, we know better. Clarity is not a result of outward experience you've gathered. In fact, experience has failed leaders because they've mistakenly thought what worked in the past will work now. The CEO of Quaker Oats had this experience in the 80-90s. Your experiences change your brain- a concept we will cover in an upcoming chapter, so we cannot discount experience. However, we need to look at the fact that the longer you are in business, the more fog or noise you have to clear when it comes time to act and the more at-risk you become with this lack of coherence.

How do leaders develop better vision?

True visionaries don't sit idle in their high rise, glass and mahogany offices developing their future vision. This ability to maintain and develop vision for the future is a result of something much bigger, something running much deeper.

1 *The New M&A Playbook* by Clayton M. Christensen, Richard Alton, Curtis Rising and Andrew Waldeck https://www.hbs.edu/faculty/Pages/item.aspx?num=39920

How do you shift from a local to a global perspective?

The high performers we talk to see inconsistency in this area more than any other. The ability to take a broad and long perspective on mergers, partnerships, business direction, and goals, is cited as being one of the most difficult aspects of high-level leadership.

Bottom line: Even when immersed in a global market, leaders have a difficult time maintaining the long or broad view, and knowing (without a doubt) when to take action or what action to take.

How much time, money, energy, ROI, key talent, and shareholder value are you losing?

Costly mistakes are inevitable when there's a lack of clarity, lack of inner fulfillment, lack of belief or investment in key people around you, lack of inner stability, inconsistent growth, and fear of failure.

The power of a leader to make or break, re-make or un-break a company is vividly clear in todays accelerated digital age. We need go no further than Microsoft to illustrate this point:

Steve Ballmer assumed the CEO role of Microsoft in September 2000, when the company was valued at $642 billion. When he left in February 2014, it was worth only $315 billion. Under the current leadership of Satya Narayana Nadella, Microsoft's value has topped $500 billion in January 2017 — the first time since 2000, when Bill Gates left the role.

Why Now?

> **If we continue to develop our technology without wisdom or prudence, our servant may prove to be our executioner.**
>
> *–Omar N. Bradley, highly distinguished senior officer of the United States Army during and after World War II.*

Where does wisdom and prudence really come from? And how do we naturally develop more of it within ourselves so technology does not get the better of us or our potential future?

Your expectations from life, yourself, your relationships, your products, your businesses, and your partnerships are higher than they've ever been.

When 'Think and Grow Rich' was published, the year was 1937. The world was beginning its ascent from a worldwide economic depression, and hope was at an all-time low. People needed to be told they could dream again. Mr. Hill inspired those dreamers to conceive, believe, and achieve; and through personal development, helped others to realize their dreams. Hope and the ability to dream were necessary then, and The Science of Protection, which requires higher awareness and more spontaneous right thought and action, is what is necessary now.

We are experiencing such rapid change in all facets of our lives that more consciousness is necessary just to be able to keep up.

Building on Think and Grow Rich

Content-rich heavy hitters like 'Think and Grow Rich' made a permanent home for themselves in the development "Hall of Fame" because people needed that content at that time. Especially coming out of the Great Depression, where all they could handle was content and habits, a new rule book was necessary, because it was a new world. The masses at that time had been barely surviving, so thriving hadn't been considered or top of mind for quite some time hence a Think and Grow Rich message was required.

Today dreaming is still necessary but isn't enough anymore. As we continue to evolve and accelerate on our path forward in time, it is evidently clear that we want/need/desire/seek more than ever before.

Consider the generations before you, or even your parents. They were probably thrilled and totally content to accept a 9-5 career with a promising pension, one car, a home in a quiet area, and a few bundles of joy. Now consider your path. As a high- performer, you've pushed yourself to grow further than most, in a career that will never be 9-5, and you haven't stopped there. Your demands and expectations of your professional life are as high as those you place on your personal life. Travel, opportunities, self-development… these are non- negotiable for you. You will undoubtedly continue to thrive and push forward, even if one day you retire, because you expect more. Seeking has replaced silence. Achievement has replaced fulfillment.

Not only are our expectations higher than ever before, we are also being outpaced by the change of everything we have created. In total irony, our attempts at efficiency have left us less efficient and less capable, while our cultures boast a lack of sleep, high impact hobbies, and wear 'stress badges' with honor.

We can see this truth of rapid growth mirrored in the way our business, technological, and intellectual markets are following an exponential 'S' curve, rather than linear growth. Markets are being disrupted quickly, with seemingly overnight takeovers. Consider AirBnB, Uber, or Amazon as present-day examples.

Let us circle back to the question of 'why now?' The answer is simple. Protection is what you need. This is what business needs. And most importantly, this is what leadership requires. Call it what you will... an awakening, a revolution, collective consciousness expanding, it's time for the next level of fulfillment, and this is your roadmap to begin understanding and applying the science of protection to:

» expand your leadership capacity to get what you want
» protect you and your business
» align you with the knowledge that allows you to be an enlightened leader

Why You?

Your constant desire for more may have left you inconsistent. In the drive for achievement and excellence, you probably find yourself in chaos more often than not, and wondering which path is the right path out. It's not just this desire for more that contributes to chaos. You also contribute to the chaos by being inconsistent in developing yourself. This inconsistency is built into your existing default settings. That means, no matter what kind of habits you attempt to develop, or what new knowledge you'll attempt to apply, eventually, when the going gets tough, you will default back into inconsistency and chaos.

It isn't only you. It's just that the buck stops with you. So even if you aren't "the problem" per se, at the end of the day, it's still your problem and the problem may be contagious. This plateau you've reached right now, in this moment, is one most cannot even imagine. Your plateau is their glass ceiling. Your insurmountable wall is their unobtainable.

As a high-level leader, you've reached heights most cannot even fathom, yet here you are, maybe wondering... what is the meaning or point of all this? Or maybe you're wondering if there is anything you can actually do that will solidify your legacy, and sustain your achievements. Or perhaps you're even wondering if there is more beyond everything you've already achieved. Is there actually a way you can protect yourself, your achievements, your business, and your people? What is this missing piece of life, of business, of leadership, that constantly nags at your subconscious mind? The answers to these questions do exist.

Why Us? (Our bragging rights)

Through our work with top CEOs and their teams; on four different continents, over the last two decades, we've helped leaders redefine success to include protection. We've:

- » Guided a CEO of one of the largest divisions of one of the biggest companies in the world to transition into a more life-supporting role. He calls this one of the toughest decisions of his life, as he realized his role and industry was having adverse effects on the health and well- being of his family.
- » Helped a high-level leader, who lost their X-factor, to a comeback that inspired the biggest multi-billion dollar deal of their career. During this transition, he described himself as 'the eye of the storm', calm, focused, and abundant in his knowledge of how to proceed.
- » Supported a leader of a new start-up franchise company, struggling to breakeven, to a Midas emporium where staff commented everything they touched turned to gold. Their business multiplied 10 fold and went IPO.
- » Rescued a luxury home developer who was on the wrong end of the GFC and experiencing suicidal thoughts, into a comeback of epic proportions. Having lost his business, luxury family home, savings, and basically drowning in debt, such a massive comeback is really unheard of. He is now back to 8-figure projects and living his best protected life.
- » Inspired a founder/CEO, who was having deep internal conflicts when he brought in a VC for his business that was serving Fortune 500 clients, into a fresh start. He walked away from the business to start another business doing what he knew best, in a more sustainable and efficient manner. This is very representative of what we call timely or spontaneous right evolutionary action. When you're in alignment and protected, change happens easily, and often, without consequence.
- » Helped transform a managing partner from a place of anger and high anxiety, only serving a few clients, to having over 25 publicly listed clients and their own office building.
- » Reinvigorated a founder/CEO, who was ready to throw in the towel and let a 9-figure business fold, on a new path of reviving their business and achieving a new level of excellence.

The only short-term clients we have are the ones who just started. Our clients maintain their work with us because the added value is obvious. Our goal with this book is to provide some of that value to you, because, as a high-performer, you need it now more than ever before. There is a clear path to protection and we want to help you find it. This knowledge is your personal development insurance policy.

See, you're already a high-level leader and performer. You're highly motivated, you have increased business and performance acumen, you possess a strong leadership prowess... we aren't here to help you in those areas, you've got that covered. We aren't here to develop your skill sets in business or to attempt to motivate you. You've mastered the Science of Achievement. Let's move onto something bigger, something Universal. Something you haven't tapped into yet.

What else is there?

This brag book of sorts validates what we're about to share with you. Forget the habits and intellectualization of development. None of that matters. Whatever it is you feel you are lacking, is merely a symptom of a deeper cause. Just like poor communication is a symptom of a lack of development, learning topical communication skills will only suffice the symptom, and mask it without ever going to the root of the problem. Putting wax over rust doesn't make everything shiny and new underneath. Buffing a bent bumper might help make it shiny for a while but it doesn't actually correct anything.

What is this new level of leadership?

There is a new type of leader emerging, and we will see this leader spearhead massive changes in how our business economy operates, what motivates growth, and especially how businesses take care of their people. This is the age of leadership, where true leaders will be the change makers of the next century.

These leaders must be independent-minded, able to take a stand for something they believe to be a better way, someone who refuses to play by the rules and instead creates new and better systems. They aren't scared to cross the line of conformity and use unorthodox tactics to get results. To summarize that: you, as a leader, must be able to recognize new Universal truth, speak to that truth, apply that truth, and take your business and people with you on this powerful journey. That is the task at hand.

This new age of leadership will require leaders to be positively disruptive by using the power of their free will to align themselves with higher Self-awareness, to unfold more infinite intelligence, which is equally just and supportive of everyone, and to align with this new Science of Protection.

The Vision of Benefits from Reading this Book

» 360-degree awareness of how to protect yourself and your progress.
» Knowing the true basis of action which truly guides you.
» Being established in the field of enlightened invincibility within you, to more spontaneously take actions that enhance, support and protect your achievement and progress without being corrupted and diminished by stresses, vices, incoherent thoughts or external challenges.
» Minimize and neutralize unforeseen events that could come and blow up your achievement.
» Reduce the need to overly Self-analyze because you have a clear understanding of why you're in a position of leadership, so you can enhance and protect it.
» Overcome and avert burnout, overwhelm, fear of loss or working crazy hours so your mental sanity, health and wealth is well protected.
» Understand the mechanics for enhancing your ability and capacity to lead so you become even more of an elite leader.

The Six Steps of the Science of Protection: How It Works

We'll elaborate on the six steps of the science in each chapter. Below is an overview of the Science of Protection with a brief definition of each component and how it works.

As mentioned in the preface growing in protected achievement and progress is a two-step process, yet most leaders skip the first step- which is the alignment with protection.

The first step is an internal protection development for enhancing and protecting yourself from within before you take external action. This helps give a secure foundation for creating better more fulfilling and assured achievement and progress. The second step is external protection integration for being and staying protected as you take the risks and actions to achieve and progress. Each step has three steps making a total of six steps.

Step I: Internal Protection Development:

1. **Purification** – Purify negativity, stress and vices to have fewer resistances, more simplicity and energy to progress.

2. **Coherence** – Greater global alpha brain coherence to have more clarity, to have the right unifying thought at the right time.

3. **Leadership State** – Fully awake truthful creative mind to proactively avert danger and see the best possibilities.

Step II: External Protection Integration:

4. **Capacity** – Heightened expanded awareness and focus to naturally handle any obstacle and opportunity.

5. **Spontaneous Right Action** – Timely evolutionary right action in tune with what is required.

6. **Deserving Power** – Having the good merit and support to get, protect and sustain what you want.

These six steps together help you reach the goal of the Science of Protection which is protecting yourself, your team and your achievements and become an enlightened leader.

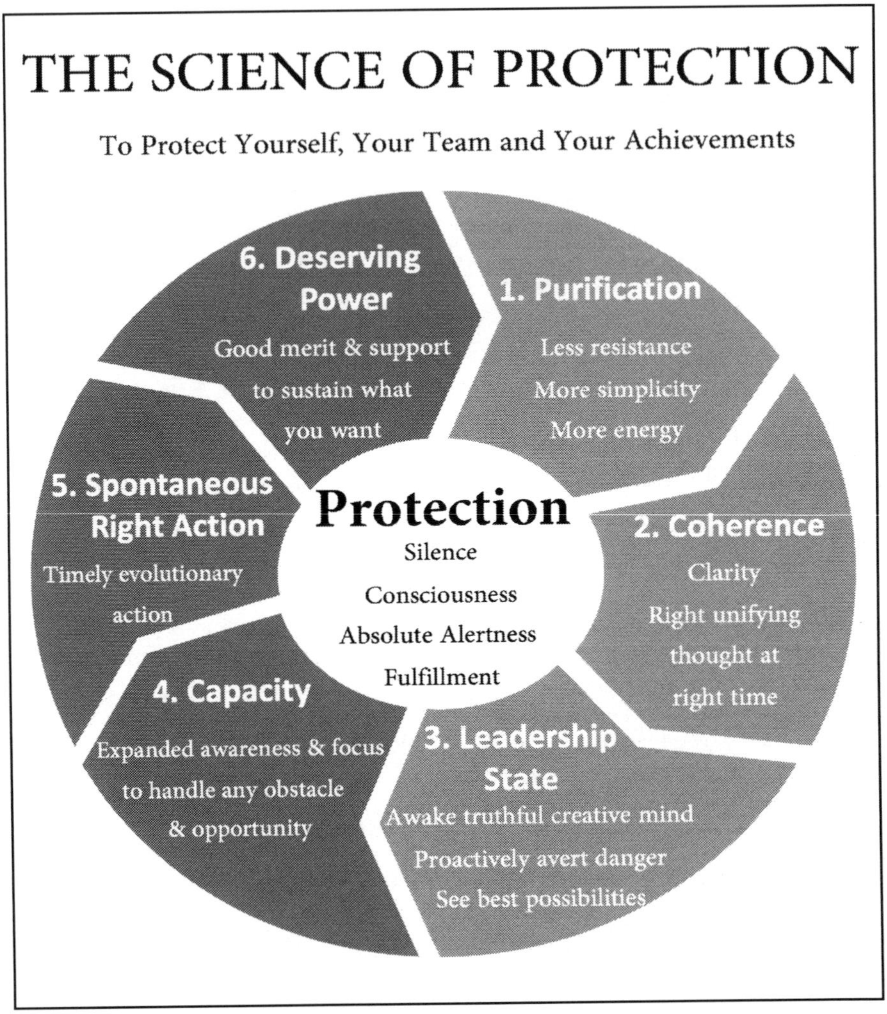

The Science of Protection gives you the ability to more easily avert problems before they arise so you can protect yourself, your team and your achievement and ultimately sustain what you want for as long as you want without burnout or overwhelm. With this process you become more of an enlightened leader who illuminates the path for others. This means your achievement also comes with fulfillment and not suffering. The source of these steps is your enlightened leader silence, consciousness, awareness and fulfillment deep within.

These steps are intimately connected and sequentially unfold to enhance and support the next component.

This process starts internally with purification of any stresses, vices and negativity that are causing a drag and resistance to you and your company's progress. Through the purification process more simplicity and energy for better progress is created.

Purification paves the way for allowing higher brain coherence to be developed, specifically global alpha coherence, which gives greater clarity to perceive the right unifying thought at the right time.

With more coherence within you and between you and those you lead, you activate being in the Leadership State, a state where you have a more fully awake truthful and creative mind to proactively avert dangers and see the best possibilities.

Being in the leadership state is the basis for having greater capacity, heightened expanded awareness and focus, to handle any situation, obstacle, opportunity or demand you face in the best way possible without feeling overwhelmed, stressed or fear of failure or success.

With enhanced capacity you have greater ability to take more spontaneous timely right evolutionary action in accord with what is required.

More spontaneous right action means you're giving more of the right value at the right time. This builds more good merit and power of reciprocity, which creates deserving power and support to avert problems before they arise and fulfill what you want.

How many times when an individual or team wins a championship has everyone pretty much said they deserved to win? The consistent sum total of all their feelings, thoughts and actions taken to develop and prepare themselves before their championship allowed them to earn and have the "deserving power and support, luck and grace to win", more so than those they are competing against. Just to be clear deserving power is really one word/phrase not two, it's not about being deserving of power it's developing and having the power of deserving to deserve what you want. Results happen because one has earned and therefore created the deserving to support them happening.

The wholeness of all these steps, or parts of protection, is what enhances and protects results. Functioning from the wholeness of protection happens through alignment with the source of protection, which is that enlightened silent, consciousness, awareness and fulfillment deep within, which is what we innately are. Without having consciousness and awareness we cannot exist, express and function. It's this pure existence that allows our minds and bodies to express. This innate, inner level of ourselves is invincible: fire can't burn it, water can't wet it, wind can't dry it—none of the elements can afflict this level of ourselves like they afflict our physical bodies.

By connecting and aligning with the source of protection and then sequentially activating the six steps of protection, you can cultivate a high degree of protection where you and your organization cannot be diminished due to incoherence or negativity. This naturally has the side benefit of a higher level of trust and belief in yourself and faith that you will achieve what you want and be able to protect and keep it.

This science goes against the grain of how most leaders approach their development, which is the constant force feeding of intellectual information. We don't call ourselves New Mavericks because we're just regurgitating something already known. Our role is to add value and positively disrupt and enhance what leaders already know.

This constant information consumption is preventative, but not in a positive way, because it is only preventing you from inner growth by distracting you and keeping your mind on the surface, consumed with busy work, so to speak. As Eckhart Tolle puts it, "*Rather than being your thoughts and emotions- be the awareness behind them.*"

Many leaders, focused on intellect, believe that education is the only key to true leadership. This is why leadership seminars and team-building camps exist in the first place. They want to educate you, to help you learn to be a better leader. But true leadership is not based in education. True leadership is a state of existence. This leadership state, along with coherence and purification, exists at progressively deeper levels inside you. The Leadership State is a fully awake and truthful mindset that proactively and creatively averts danger, while simultaneously enhancing progress.

To be clear, there is nothing wrong with educating yourself, but there is an entire foundation, deeper than education and intellectual growth, that you must first experience, understand, and master. Focusing first and foremost on education is actually just another one of those backward business processes we mentioned at the beginning of the book.

Imagine trying to complete a math problem without the proper formula. You might toil away for hours, attempting to figure out how to go about solving the problem. You might ask everyone how they think you should solve the problem or if they know the formula. You might spend every waking second attempting to figure out how you can solve this problem, or figure out the right formula, because without the answer, it is driving you to the brink of insanity. You might make it your mission in life to find the formula and then share it with the world so nobody ever has to rack their brain for so long ever again. You might go gray and wrinkle up before you figure out that the formula was the most obvious answer. So much so, that you overlooked it. The current state of leadership is like this, except the formula is not unknown—it has just been forgotten.

Thousands of research findings mentioned in the book *World Class Brain* by Dr. Harald Harung and Dr. Fred Travis found that once someone reaches adulthood, around age 25, things like age, education, practice, incentives and genes contribute very little, like 1%, to improving performance.

What really enhances performance is inner self-development that allows you to have a more global alpha coherent brain. Developing this more integrated style of brain functioning should come first, because that is how you expand your capacity in all areas of life. Plenty of education and training is wasted on individuals who either lack the capacity or ability to understand, and never fully apply the content they've learned because they weren't given the tools to develop a more integrated coherent brain. If a leader cannot exist in the leadership state, any knowledge or training they receive will only be surface level. General Electric proved this by spending $1 billion on education and training of their people worldwide only to experience falling revenues and profits for 10 years, culminating in its delisting from the Dow Jones Industrial Index, of the top 30 industrial companies in America in 2018.

Length Disclosure

A few of the chapters in this book are lengthy so you should expect that. The knowledge shared in these pages is profound and Universal. That means, the process of you remembering the truth of what we are sharing is more complex than us attempting to instill new habits into your daily routine. We have worked endlessly on simplifying this knowledge for cutting edge leaders who understand the changing world we live in and the need for a new fresh approach to leading. That being said, we had a lot of ground to cover. So, take your time and enjoy the wisdom, knowledge, and truth packed into every page.

PART 1

THE PRIMARY IMPORTANCE OF PROTECTION

1) The Universal Force of Protection
2) The Myths, Reality and Future of Leadership

1 The Universal Force of Protection

What Protection Really Is

Protection is a universal force that creates, preserves or dissolves based on what is best for the whole to continue to survive, thrive and evolve.

The protection we're bringing to light is like a universal immune system that protects your whole life (inner and outer), your development as a person and a leader, and your achievement and progress. Enhance and take care of this universal protective immune system and it will enhance and take care of you so you can accomplish as much as you want for as long as you want. If we and our families don't have strong immune systems we don't have the foundation to protect ourselves, our team, and what we achieve.

There are approximately 100 trillion live microorganisms in our gut that help us digest and metabolize. These make up the mucosal immune system that is more than 75% of our total immune system that protects our body from infection. In addition, 95% of our body's serotonin and most of our neurotransmitters are created and stored in the gut. So, ensuring we have a healthy gut and digestive system is super important to support your body's ability to resist viruses and any form of negativity, stress and incoherence.

A strong immune system provides a protective shield to protect what is positive while neutralizing stress, vices and negativity that can come up when achieving. Protection is the antidote to many things that can ail a leader like the fear of loss, vices, stress, bad impressions, compromised health, wealth, happiness, relationships and reputation, which we'll elaborate more on in chapter 3.

This universal protection is what allows leaders to remain at the top of the mountain, regardless of weather conditions, shifts in the economy, potential stressors, and avalanches of change and disruption. The leaders at the top don't spend their lives avoiding the world around them. They maintain their own state, their own protection, so when the world around them is shifting, they are immune to the dangers, able to see what is coming their way and adapt, while maintaining their ability to recover quickly when they miss a beat.

The Destructive Duo: Fear and Ego

When we started offering our consulting services to leaders, we were fresh out of a combined total of 25 years of being full-time meditating monks. Having spent thousands of hours in meditation, we were eager to take our well-established foundation of inner peace to the high-level executives of the world. But all of the stillness inside could not contain the shock and surprise we felt, as we learned the dire state of business leaders around the world. We spent the following decade immersing ourselves in the global business economy, identifying the largest issues plaguing modern leaders. We saw and felt the massive disconnect from silence- that gives leaders the awareness, energy, capacity, coherence, clarity, stability and agility to be more in tune with change. This journey led us to eventually translate everything we learned into the knowledge you will find in this book.

It became immediately clear to us in our work that something crucial was missing from the mindsets of leaders driving the business economy. The truth is the same now, almost a decade later. Most leaders don't realize their full power and potential, both individually and in terms of their capacity to inspire their organizations. Many, as a result of this, operate from a place of fear rather than joy. In addition, a large majority of these same leaders have their ego in the driver's seat, ultimately pushing an agenda few will ever benefit from. We see the results of this approach in the tumultuous economy and state of business today.

This destructive combination of both ego and fear is constantly churning under the surface. If you are a leader in this position, this destructive duo is affecting every economic movement your business makes under your leadership.

In addition, the amount of responsibility placed on leaders today is almost unbelievable. Authors Rasmus Hougaard and Jacqueline Carter, in their book *The Mind of the Leader*, wrote about how leaders are responsible for leading themselves, their people, and their organizations: *The Mind of the Leader* concludes that, "organizations and leaders aren't meeting employees' basic human needs of finding meaning, purpose, connection, and genuine happiness in their work..."

Think about that statement for a moment. It is now considered a basic necessity and certainly a responsibility for you, as a leader, to ensure your people have found their meaning, purpose, and genuine happiness or at least given opportunities to do that for themselves. That's quite a tall order for any one person, especially considering many leaders are unable to achieve this for themselves, let alone entire teams of people.

One leader who clearly was able to meet employees' and customers' basic human needs is Michael Eisner, the legendary CEO of The Walt Disney Company. Eisner served in this role from 1984 to 2005, a period when his leadership helped grow Disney's annual revenues from $1.5 billion to $30.75 billion. Under his command, the company opened new theme parks worldwide and grew the number of employees from 28,000 to 129,000. He led the development of the Disney cruise ship line, a stage play division, and multiple domestic cable channels, including ESPN.

The legacy of Eisner's progress was carried on by another great leader, Bob Iger, who in 2006 led Disney in the acquisition of Pixar for $7.4 billion. Iger struck gold once again, in 2009, when Disney acquired Marvel Entertainment for $4 billion, and once more when it acquired Lucasfilm for $4 billion in 2012. The ability to be able to pull off these great feats of business is ultimately due to an underlying level of support and protection that these leaders had and have. You'll find that each of the six steps of the Science of Protection, purification, coherence, leadership state, capacity, right action and deserving power, were lively to a high degree for both of these leaders.

The story of Atlas, in Greek mythology also comes to mind. Atlas was tasked by Zeus with standing at the edge of the world and holding up the entire heavens for eternity. The actual weight of leadership on your shoulders is something you have been tasked with, and the responsibility is great. The only way out is achievement or failure, or *so you've been told.*

More and more we are seeing leadership training content and materials shift their focus to the people of an organization, encouraging leaders to be selfless and compassionate. While that is not wrong, it also is not right because this is not the first step. Being selfless and compassionate is based on a deeper development of consciousness. Jumping steps in development can be detrimental because the foundation and protection a leader needs themselves is missing.

Yes, we agree, the people and the organization are of massive importance, but what about the leader? What about you? What is it that you need to help you carry the weight of your organization on your shoulders? When we focus solely on the people of an organization, we are leaving the leaders out—all while placing great expectations on them, expecting them to focus on making everyone else happy. This is not the way of the future for leadership. We need to bring high performance leaders back into focus, and guide them into untouchable territory, where they are protected from the negative effects and influences of the stresses, strains and pressures that come with being a leader. Then they are even more capable of providing and giving what their people and organizations need with the security of knowing, not guessing based on limited information.

You can only give to others what you've cultivated inside yourself. If you want to work better on and in your business, and with your people, you must work on yourself to bring more abundant energy, intelligence, happiness, and even love. You are the subject, the leader, the cause, the humanware that creates and is the primary influence on your organization's people, processes, systems, products, and customer philosophy.

What Is Protection?

Protection is an intelligence designed to ensure you're on the most evolutionary path, like your immune system which does its best to protect your health, so long as you don't compromise its natural functioning. This protection is everything you have been seeking, and the reason for the longing you felt when everything else fell short. Every quality, accelerant, or habit you've pursued, they are all by-products serving the value protection. This protection encompasses your health, wealth, happiness, relationships and reputation.

You've been led to believe that in order to be fulfilled, you must achieve. You've been pushed into a false reality, where true fulfillment is just around the corner, in the next big thing you accomplish. And because you've believed that fulfillment exists just around the corner… in that next big thing… it's never existed within you.

We hate to tell you that you've wasted your time chasing the cart when you could have just ridden in on the horse, but we figure it's better to go ahead and rip that bandage off now so we can get down to business. Our entire basis for writing this book is to shed light on the fact that you've been misinformed. Not just you, but the majority of leaders around the world.

Every single self-help book you've ever read has stopped short of identifying your full capacity as a conscious human being.

We're not talking about protection by way of an external body guard or an alarm system. Our concept, The Science of Protection, will show you that protection is an internal proactive, not reactive, process. Protection is offensive rather than defensive. Protection exists in everything all the time, a constant force working below the surface, both awake and silent, and all you have to do is align with it. Protection is freedom.

Protection can only be gained by inner self-development.

Perhaps those bold words don't read like a profound statement, but given the amount of money businesses spend on professional development, that statement should, at the very least, intrigue you. All the time and resources poured into outer self-development (like learning to be better at speaking, body language, dress better, relate better, sell better, communicate better) for leaders this adds up to astounding amounts. And when we take a look at what organizations and leaders are getting for their money, we have to begin to question this approach, its efficacy, and why it isn't working.

General Electric prides itself in spending $1 billion per year on training and development of its people worldwide- yet was delisted from the Dow Jones Industrial in 2018 due to falling revenues and profits. We can only conclude the leadership development didn't go deep enough and remained surface level. Let's veer into the category of professional development for a *moment* because this heavy shift into surface level fixes has contributed largely to where we are today, and the clear lack of protection we are currently suffering from.

> **"American companies spend over $15 billion annually on leadership development training."**
>
> *–Bersin by Deloitte study conducted in 2013*

» 84% of organizations anticipate a shortfall of leaders in the next 5 years.

» 83% of organizations say it is important to develop leaders at all levels.

- 5% have fully implemented leadership development training at all levels.
- 25% of organizations say fewer than 10% of critical leadership positions have ready and willing successors.
- 58% of organizations' top priority is closing leadership skill gaps.
- 43% of organizations' top priority is closing gaps across all leader levels.
- 18% of organizations say their leaders are "very effective" at meeting business goals.
- 19% of organizations say they are "very effective" at developing leaders.

–Statistics from "Future Leadership Adventures: Transforming Leaders to Excel in the Digital Age" a blog by Kathy Sherwood

IBM conducted in-person interviews with more than 1,500 CEOs from 60 countries and 33 industries globally to find out what leaders thought were the most crucial factors for future success in business. IBM discovered that fewer than half of those interviewees thought their organizations were adequately prepared to handle a highly volatile, increasingly complex business environment.

Further, they stated, "CEOs are confronted with massive shifts—new government regulations, changes in global economic power centers, accelerated industry transformation, growing volumes of data, rapidly evolving customer preferences."

A quick Google search will pull enough statistics to fill this entire book and then some. We chose a handful to solidify the truth of why leaders require a deeper level of development and protection than ever before, to survive and thrive in the ever evolving global business landscape. Everyone might not agree on the solution or approach, but everyone is in absolute agreement that we are in a state of massive, fast-paced change, making the need for sustainable / protection practices more important now than ever before.

Simply put, there is no better time for you to have this in your hands, because the business economy is eating leaders alive. For the future of business, development of outer skills like communication or emotional intelligence must be based on the foundation of inner development and protection.

Average Learning and Development Budget Based on Company Size

- Large (10,000+ employees): $85 million
- Mid-size (1,000-9,999 employees): $6 million
- Small (under 1,000 employees): $1.1 million

Source: Brandon Hall Group 2020 Learning and Development Benchmarking Study

The current training practices in the business world encourage professionals to work tirelessly on perfecting specific skill sets or habits. The number of workshops you can take with your staff right now on communication, leadership development, personality types, etiquette, conflict management, conflict resolution, training to train the trainer to be a trainer (okay, maybe we made the last one up, but you get the point nonetheless) are endless.

A few years ago, we landed a large contract with a healthcare organization to bring their B-level managers up to par with the market competition. We were tasked with creating content on everything from etiquette to harnessing the power of each executive's personality strengths. But the blatantly obvious truth was staring us in the face from the beginning: these leaders didn't need etiquette training. The actual problem was they weren't happy, they didn't know why they weren't happy, and they had no idea what might make them happy. At the basis of this truth was another truth: no matter how developed an executive's external skills are, if the internals aren't right, that overshadows everything else. And perhaps an even further truth: in leadership, we are skipping over the very basic, foundational elements needed for a leader to thrive, elements that pertain to protecting a leader's inner happiness and coherence.

Remember, buffing a bent-up bumper might help it shine for a little while, but the problem or the damage is still there, so you haven't really fixed anything. We are all bent-up bumpers. We have all survived negative experiences or held onto fears, sometimes rational, mostly irrational. Those fears and those negative experiences lurk below the surface at all times. Somehow once those events are over, we forget their impact. We find ourselves asking, "What's wrong with me?" What's wrong has already happened, you just haven't made it right yet. And your attempts to make it right focus on the symptoms and not the cause.

Our obsession to perfect these pieces and parts of who we are reaches from one side of the globe to the other. So we listen to audiobooks while we're in the car on how to be a stronger leader. And we take meetings from coaches who promise us they will amp up the attitude of our sales force. And we buy books that regurgitate habits because if we can just get to that 30-day mark, we will naturally commit to this habit or that habit, just in time to start obsessing about a new habit.

We sacrifice everything that is important in our lives to achieve success, or fame, or awards, or wealth.

We believe the mistruths about achievement, and how that will bring us to a place where the "art of fulfillment" becomes a real part of our lives. But the truth is, fulfillment is a state, not an art, and achievement doesn't get you there. We will explore this concept further throughout the next few chapters.

Let's go back for a moment, and reiterate the awful truth many leaders choose, which is that we sacrifice everything that is important in our lives to achieve our objectives. Then, when the day that changes everything is upon us, we are left wondering: where did I go wrong? What did I do that I shouldn't have done? What should I have done that I didn't do?

This shift, from the pieces and parts to the whole, is the future for high performance leaders. It isn't compassion, or selflessness, or some hidden form of communication that will "change everything for you." Rather than trying to wet the leaves on your tree of life, you can water the roots. This is the most simple and sensible solution.

Just to be absolutely clear on what we are saying, no amount of habits or training will protect you or take you to the level of true leadership you are seeking. No amount of coaching or reading will teach you inner fulfillment that is real and lasting. No amount of compassion will identify purpose. No amount of selflessness will help you carry the weight of your responsibility as a leader. No amount of wealth can protect you.

No amount of defensive behavior makes the offense obsolete.

The reason we are so adamant to debunk this approach of learning or practicing habits and going through endless amounts of training is simple. We have watched too many leaders suffer for too long. We know, firsthand, and our clients know, firsthand, that all of this can be achieved; healthy strong habits, an excellent positive attitude, good health, growing wealth, all of this can be achieved as a by-product of inner development that builds alignment with protection. You must develop the capacity and coherence of the mind to comprehend even better possibilities rather than just training, managing and trying to get the most out of the current capacity and coherence of the mind.

In neuroscience speak, this specifically means developing more Global Alpha brain coherence. Brain coherence means the degree of orderliness and connectivity the brain has between its different parts. A more orderly connected and coherent brain is able to integrate the parts with the whole much better and quicker. A Global Alpha coherent brain, which we'll discuss in more depth in chapter 4, is a highly integrated world-class brain. The author of *World-Class Brain*, Harald Harung, describes it this way:

> **"A world class brain has one feature that makes it stand out: More integrated functioning. A world-class brain works in a more coherent, relaxed, wakeful, and efficient way. Plus, it has more intensely happy and fulfilling peak experiences and a greater moral sense, making top performers happier, more intelligent and effective."**

That means every single piece and part you are working on will naturally become even more right, strong, and positive, just by you focusing on your inner connection and development. Protection is freedom from everything that doesn't matter, from everything that weighs you down, and from everything that negatively diminishes your life and your business.

You are responsible to yourself, to your business, and to your people to expand your personal capacity, to ascend to this new level of leadership, to gain protection, and to protect those around you. Protection is the long-lost, under-recognized role of a leader. Without protection, achievement becomes more difficult (dangerous even, given the risk of one unfortunate event destroying years' worth of achievements). This is greater than any act of compassion towards your people because, with protection, you will automatically create an environment where they can flourish in security, should they choose to do so.

What does protection look like in action?

Let's think about protection in terms of events, because this is a more easily understood application. Think about your day and every action you have taken today: right before you said yes to that new partnership, right before you agreed to a new sales process, right before you settled on how you would streamline your marketing, right before you took that lunch meeting. The moment right before every action you take is when everything matters.

We must learn to recognize that the most important moments in our lives are the moments right before anything happens. These moments preceding actions and decisions are constantly deciding our next steps, our path forward, and our actions taken. And to take this concept one step further, the state you are in, in those moments right before anything happens, is shaping your reality.

In these moments we see protection take form through a leader's actions. Protection is a constant stream of inner wakeful intelligence occurring below the surface of the conscious mind. True leaders have the ability to manifest this protection as they go about their day making decisions, to inherently know what is right and truthful. If you think it doesn't matter, if you think these preceding moments do not equate to your outcomes and the direction of your entire life, you need to look deeper.

Review your day, think about every action you've taken, every yes or no you've given, every decision you've made, every thought you've had. In each one of those occurrences, did you inherently know what was right? Did you inherently know the best decision you needed to make, not only for yourself, but for everyone? Did you naturally take a broad perspective? Did your thoughts and actions align in every instance?

If so, good! This is what happens when you are protected. Leaders who align with this Universal protection don't worry about sales techniques, negotiating skills, or likeability because they are in a state of equanimity and coherence, where their ingenuity acts as a magnet and business becomes more effortless.

There is no inner struggle for leaders who are protected because they have aligned with the inherent knowledge of the Universe or as one of our clients put it:

> **"I used to lie in bed at night worrying. I used to get stopped by roadblocks I couldn't see past. I used to be stressed all the time. Now I don't.** ***It seems***

> ***counterintuitive, but the less I've struggled the more successful my team has become.* I owe much of this to New Mavericks."**
>
> –*Kelvin Hyland, Former GM EBOS,*
> *Now Managing Director, Ossis*

There are no attempts at getting others to connect or like them, because protected leaders draw people to them with their X-factor. Their high level of coherence, global alpha coherence, makes them a magnet, consistently drawing in and seeing better possibilities. Leaders with protection negotiate with ease, and grow their businesses with a smile.

Your capacity to look at everything, effortlessly, from a broad perspective, where your thoughts and actions are supportive of the whole—*this is protection*. It's the wholeness that is greater than the sum of the parts that gives protection to the parts. The great spiritual teacher Maharishi Mahesh Yogi used to say that ideal leadership and management is "wholeness on the move."

Top leaders we've worked with from around the world tend to have a high degree of development and skill; not only in one area, but in all areas, they compete or exist within. This is easily observable. Look at someone like Roger Federer, who may not have the best serve in the game. But what he does have is a *strong* serve, forehand, backhand, drop shot, court speed, and return of serve. You can't win 20 grand slams just having the best serve. There's a well-rounded wholeness to who he is as a player and a person. We see this idea about wholeness to be true, not only in sports, but in all areas of high-level performance.

This wholeness approach—of focusing not on individual parts but on a person's whole being—has helped us develop our Science of Protection. This is vitally important because CEOs and leaders have to be able to integrate and create coherence and wholeness between the what, why, how, who, when, and where of their business.

1. At great example of a leader who is currently demonstrating a high degree of competence in protecting her company's progress is General Motors Chairwoman and CEO Mary Barra. In 2017, Barra was crowned No. 1 on *Fortune*'s list of the most powerful women. Appointed CEO in 2014, she was called by some a "lightweight," but she most certainly proved her naysayers wrong.

Barra has lead GM through its post-bankruptcy recovery, navigated a widespread vehicle recall and public relations crisis, and helped the company turn a consistent profit. GM has started a ride-sharing service called Maven, invested in self-driving technology, and came out on top in the affordably priced electric car market. In Q2 of 2018, GM earned $36.76 billion in revenue—beating estimates—and its China division reached an all-time high of 858,000 deliveries.

Despite the negativity and incoherence, she's had to deal with, Barra has had enough protection and coherence to not allow it to corrupt or diminish her clarity of vision and focus to make the required changes. This is protection in action.

What Needs Protection?

The short answer is everything. But for the sake of this book and to develop your understanding of how every single thing affects your ability to be protected, let's get specific. We've created a list of the most important areas you need protection and what each area looks like when protection is lacking.

1. **Your thoughts.** Our society generates massive amounts of information daily. We are conditioned and programmed to consume that information, and in response to that information, we generate thoughts and opinions. This is a constant process you are participating in, a process which prevents you from establishing an inner connection because you can't get past all of the noise. We become so accustomed to the noise that silence, for many leaders, is a very uncomfortable thing to deal with. What's even more interesting about our constant consumption of information is what our brain does with all of that content. Because we don't allow ourselves a chance to separate from this information onslaught, we don't allow time for growth from old thoughts or experiences. Our brains can only attach new information to something we've already experienced, and, ironically, we tend to especially hang on to negative events throughout life as a form of protection. So here we are, consuming information, our brains working overtime to attach that information to something we've already experienced, something that may well be negative. The result is we are creating more negative energy and fear without actually doing anything.

- Swisscom CEO Carsten Schloter was found dead[2] in an apparent suicide. The executive reportedly left a note[3] explaining that he was depressed about his failed marriage and living separately from his children.
- Pierre Wauthier was found dead at his home in August 2013. He served as the CFO of Zurich Insurance Group. In a suicide note, Wauthier reportedly blamed Zurich Insurance chairman Josef Ackermann (who resigned after Wauthier's suicide) for putting him under pressure.

These thoughts that are generated from the constant consumption of information are the same exact thoughts that are firing in the moments before you act, or decide, or speak. You know, those moments we earlier deemed "the most important moments in your life"... the moments right before anything occurs. These thoughts and thought patterns are subconsciously being influenced by a massive under layer, and you don't even realize it because on the surface it seems you are the one in control. We will discuss this further in chapter three, to help you fully understand what is happening in your brain and to show how you can create new pathways, separate from the old, and create a new process of healthy, productive thinking.

2. **Your health.** It's no secret that high level leaders, more often than not, sacrifice their health for the growth of their business—something that is utterly insane. Unwanted health consequences should not be the price you have to pay for success and achievement. Nobody should be 35-45-years old and suffering from their first heart attack or stroke. The problem for most leaders is that their environment supports the generation of stress over calm. In addition, most leaders don't realize they have the capacity to exert power over their environment, rather than letting their environment control them. The creation of a supportive protective environment that allows individuals to fully express their full potential without fear of negative judgment is your responsibility as a leader. At the very least,

---

2 http://www.reuters.com/article/2013/07/23/us-swisscom-ceo-idUSBRE96M0EA20130723
3 http://www.thelocal.ch/20130820/swisscom-chief-exec-left-suicide-note-report

you owe this to your people as you have a major influence on their well-being.

- Corwin Hardham was co-founder and chief executive of Makani Power before it was acquired by Google. His leadership ended when he died unexpectedly in October 2012. The 38-year-old executive reportedly died of cardiac insufficiency.

Fifty percent of a worker's satisfaction comes from the quality of the relationship they have with their boss. Our clients have found that an environment that is protected is also positive, creative, and innovative, and accelerates growth. Stress is a major health and happiness influencer. It wreaks havoc on today's leaders, its toxicity carrying a long list of side effects that are detrimental to your health.

The biggest fraud ever sold was that we could just manage our stress. Fine, manage it, but it's still bubbling disruptively below the surface, creating ecosystems ripe for chaos and detriment. Whereas coherence is one of the six foundational steps of the science of protection, incoherence is foundational to disease, failure, and corruption. Your goal should be to eliminate stress and incoherence altogether. There is now confirmed research showing us how establishing this inner connection and protection actually eliminates stress, which we will discuss in a later chapter. Elimination of stress is a byproduct of gaining protection. Protection is freedom from this toxic stress and the myriad health issues business leaders continually fall victim to.

3. **Your energy.** A quick physics lesson will remind us that everything can be measured in terms of energy. Nikola Tesla, who was influenced by Vedic philosophies, said, "The day science begins to study non-physical phenomena; it will make more progress in one decade than in all previous centuries of its existence. To understand the true nature of the universe, one must think in terms of energy, frequency, and sound vibration." Scientist can now make small objects levitate through sound frequency. Tesla understood that energy not only made the world go round, energy was the world. Energy is you and you are energy. Your level of energy depends solely on your level of development. If you wish to expand into a higher level of inner energy and capacity, you must establish this inner connection. Think about what happens when you walk into a gathering, meeting, or

business affair. You immediately connect with other people who are on the same energy level as you. You probably make eye contact with them, even if you don't know them, and most certainly feel drawn to those who are on your same level. This is energy. Additionally, when you maintain a higher energy level than those around you, they suddenly want what you have. This energy is intriguing, and it draws people in. This x-factor leaves others craving your presence. They can't help but want to be near you. This is also energy.

Einstein wholeheartedly agreed with Tesla, saying, "Everything is energy and that's all there is to it. Match the frequency of the reality you want and you cannot help but get that reality." Science tells us that one of the major functions of your DNA is to receive and transmit energy.

True leaders exist on a higher energy level, and because of that they inspire change and growth, not only around themselves, but also within themselves. More and more the quality of energy, positive or negative, is being found to influence the perception of the quality of a CEO's leadership.

In 2016, *Notre Dame News* published an article[4] titled "Market reactions to sudden CEO deaths highlight CEOs' importance," which described the University of Notre Dame's Mendoza College of Business's published research on the subject. The researchers looked at the market reactions to unexpected CEO deaths over three 20-year periods: 1950-1969; 1970-1989; 1990-2009. Professor Craig Crossland was quoted in the article:

"The market response was larger in later periods. In other words, the negative reactions were more negative after the death of a highly regarded CEO, and the positive reactions were more positive after the death of an underperforming CEO. The average firm in our sample had a market capitalization of $1.3 billion (in 2009 dollars). Thus, over the course of 60 years, the shift in market value caused by an unexpected death increased by approximately $65 million (in 2009 dollars)."

4 https://news.nd.edu/news/market-reactions-to-sudden-ceo-deaths-highlight-ceos-importance/

The article went on to say, "Although it's difficult to prove why perceptions of CEO influence have changed over time, the researchers suggest the most likely explanation is simply because CEOs are becoming more important to a company's performance."

Carly Fiorina was CEO of Hewlett-Packard from 1999 until 2005. She was the first woman to lead a Fortune 100 company and created a merger with Compaq which resulted in sizable layoffs and a steep plunge in the company's stock price. She wasn't popular as HP's leader, so when news broke of her leaving the company stock prices immediately soared nearly 11 percent. As Fiorina went on to run in for political office, her history in business followed her, and this red mark on her record heavily affected how the public perceived her capacity.

4. **Your achievements.** It's important to be honest about the potential for failure. For many, success is fleeting. You've been made to believe that achievement for the sake of achievement is sustainable—that simply isn't true. Read that again: achievement for the sake of achievement is not a sustainable model. Our cultures spread the lie that if we succeed and find ourselves on top, that's it, we've made it, we're there. But that top position isn't a forever position for many. Here's another real-life example for you to chew on:

   - After co-founding Uber in 2009, Travis Kalanick grew the business to a value of $72 billion as of August 2018. In 2017, Kalanick's leadership skills culminated in several public relations nightmares and he ended up resigning in June 2017.

Just because you've found success, does not mean you will always be successful. How many examples do we, as high performers, need to see before we accept this simple yet startling truth?

And where does the achievement cycle end? Once you've achieved, are you supposed to remain in a perpetual cycle of achievement thereafter in order to maintain your success? Our approach in this book will change the way you view achievement, because your achievements will no longer be based on seeking fulfillment; rather, they will be based on your efforts to create something better for the whole. Once you develop your ability to naturally, effortlessly, take a broad perspective, this shift will also occur, and you will see your level of achievement change as a byproduct. Protection is freedom from the exhausting cycle of achievement, and it will transform achievement into a more effortless byproduct of your happiness, alignment, coherence, and bliss.

5. **Your business.** Not only the business but everyone involved in the business, and everyone relying on the business, needs protection. We don't want you to think about your position as a leader as a path to success. We want you to think about your position as a leader as a path to advancing the human race. We believe that leaders have forgotten their influence, their capacity to magnify change, their ability to evolve and bring others with them, their ability to change the status of our future, their ability to protect what is important... their people. Businesses are nothing without people, and to protect your business you must protect your people. To protect your people, you must create a supportive environment where they can grow and develop themselves. Your job is not to be the boss; it's to be the leader. The leader to/of what? What are you leading your people to? More profits for your business? And how much do you lose in the process? If you are not protecting your business by protecting your people, you are failing them. Here's a great example of this:

    - In 30 years of leadership, John Schnatter of Papa John's Pizza grew his business to $1.7 billion in revenue and 5,000 stores as of July 2018. But 2017 was a rough year for both Schnatter and Papa John's. When Schnatter criticized the NFL's approach to the national anthem protests, used a racial slur, and made controversial statements on a conference call, he probably could have never imaged the storm about to rain down on him. Then, in May 2018, Schnatter was accused of sexually inappropriate conduct, as well as spying on his employees. When Schnatter stepped out of his primary roles within the company, shares fell rapidly, more than 17 percent, and everybody could see that coming...but why couldn't Schnatter? Why couldn't he quit while he was ahead, so to speak? The answer is simple: he lacked protection. Sure, hindsight is 20-20, but what about foresight?

True leaders make it their first and foremost responsibility to develop their own consciousness, and then the consciousness of their people. They do this so everyone has the possibility of maximum protection.

6. **Your wealth.** The only reason leaders lose their wealth and diminish their legacy is because of a lack of protection in some area of their life. Whether their health fails, or their decision-making is clouded, or their merger goes wrong, or their buyout falls through, or their corporation collapses, or their people constantly leave them, or their sales aren't sustainable—no matter what, the only reason leaders lose their wealth and diminish their legacy is because of a lack of protection from these pitfalls. Kenneth Lay, former CEO of Enron, is a great example:

    - He became CEO of natural gas provider Enron in 1986, and had grown the company into an energy giant valued at roughly $68 billion at its peak. In December 2001, Enron filed the then-largest corporate bankruptcy in U.S. history. The Securities and Exchange Commission charged Lay with fraud and insider trading in July 2004. Among other allegations, he was accused of garnering illegal proceeds totaling more than $90 million in 2001. One of the most legendary failed CEOs of all time, Lay was convicted on six counts of fraud and conspiracy in May 2006.

We will discuss protecting wealth further in a later chapter, and address the lack of mindset development that kills success for many business leaders.

Does all this talk of protection and coherence and development seem overwhelming? Well, before you take off running as far away from this book as you possibly can, know this: While in essence, everything needs to be protected, the good news is that this all-encompassing protection exists in one place. When you've developed your inner connection and you align with protection- that protection spans across every part of your life. This is what we mean by all-encompassing.

It's not on the level of the mind, because that fluctuates, nor is it on the level of the body, intellect, feeling or ego. These are all the relative changing parts of our self. The source of protection exists on the level of existence itself, on the level of the indestructible all-pervading invincible consciousness that governs the creation, maintenance and dissolving of everything. Consciousness is that which is aware of itself and is what allows us to have awareness. Within consciousness is fulfillment of who you are and what allows us to create again and again and again assuming we're connected to it. Hence why in the Science of Protection diagram below the source of protection is denoted as invincible leader consciousness, awareness and fulfillment. This is what we want to inspire you to be in tune with.

Rather than send you on a wild goose chase to protect this or protect that, or to develop this habit or that habit, we're here to show you all-encompassing protection in one science, to infuse protection into all areas of your life.

This shift is turning your focus from your outward expression to your inner connection, something few leaders pursue, yet something the highest performers cite as being their magic formula.

7. **Your environment and world.** Even though we believe we are so smart and technologically advanced this still doesn't top the organizing intelligence of nature. Either we're in tune with nature, which makes us orderly and protected, or nature is having to teach us a lesson, as the corona virus has.

   The virus is the effect of the underlying cause that is incoherent human behavior, which allows negativity like this to arise. Nature has been giving us strong signals for a while now in the form of intense bushfires, floods, and climate change. Nature is showing us we have created imbalance in our environment and has been doing something to correct it. These signals from nature have been localized in different parts of the world and now nature has conjured up something that is having a rapid global impact to really get our attention.

   What are we doing to ourselves, animals and the environment to cause nature to produce such a hidden all-pervasive negative global impact? Are leaders in denial, not listening and ignoring these signals? What else has to happen to realize we have to change the way we are treating ourselves, others and the planet? What is the big lesson in all this?

   We believe the BIG lesson is implied and symbolic in what is already happening. We're literally being forced to take recourse back to ourselves, back to silence, orderliness and coherence to have protection from within through having strong immune and nervous systems that can avert and neutralize highly contagious incoherent viruses and negativity. The virus is actually doing us a favor in making us retreat back to ourselves. It's realigning us with nature's higher evolutionary intelligence, which we are intimately a part of, so we are protected and don't create more damage than we already have.

Coming back to ourselves, silence and coherence is the only thing that is truly going to purify and prevent us from being a fertile ground and susceptible host for viruses. It's also helping us purify and avert negativity and bad decisions and actions that hurt ourselves, others and the planet. Silence, peace and coherent behavior have to be restored as the foundation of activity, achievement, progress and leadership. Otherwise these continue to be motivated by fear, selfishness and greed.

Learning the lesson nature is teaching us we'll progress in a better more sustainable way. Not learning or resisting the lesson then nature can only continue to dish up more suffering and negative influences until we do.

It's time to make the Science of Protection the foundation and basis for sustaining the Science of Achievement.

The Truth About Achievement

As you can see from the examples we've shared, achievement and progress require protection. We've invested countless hours and surveyed business leaders from around the world while writing this book, and discovered a common theme on the topic of achievement. The majority of leaders we surveyed were most often taking action based on what they wanted or what they felt would be fulfilling. For example, one award winning CEO, when asked how he was going to achieve something, would give the short yet truthful answer, "I don't know, but we will". It isn't short-sighted; it's just the way things are. That's not to say no achievement is deliberate, but for the most part, a lot of achievement happens for surface level self-fulfillment. This is true on one level of thinking but superficial on another, and possibly one of the biggest lies that exist in business. Fulfillment, true fulfillment that goes beyond the surface, is not something you achieve or create, it's something you are. Hence why we have it as the foundation source, course, and main goal of the Science of Protection.

To reiterate an earlier point, achievement does not bring sustainable fulfillment or success. Achievement does not create better, more balanced, or calmer leaders. Achievement does not create a pipeline to sustainability as you've been told. Your push to achieve for the sake of self-fulfillment is not long-term or permanent. Making decisions based on short-term fulfillment is the norm, and also part of the reason so many leaders fail quick and often.

Proper achievement is not some lost art in need of rediscovering. Achievement is a byproduct of a developed and stable leader. Protected achievement is the next level of leadership you've been seeking.

The process of sustainable growth and true fulfillment begins with inner development, not achievement. Yet it never fails, every leader we talk to has spent thousands of dollars perfecting problem-solving abilities and communication skills, when realistically, most of the problems they encountered would have probably been avoided in the first place if protection was in play. An underdeveloped leader can achieve all day, but that doesn't change their capacity or ability as a leader. That might sound harsh, so let's look at it this way:

Imagine a climber scaling a mountain. He is new to this mountain and he wishes to climb all the way to its peak. The climber has spent thousands of dollars on new gear and has spent weeks reading about the mountain in preparation for this climb (outer development). Once the climber reaches the base of the mountain, he realizes something incredible. He has no idea how to climb. He has never learned the proper knots or anchors or even the proper steps or positions. So even with all of the right gear and resources, his skill level is not developed enough for the task at hand, and that spells trouble.

The climber might attempt to rely on past experiences or knowledge to make the climb, and will inevitably fail because he is out of his experience zone, operating with less than sufficient capacity.

The same is true in leadership. You may want to ascend into a new level of leadership, or even just maintain your current level of leadership and achievement, but if you are not developed enough to do so, either you won't make it, or your success won't last.

Again, protection is what allows leaders to remain at the top of the mountain, regardless of weather conditions, shifts in the economy, potential stressors, and avalanches. The leaders at the top don't spend their lives avoiding the world around them. They maintain their own state, their own protection, so when the world around them is shifting, they are immune to the dangers, able to see what is coming their way, and able to recover quickly.

When you develop and expand your inner capacity (coherence, alertness, wakefulness, consciousness), you enliven the unified source of all the great leadership and high performance qualities and habits we are discussing. This enlivens protection for you.

With more capacity, you are naturally more courageous and truthful, not only with yourself, but also with others. You don't need to seek courage as you expand your capacity; courage is a byproduct. You don't need to work to be more honest or transparent, as these things are by-products of your expanding capacity. As you'll see from our research at the end of this chapter, the majority of high-level leaders we spoke to, from around the world, named honesty as one of their biggest challenges. We understand. With the weight of the world on your shoulders, along with performance expectations, not to mention the added expectation that you'll be a so-called yes man or woman, honesty falls to the bottom of the list. But this puts you at risk, unprotected, and we've seen what that leads to.

With more capacity, and by following the Science of Protection presented in this book, you're naturally 'more' of the qualities you are seeking to be a true leader.

Expanded capacity also equals more clarity and better perspective, one that is broad and encapsulates all of the moving pieces you may not have otherwise factored in. You'll know what is most important right now, have a higher energy frequency, and you'll find yourself connecting the dots more quickly than ever before.

All of these new or enhanced characteristics will allow you to be more convincing to others, connect with others more easily, and to serve as a more inspirational leader. This is protection delivers, and why the need for The Science of Protection and its fundamental properties exists. With that, let's dig into this new science and begin focusing on the six fundamental qualities now required of high-level leaders and top performers to align with protection-based achievement, which is really fulfillment-based achievement because you and others don't suffer, or at least minimize it. Achievement that causes suffering does not create fulfillment, it's simply achievement that comes and goes with negativity attached.

Interesting Data from Our Most Recent Research with CEO clients using the Science of Protection

Here are the most significant changes identified by shifting to The Science of Protection approach:

#1 Answer: Ability to be completely honest about everything.

This is an interesting response because honesty, in and of itself, is a form of protection. When you exist in total honesty, you eliminate gray areas, which will prevent you from dealing with unnecessary negativity and potentially negative situations, both personally and professionally.

#2 Answer: Ability to almost effortlessly connect with people.

Building connections with employees, clients, and executives creates a culture around you that is fully supportive of your growth. We had one client who was about to be ousted from his position. After making this Science of Protection shift, his entire staff, hundreds of people, stood behind him. Eventually they won, and so did he. As you can see, this is also a form of protection. This only happened because of the connections he built, connections which were genuine and strong, and a result of his shift to The Science of Protection.

YOUR TURN

How is Protection Important to You Right Now?

1. What is the most important thing you really want protection around right now?
2. Why do you want this thing to be well protected?
3. How can you go about ensuring this is well protected without creating fear?
4. Who can you align with to support you in what you want to protect?

Share this with others so they are aware how they can support and protect what is most important to you. Better still, share it with us at support@newmavericks.com and we promise to acknowledge it, protect it (that's what we're about) and even give you some input to support you on it.

2 The Myths, Reality, and Future of Leadership

Busting the Myths and Exposing the New Reality

"The secret to change is to focus all of your energy, not on fighting the old, but on building the new." —Socrates

The word *existence* is derived from the Latin word existere, which means to appear, become, or be. But the literal translation means "to stand out." As is true with the literal definition of existence, leadership is "to stand out." Your ability to lead and to stand out is inherent in your natural abilities and in your existence, but do you let everything else get in the way of your existence, your leadership, and your alignment?

In our research efforts to identify and define leadership, we have realized a few major common misconceptions regarding leadership. In fact, the truth is so far from what is now preached to leaders that we have dedicated this entire chapter to debunking leadership myths and setting the record straight.

What Is Leadership?

To answer this question, we need to first understand the definition of consciousness, as this is the foundation to everything.

One of our favorite answers to this difficult question comes from Dr. Tony Nader. Dr. Nader, a Ph.D. in brain and cognitive sciences from MIT, who also served as Assistant Director of Clinical Research at MIT, set out to help solve the mystery surrounding consciousness. Nader presented 'Hacking Consciousness' to the students at Stanford University, and used tangible methods to explain a very abstract concept. Through human physiology, quantum mechanics in physics, and Vedic philosophies, he explained that consciousness was essentially the foundation of everything:

> **"Consciousness is the source, not only of the human mind, and our ability to experience, know, innovate, and create, but also the source of all physical structures and functions, from fine particles and DNA to galaxies."**

Another clear explanation for this question comes from Dr. Harald Harung PhD, Associate Professor of Management and Performance at Akershus University College of Applied Sciences in Oslo, Norway, a true expert on the topic of brain cognition:

> **"Consciousness, fundamentally, we believe is the substance of the world. To elaborate on that, it's what everything is made of. We look at consciousness as a field that penetrates everything."**

The extent to which we reflect this universal consciousness as individual humans depends on our level of Global Alpha Brain Coherence a unique style of orderly total brain functioning found in world class athletes, business leaders, and musicians. This high level of coherence allows them (and you) to be very settled, and simultaneously alert, enabling more efficient thought processes, which equates to having more of the right thoughts at the right time. In addition to that, it is well known that there are different states of consciousness we experience. Just like sleeping is a state of consciousness, leadership is as well. Leadership is not just something you think or feel. Much like sleeping and other states of consciousness, leadership is a state of existence you experience.

These definitions of consciousness and leadership serve as incredibly important groundwork for the remainder of this book. We will continue to explore and debunk the mystery surrounding consciousness and high levels of performance, as we take you through the story and truth of your very unique existence, with the goal of defining a new way of leadership for you. In the spirit of debunking, let's look at leadership myths whose shelf life has long been expired:

Myth #1:
Leadership is a person or set of qualities and habits.

True leadership is not a person, or a set of qualities you can learn, or daily habits you can exhibit. True leadership is a state you achieve by developing yourself.

Myth #2:
People are either born leaders or they are not.

True leadership is not something you are born with, it is something you have to develop. You have the capacity to lead within you, inherent in your existence, but you have to develop it.

Most business leaders do not approach leadership like this. What most leaders do is identify someone in a moment of success, and ask, "How did they do it?" Then make a list of the things they said or did to achieve that success. Of course, everyone else wants that success, so we try to do those same things, without ever going an ounce deeper in our understanding of the actual source of that leader's capacity.

That leader might tell you, "Well, I get up at 5 am and I drink carrot juice." So you go and do that, and your results don't really change. Internally you label that as a failure on your behalf and move on, but the truth is that it isn't you. It also isn't the 5 am wake-up or the carrot juice. That's because leadership is a state, not a person, or qualities, or habits.

When you go to sleep, what happens? Are you deliberately thinking, "I'm asleep, I'm asleep"? No. You are in the state of sleep. It's not a feeling, or a thought, or a quality. It's a state. You aren't thinking you're sleeping or feeling that you're sleeping. You are sleeping. You are existing in a specific state of consciousness where you are able to experience sleep. In order to experience sleep, you have to be in that state.

The same is true for leadership. The irony of this truth is that plenty of leaders already experience this leadership state, but they aren't aware of it. So as in the example above, they chalk their success up to good qualities, habits, and carrot juice, never understanding that the state of consciousness they have or experienced is primarily driving their moments of success. This is important for you as a leader because when you're able to identify this state, you're more able to stabilize and enhance this state to unfold more consistent success.

"In the Zone"

In sports, we give credit for high-level performances by an athlete to being "in the zone." When an athlete brings home gold or breaks a world record, we say, "They were in the zone." While there are plenty of articles and books written about this zone, we still haven't clearly defined what the zone is, how to get there more often, or how to maintain this elevated state.

Your focus on all the pieces and parts of your organization can interfere with your ability to go to the source of everything that is you. This prevents or limits you from stabilizing high-level performance over long periods of time. We could describe this pattern of stable, high-level performance as being "in the zone," or in the leadership state. They are one in the same; the holy grail of performance, the state where ultimate clarity of vision of the whole is coherent with your focus on the parts while being aligned with your true nature and existence. This is what makes your ability to display leadership stand out.

However, this leadership state is always being undermined. Your constant consumption of information interferes with your ability to inherently know what is right, what the next best decision should be. Your constant push to achieve, to meet quarterly goals, and your constant fluctuations at the mercy of your environment, all of these things prevent you from stabilizing your leadership state and staying in the zone. Before we look at this wholly, let's identify the types of leaders we currently see in business.

There Are Two Types of Leaders

We work with leaders from all around the world, and while everyone is individually unique, we can generally, within minutes, place each leader into one of two categories. By identifying the categories in the following chart, we can easily know how developed and therefore protected a leader is. Leaders can fool themselves and others about how good they are, but their development is reflected in their language and behaviors, therefore it is easy to recognize whether they are reactive or proactive in protecting the progress of themselves and those they lead. The following chart contrasts what these are.

Reactive	Proactive
LOOK AT ME	LOOK AT YOU
Commands	Communicates
The Individual/Me/Mine	The Whole/Us/Ours
Detracts	Attracts
Tension & Conflict	Calm & Peace
Intellect	Consciousness
Achievement	Awareness
Fear & Ego	Love & Light

Command vs. Communicate: Communication is one of the most difficult tasks a true leader must develop. The only way you could possibly entertain the idea of mastering communication is by first developing yourself. Strong, effortless, kind, productive, coherent communication is a byproduct of your own inner development.

- Consider how differently everyone communicates, just based on the immeasurable variables affecting their thoughts, perception, and words. You could, realistically, never learn a skill or a set of skills based on communication that would ensure you get this right with every different person you communicate with, on every topic, every time.
- Body language is another form of communication that we all participate in, most of the time unknowingly. We are just responding with our movements, gestures, and even how we position ourselves in a room. Body language is also decided by the

level of stress in your body, past or current trauma, and your level of development or lack thereof.

- Leaders who are not developed do not understand communication on a deeper level, and are left to command in order to make things happen or to get their way. Over time, this approach is destructive, costly, and growth-inhibiting, as it results in you losing talent, time, potential partnerships, and profit.

The Individual vs. The Whole: An undeveloped leader cannot focus on the whole because they are consumed with themselves, and most of the time they don't even realize this. Their lack of development also prevents them from making decisions that will benefit the whole.

- Lacking coherence prevents an underdeveloped leader from knowing the needs or desires of the whole, and can only see their own needs and desires.
- A leader's inability to take a broad view will lead to failures and setbacks, and probably already has, even if they don't realize it yet. It is common among our clients to have this realization much too late, after the failure or setback has occurred.
- Once a leader does spend time developing their consciousness, they begin to clearly understand the true root causes for why things have happened in their lives. For many of these leaders, the root cause has been an inability to take a broader view and to intuitively understand the best decision for everyone.

Detract vs. Attract: An underdeveloped leader takes away value, meaning they might make some gain for themselves and shareholders while causing damage to the quality of service to customers, quality of life of employees and quality of environment. This will undoubtedly cause an overall net loss. On the other hand, a developed leader attracts and adds value, uplifting everyone involved within the company and the environment. There's no point improving a part while detracting from the whole. This isn't always intentional; it is just a side effect of being underdeveloped, just as adding value is a side effect of being developed and in alignment with *The Science of Protection.*

Conflict vs. Peace: A leader busy dealing with conflict resolution isn't a real leader. The underlying issue is that the leader has fostered a toxic environment wherein conflict arises easily and often. Where there is conflict, there is eventually war, and a leader in this type of environment is not protected.

- A leader who is developed brings a level of peace and calm to any situation. They are, in the words of one of our clients, "the eye of the storm."
- A leader who is developed exists in a state of peace and calm, and that flows into their environment, their interactions with others, and even their business dealings.
- Business and life are like one big hurricane with constant dynamic change and transformation going on around you. Your goal is to be protected by being centered in the eye of the hurricane, in yourself, where it is calm and where you draw maximum coherent energy, so you may guide that hurricane in the most life-supporting direction for everyone.

Intellect vs. Consciousness: We've already touched on the differences between leaders who lead from consciousness over leaders who lead from intellect.

- A leader who leads from intellect is always limited, while the conscious leader leads from a place of infinite opportunity. UCLA Basketball Coach John Wooden understood the limitations of intellect and summed this up by saying, "It's what you learn after you know it all that counts."

Achievement vs. Awareness: You can gain awareness through achievement, but this is what we call hard earned partial awareness. Awareness is more easily and better gained by becoming more internally awake within yourself, which then allows you to be more awake to your environment and the people in it. Achievement is really a byproduct of inner development. Achievement can be something you work endlessly for without ever knowing if your achievement will be protected or bring fulfillment. Achievement fundamentally doesn't bring complete fulfillment because fulfillment isn't something you achieve, it's something you align with and wake up to within yourself. However, inner development brings and supports both fulfillment and achievement.

Ego vs. Love: As Buddha says, "Ego is like dust in the eyes. Without clearing the dust, you cannot see clearly." Your ego manipulates you to covet power without ever realizing that true power exists in love.

- This egoist-based functioning is a disease of the mind, tempting you to make choices based on false information, encouraging you to only focus on the individual experience and sense of self, and constantly pulling your attention away from others. This doesn't foster unity around you. In fact, it has the opposite effect.
- The ego withholds love and thrives on control. The ego wants to be in control because of fear of losing its position. Wanting to hold on to your position you're lost, because you're too focused on that rather than genuinely serving a higher purpose. Being in control is not what we want, we want to be balanced and settled so our perception is supportive not defensive. It's being yourself without ego is when you're coming from the right place.
- The ego lives and rules by ulterior motives, which leaves a wake of chaos and a life that is unfulfilling. The ego judges and criticizes, while love does neither.
- Love encourages us toward the good. Within love is kindness and understanding. Love allows us to recognize that we are love and are connected by love.
- A developed leader allows love to flow freely to and from them without being intimidated. They greet and meet people with love and they see the same love in others as they see in themselves.
- You are a source of infinite love, and to turn off the flow is damaging to your success as a leader. In business, love got a bad rap. You have to change that narrative. Love is not a symptom of weakness, but rather a benefit of strength, development, and your leadership state.

Reactive vs. Proactive: A reactive leader is always one or two steps behind the ball. They don't have the coherence to see the bigger picture or finer details, and are often stuck in a cycle of reacting to constant change. When you have developed Global Alpha Brain Coherence, you're able to be proactive because you more clearly see the entire picture, with all its many details, and you're in tune with or creating change, rather than reacting to it.

A Story about Conflict

One of our first clients in the States came to us with a multitude of problems she needed to solve. The most important and pressing issue, according to her, was her inability to keep staff long-term. I still remember her saying, "It's just so difficult to find good help these days, ya know? It seems like there aren't a ton of qualified executives out there, willing to put in the time, and really engage." So we talked, and held sessions where we began digging deep into the everyday inner-workings of her company, the most recent employee losses, and the stories behind each loss. Through all of this, we had a pretty good idea of what was happening, but wanted to gather perspective from the other side.

With our client's permission, we spoke to executives who had moved on from the company to find out why they really left, and what made it so unbearable for them to stay. Keep in mind, during this time, the economy was pretty well tanking, so it seemed risky for these executives to be jumping ship when a replacement position was not a guarantee. Our conversations with the executives confirmed what we were certain was happening. Our client, who gave her blessing for us to share her story in this book, could not connect with her staff, and it was creating conflict. Her ego was overshadowing the truth of the situation, and she assumed it was the hires, not herself, who was the source of the conflict. As her frustration grew, the work environment became toxic, the stress level rose, and this perfect storm created a company people did not want to be a part of. As we worked with our client to develop her inner stability, her protection grew, and her connections with people flourished.

This shift opened her eyes to the ego-driven world she had created and existed in before she started working on herself. She noticed that now executives wouldn't abruptly leave the room when she entered and now offer to pick up the slack when necessary. These changes, along with many other small shifts, combined to create a culture within the company that felt good, stable, and supportive. This is a common occurrence when a leader releases their ego and embraces inner development.

Your Ego Is Fighting to Survive

There is so much action happening below the surface inside you, and much of this action is happening unbeknownst to you. The action on the surface, which is the result of these internal processes, is being driven by your ego, because your ego is subtler than your mind and emotions. These delicately complex and often understated processes are powerful and all-pervading. Now that we can identify where the action stems from, it is time to look deeper at the thought process of the ego so we can begin to understand the role the ego plays in your everyday life. Let's break out a few of the characteristics of the ego, point by point, for easy understanding.

1. Without coherence, your ego acts without your permission because it wants to experience what it wants to experience, like a demanding and unruly child. Ulterior motives and intentions you are creating (that you might not realize you are creating) are being acted upon by your ego without much consideration for the effect it may have on others and the environment. This reason alone really drives home why it is so important to be developed. Having thoughts and intentions you are unaware of, because you aren't connected to your true inner self, will ultimately lead to your downfall. This seems a risky state of being at best. To illustrate, let's imagine those ulterior motives and actions in the form of a business partner who constantly undermines your deepest desires and loftiest goals in life. You would never stand for that, especially not for a long period of time. You would get that partner out of your life, no matter what the cost, because you would understand the amount of damage that could potentially happen at any moment.

2. The ego abuses everything and everyone. Your ego will abuse money, power, and people to survive and gain space and command of your subconscious mind.

3. The ego is strengthened by attachment. Taking credit and being attached feeds the different vicious cycles we pointed out earlier, never really allowing you to grow beyond those experiences. Once you achieve something grand, your ego will convince you that in order to be happy or fulfilled, you must continue achieving—at any cost. If your achievement affords you a sports car, your ego will not

stop there. It will expect a second sports car, and this cycle of attachment does not stop unless you develop enough coherence to stop it.

4. The ego needs to be right. To satisfy this constant need to be right, the ego will tell lies, manipulate situations, and allow you to believe a false perception as the truth. It will even encourage you to participate in an altered and skewed reality, all in the name of false righteousness.

5. The small individual ego is driven by what it wants to experience, regardless of how this affects others. When this small ego is integrated with the higher brain through the inner development of coherence, something we'll talk about in Chapter 3, it can still experience what it wants, but in a way that is no longer harmful.

6. The ego is not you. Although your ego whispers "I am you," this is a lie. Your ego is a false construct of your mind, and in order to escape it, you must know yourself. To know yourself, you must look inward, beyond the ego.

7. The ego is all of the emotional distress in your life. Jealousies, anger, righteousness, hatred, insecurities, judgments, greed, self-loathing—these are all qualities derived from the ego and are unnecessary.

All of this can be boiled down to one or two results: You are either a developed leader, or you are still getting there. Developed leaders are aligned with the fundamental qualities of The Science of Protection.

A Story about Greed

A combination of ego, and its by-product greed, caused this experience for Bernard Ebbers, the CEO of WorldCom Inc. from 1985 to 2002:

In March 2004, Ebbers was charged with conspiracy and securities fraud for his role in a scandal to falsely inflate WorldCom common stock prices, totaling $11 billion in fraud. He was found guilty on nine counts of accounting fraud and has been serving a 25-year prison sentence since 2006. This outrageous lack of protection is just another case study in the books, sure, but it's also a blatant example of leadership gone wrong. Rather than devalue life, we need to begin devaluing the inconsistent processes that lead life in these corrupted directions. Rather than call for heads to roll, we must begin calling for the high-level change needed to protect the very system we rely upon to continue evolving our economy and business ecosystems. Rather than cry out at foul behavior, let's get in front of it, preemptively strike at it, and proactively change it. Rather than watch our leaders die young, let's open our minds to this next level of leadership growth and begin making the changes necessary to live fully, where leadership is an internally joyful, harmonious, peaceful and rewarding experience even with all the external challenges that come with it.

Beyond the Two Types of Leaders

Remember, consciousness is the leader of everything, even your leadership. So in order for you to be an effective, powerful, and true leader, you have to be developed based on consciousness, not just mind, intellect, ego and feeling. In order for your success to be sustainable, you must have protection by way of inner development. Your inner self is the source of everything you are capable of. Your outward expression is everything you have accepted as truth, and so it exists in your life.

The best leaders in the world are not just those with the most developed skill sets. They are those with the most developed inner selves and the most expanded capacity. The best leaders in the world are those who have the capacity to get what they want, and protect it. Ingrained, within that capacity, is every quality you could ever need to progress, to lead, to achieve, and to sustain your achievements.

The simplest answer has been misidentified as the most complex because we let terms like "consciousness" or "Global Alpha Coherence" scare us away.

Within the simple unified source (consciousness) exists every other quality and skill you could ever want or need as a leader. The whole takes care of the parts, just as the roots take care of the leaves. If we go back to our definitions of consciousness to understand how consciousness works as a foundation for every single part of our lives, this process seems much clearer. This definition also proves the common sense approach, presented here, to water the roots instead of wetting the leaves.

You can call this inner source anything you would like. Whether you call it your capacity, your consciousness, your source, the leadership state, the zone, it doesn't matter. The only thing that matters is that you recognize the importance of learning to connect to this source effortlessly. This is how you gain protection.

The answers to your questions about ascending to a new level of leadership are within you. How do I progress? How do I know which path is the right one? How do I know if this partnership will be successful? How do I get ahead? How do I take my business to a new level? How do I get rid of the bad impressions I've suffered in the past so they stop affecting my business decisions? How do I make my achievements sustainable? How do I stabilize this new growth? How do I become a better negotiator? How do I get more people on my side?

Speaking of questions, let's present a new question we know lives in your brain: How do I know if I will fail?

It's important for you to understand that true leaders maintain a process of constant growth. Once you go down this path of universal leadership, you will find that you are always in a state of growth, failure, or reflection.

First, let's talk about failure, because it's important as you grow into this new level of leadership, that you also begin to reframe and redefine what is true in high level leadership.

Failure Is Never a Stopping Point

It has almost become cliché that, to succeed you have to fail forward fast; but I think people lose sight of their focus here. Your focus shouldn't be on the failing. Your focus should be on what that failure is trying to show you. That failure is trying to show you where you are so you can focus on becoming even more coherent on the inside, allowing you to achieve better on the outside.

> **"One of the lies would make it out that nothing ever presents itself before us twice. Where would we be at last if that were so? Our very life depends on everything's recurring till we answer from within."**
>
> *—Robert Frost*

Failure provides rare and valuable moments for gaining wisdom, clarity, and vision. Wisdom, clarity, and vision are not free; wisdom grows through lessons we experience, clarity forms when we step to every outer edge of that experience, and vision reveals purpose after we fully understand the experience.

When we look at this process, failure seems necessary for growth, especially when we arrive in a place of leadership where we need wisdom or clarity of vision to proceed.

A few more important points to reiterate about this truth before we move on:

- When you are not clear on your vision, you will question everything you are doing, which initiates more failure, until you gain the clarity necessary to move forward.
- A clear vision grounds you, and everything around you will also have an instilled sense of purpose.
- Your own truth, vision, and purpose exist within you, and it is up to you to discover them fully.
- Sometimes, failure is the vehicle on this path to discovery. As you discover yourself, what is hidden comes to the surface.
- Having a profound vision pulls you forward.
- Without vision, we perish.
- By more deeply discovering your purpose and vision, you become more coherent and therefore more protected.

If failure happens, you are left with a valuable opportunity to dig deeper, to step to every outer edge of that experience, to gain clarity and wisdom, to reveal purpose, to increase coherence, and to expand protection.

> **"Sometimes, failure, setbacks, or drastic journey changes are necessary to align with what is more evolutionary for ourselves, others and the environment. This is where leaders need protection so they minimize the damage that setback has on them and have the mental steadiness and agility to bounce back in a better way."**
>
> *—Raamon Newman, co-founder/CEO of New Mavericks*

Failure is not a stop point, failure is an opportunity to grow, to pivot, and ultimately to expand your consciousness, i.e. the foundation of your life and your business. Of course, it is true that no one wants to fail, even when failure is necessary for success. The reason leaders do not want to experience necessary failures is simply because of fear.

Most fear is irrational, and causes leaders to do crazy things, take rash actions, or sabotage their own success. Of course, we don't know that it is irrational until months or even years later, and by then it is always too late. Fear is like the gum on your shoe that kind of melts down into the crevices of your tread. It's annoying and messy, but over time you kind of forget about it. Then, a sticky edge will break free and all of the sudden you are picking up trash with that sticky edge and getting annoyed. You attempt to scrape it away, and you get most of it, until the next sticky edge breaks free, and there you are, dealing with that gum all over again.

Fear is like this. It never really goes away completely. Every now and then, a new edge breaks free, and there you are, gathering negativity while simultaneously desperately trying to get rid of negativity. Fear works against you, and to get to the bottom of this fear, especially in leadership, you have to go deeper. We point this out because fear frequently precedes failure.

Note: Not all failure is necessary. Yes, we learn from failure, gain wisdom, and discover our purpose. However, it is also a possibility that some wisdom could be gained sooner, some pitfalls avoided altogether.

What Is Failure Anyway?

For you, in your life, in leadership, what do you consider failure to be? It is an important question leaders either skip over or willingly adopt someone else's definition. But defining failure also helps us understand our growth as well.

So if all failure isn't necessary, but some serves a purpose, how do you discern between the two? Which failure is necessary? Now that's a question.

And the answer is: alignment with protection.

The only way you could possibly discern between necessary and unnecessary failures is to align with protection and the knowingness that goes along with that level of development.

Protection allows you to do two things with failure:

1. Protection allows you to experience necessary failure and land softly, avoiding or minimizing damage, and grow from it.

2. Protection allows you to avoid unnecessary failure.

The truth leaders usually lose sight of is that life is innately abundant. When a leader comes with a scarcity mentality and cares more about what is best for their agenda, identity, and image rather than creating abundance, they are starting a time bomb for their failure.

We lose sight of abundance because we get caught up in the routine of life, and being bound by that routine, and our unhealthy cycles, is exactly what stagnates abundance.

Developing your (and others') ability to expand your capacity, coherence, and connectivity to abundance is where you are truly protected from failure.

Case Study: The GE Dow Jones Delisting

We mentioned, earlier in this book, that GE proudly spends more than $1 billion per year on training, development, and education of their people worldwide. Yet, in the last 10 years, GE's revenue has gone from approximately $180 billion to $120 billion, with their net income going from $21 billion to -$5 billion. This decline caused GE to be delisted from the Dow Jones Index of the top 30 biggest industrial companies in the US.

The problem is not a lack of money and effort put into training and development, as we can clearly see in the numbers spent. It is the lack of deeper, more truthful knowledge, which expands the leader's capacity of abundance awareness. Leaders can be well trained and still think small because they don't have the capacity to realize how abundant they are.

Too much focus on achievement, progress, and success, without connecting to the greater capacity of abundance, will lead to eventual failure. Our mind easily falls into the habit of thinking on the level of what we lack, rather than abundance. When we are just pursuing success for the sake of success we are open to threats, unprotected, in a landscape that is exponentially changing at a more rapid pace than we've ever seen.

» Focusing on the wrong things at the wrong time is not being in tune with abundance.
» Success and achievement are limited and come and go as often as the seasons.
» Abundance awareness is not limited and does not come and go.
» We fail when we lose sight of abundance because of stress, ego, lack of alignment, or lack of development.

- When we're happy we have abundance awareness, regardless of the circumstances.
- Being happy is not based on what you have or don't have.
- You can be happy regardless of circumstance or what you think is wrong with you.
- Money is an expression of abundance awareness, which allows you to find ways to attract money.
- When you're happy, you're abundant and you become a magnet to attract good things to you, not failures.
- How you perceive yourself determines when you succeed and fail.
- Abundance is love.
- We suffer and fail when we abandon what is true; the mistake that causes the suffering is just a by-product of doing this.
- We don't suffer when we focus on what is the highest, fullest truth.
- We suffer and fail when we act based on some fleeting experience, temptation, circumstance, or partial truth.

As a child, I remember playing the same video game levels for hours upon hours with neighborhood friends, attempting to beat level after level, most often failing repeatedly. Comparing life to a video game, you only get to move onto the next level once your current level becomes effortless, you've learned where all the secret doors are, and the level has nothing left to offer you. Unless you get cheat codes and skip ahead. Then, you always spend longer (way too long) attempting to fight your way through the level until you've failed enough times to figure it out.

Except in life, you don't have to master the levels, if you master the self-first. Why waste time and energy trying to capture all the mines when you can just capture the fort that owns all the mines?

Stop wasting your own time searching for secret doors you hope will lead to achievement—and seek protection instead. Once you do that, the secrets of the levels reveal themselves to you willingly. That doesn't mean you skip the levels, but it means you see the potential failures coming, and you learn to thrive through them, experiencing more bliss and abundance along the way.

There are two kinds of leaders in this world.
Which one do you think fails (unnecessarily) more often?

Evolving from Failure to Protected Success

The list of Fortune 500 companies from decade to decade paints a scary portrait of failure and rapid change in business. For example, 88% of the companies on the list in 1955 were no longer on the list by 2015. We predict that from 2015 through 2050 we will see even more drastic changes in the Fortune 500 listings because market disruption is happening at the most rapid and exponential rate we've seen yet. Being cognizant of this amazing rate of change is so important because leaders believe they are making the right decisions, but they aren't coherent and developed enough to realize all of the possibilities.

You would never choose a car if you could only see half the features each option provided. The same is true in business. You are playing a dangerous game of risk by constantly making decisions while only being able to recognize or see some of the possibilities. That's why this vision we talk about is so necessary to your success. Your mind has to be open to the field of all possibilities, so that you can perceive the best option to protect what you're building. Being in a position of leadership and primarily responsible for results and progress is irrelevant if there is no true leadership intelligence.

Imagine if every cell in your body had no nucleus, and therefore no DNA or central leadership intelligence. The cells would have no coherence or clarity on what to do or what direction to take. There would be no protein synthesis or cell division. Because of this, the cells would not coordinate with other cells or the body's whole physiology. This destructive lack of direction, or coherence, in the nucleus—the "brain" of the cell—would inevitably lead to the decline and eventual death of the cell.

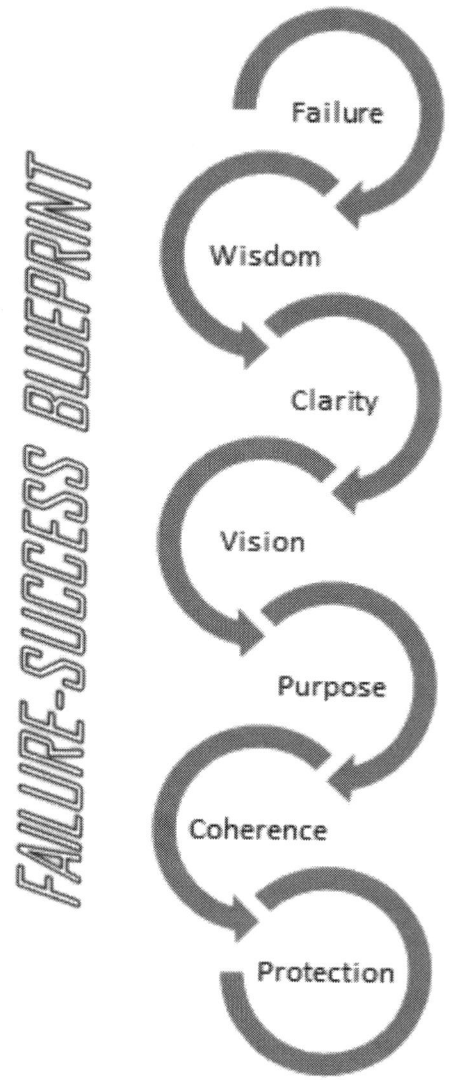

Dying Leadership

According to Stanford Professor Jeffrey Pfeffer, the workplace is the fifth leading cause of death in the United States. In his book *Dying for a Paycheck*, Pfeffer confirms what we have also experienced in our research and consulting work: "Many modern management commonalities such as long work hours, work-family conflict, and economic insecurity are toxic to employees—hurting engagement, increasing turnover, and destroying people's physical and emotional health—and also inimical to company performance."

Harper Business published Dying for a Paycheck early in 2018, calling for CEOs and leaders to wake up to the harsh impact of our business economy on their own and their employees' lives, recognize their part in all of it, and to, at the very least, admit that the physical, emotional, and psychological effects were literally killing people.

Here's where the Science of Protection comes into play. Rather than blame, rather than place the weight of the world on the shoulders of leaders, like a modern day Atlas, we must recognize the necessary point that there is a better path. Thousands of hours of meditative silence have taught us that true leadership is something we align with through coherence, not something we achieve through habits and routines.

Leadership is the nucleus, the center of everything occurring, and if it is not operating properly, there will be chaos. Leadership is totality, not a part. Leadership is existence plus expression, not only expression, as most think. This means that leadership is a state of existence within a person, not a set of habits or qualities.

Love Is Universal. Leadership is Universal. Protection Is Universal.

This direction of thought brings us to wonder, what is leading you? What is your source of leadership? What type of leader are you? Have you experienced the leadership state? If not, do you want to? And if so, do you want to more often? Do you want to learn how to stabilize your "zone" so high performance is a by-product of your development, capacity, and coherence?

The answer is protection.

Protection is freedom…

…Freedom of thought, creativity, and growth.

…Freedom to achieve, connect, and expand.

…Freedom from stress, failure, and negativity.

…Freedom from what ails modern day leaders.

…Freedom from a potentially early downfall.

This leadership state provides protection by creating space for more moments of ultimate clarity, where the pieces connect effortlessly and work fully in-sync with the outcome desired. For the first time ever, we can tell you how to get there, how to harness the power of "the zone" and how to lead from this state, where infinite possibilities exist and high performance becomes normal.

This isn't about strength or making the most power plays or achieving the most. The Universe will enable that which is morally right and just, which means you will just be along for the ride. Unless you decide to connect with that world, with that inner source, with that consciousness, because when you do this, you are less along for the ride and more in the know of what will and must happen, in every situation, all the time. This shift takes you from control to alignment. You could never possibly control the potentiality of the entire Universe. But you could align with that knowledge and fluctuate with the changes, putting yourself into a territory inhabited by truly elite leaders.

This is how protection works in leadership, and we don't know one leader, right now, who wouldn't benefit from making this shift.

The State You Exist in, in Every Moment, *Will* Strongly Influence the Outcome of that Moment

This shift allows you to develop the unique ability to operate from anywhere, anytime, under any conditions. To be the eye of the storm, no matter what is happening around you. Your ability to lead and make the right decisions, while remaining calm, with a clear mind, and taking a broad perspective, is something most leaders do not experience.

This is why we see high performers begin to breakdown, physically, around the age of 50. The stress of leading, making powerful decisions, having to bear the weight of numbers and expectations, and being in semi-constant chaos takes its toll. But it doesn't have to. Are you dying for your paycheck? Is your desire to put one more car in the garage, one more trophy in the case, killing you? At some point, we have to recognize the fact that this is not true leadership, nor is it worth the destruction. When the high of achievement wears off, and the noise fades, and the silence takes over, what foundation are you standing on? What state do you exist in?

Breaking the Cycle

Our societies tend to favor the outside, rather than taking care of the inside. There is a definite fear of loss that is driving this business culture. We think, "If I don't keep my attention outward, I'm going to lose something." And when you do this, you lose protection and you leave your leadership state. Even worse, if you do fail, you will not benefit from the Failure Success Blueprint we illustrated, because you aren't in a state to receive new wisdom, and your time will be spent on cleanup and chaos control.

You have to learn to stop relying on your capabilities and past experiences and instead focus on expanding your capacity.

Think about all the time you spend trying to come up with the right answer, calculating movements, trying to predict others' motivations or actions, trying to avoid failure, and brainstorming to come up with creative ideas. All the time spent looking over your shoulder, succumbing to fear, seeking external protection, and acting from a state of chaos probably taught you a lot, maybe even left some scars—but it's time to move on from this way of dying leadership.

Every single answer or solution exists within you. When you expand your capacity, you will have access to those potential answers or solutions. Imagine how much more productive you would be if you were not only able to go to that state, but if you were expanded enough to exist in that state consistently. You could easily pick up on the right insights at the right time. Think of how much time you would stop wasting trying to always figure things out. There's an entire world happening around you right now, and you can't see it. This leadership state we are talking about, when stabilized, will open your eyes like you can't imagine. We want this for you because this is what's best for you. And you should want this for yourself because this is the path to the absolute most fulfilling life you can lead. This is the true path to expanded leadership.

Accountability Disclaimer

If you think this approach hands all accountability over to the Universe, you couldn't be more wrong. The topic of protection carries with it a heavy dose of accountability because this is what is necessary for you to expand. There is a Universal law of truthfulness which reminds us that the truth always prevails. Accountability is rooted in brutal honesty, and in order for you to gain this honesty that applies to everything, you have to first and foremost be honest about who you are, your motives, your desires, your goals, and so on. A person of accountability can get a negative reputation as the bad guy or kill joy, but in all reality, a person of accountability is ultimately admired and respected because they help you see where you can grow more, ultimately leading to more success.

There's a quote that says, "Some people create their own storms and then get angry when it rains." As you explore The Science of Protection vertically and horizontally, you will see that both the depth and the width belong to you. You are not the waves, you are the ocean. The waves come and go, the ocean doesn't, and your experiences in your life reflect this.

It is easy to accept responsibility for our achievements, but it takes a much more developed leader to also accept accountability for pitfalls along the way. The point is not to be a martyr or to punish yourself, but so you can understand what happened, what went wrong, and how you can grow from the experience. Refer back to the Failure Success Blueprint to be clear on the process.

Think about a time you felt the sting of failure and mentally walk yourself back through that experience. Did you gain wisdom and clarity from that failure? Did you have a clearer vision moving forward? Was a purpose revealed to you? Did you experience increased coherence as a result of the failure? Did you feel more protected moving forward? If the answer is no to each step in the Failure Success Blueprint, be cautious. The lesson in that failure will revisit you, again and again, until you have enough protection and capacity to move forward.

Protection provides the platform for this process to take place effortlessly for you, day in and day out, so that you are always in a state of accelerated growth without applying all of your energy and effort. This allows you to apply your energy, creativity, and capacity to other things in your life.

We also know, based on that Universal law of truthfulness, when the truth is on our side, and we are living in that truth, triumph will also be ours. This creates deserving power (or power of deserving), *the sixth step of the Science of Protection.*

Leadership, Failure, and Future Success

We've talked about the leadership state, real leadership, the different types of leaders, and even the benefits of failure. Let's close this chapter out by discussing success. This point is important because once leaders find success; they usually ride the wave all the way until it crashes down on the shore.

As a leader, you need to know that the higher you go, the harder your wave will potentially crash down, and the more coherent you have to be to ensure you don't suffer from a crash. Achieving and progressing without simultaneously developing ever-increasing coherence inside yourself could create a potentially devastating crash that may be hard to recover from.

How many leaders and celebrities have had their status stripped from them virtually overnight in the last few years? We've lost count. A failure to develop more coherence in their prefrontal cortex, CEO of the brain, in their process of achieving and progressing has eventually caught up with them and, one by one, they end up right back at square one. The choice is simple: either develop your inner coherence as you achieve and progress, to be in tune with evolutionary life supporting change and growth, or don't, and be a victim of that change.

Protected coherent change and progress starts from within, at the most settled yet dynamic, alert, truthful, and powerful level of the mind. Like an arrow pulled back fully on a bow, with the power and intelligence to change and progress existing in this silent dynamic state of potential energy, this is the moment preceding decision and action that determines how effective a decision and action will be. Where the arrow lands, the speed at which it travels, and the accuracy of its destiny all depend on the moment right before the arrow takes flight, as the bow is positioned and the arrow pulled back.

The key to making changes is by first making the changes from within, and then going out. By taking one step back you gain coherence, energy, and the ability to take two-three-four-five steps forward. This is the inner foundation for stabilized and protected achievement and progress.

If you don't regularly pull the arrow back—meaning taking your mind back to its coherent and silent source, and making needed changes and adjustments from within—you won't have as much coherence to support and protect more achievement and progress.

If you lack this coherence, you won't benefit from the experience of failure, either, because you won't be in tune with any of the changes happening or required. Your success requires this coherence, and the only way to get it is through inner development.

The leadership state, the ultimate zone of clarity and right-thought/right-action coherence, is the future of business. This is your opportunity to align with the changes coming, rather than falling victim to the accelerated changes that are headed your way. This will be the new definition of success for the future of business.

YOUR TURN

Where is Your Leadership?

1. What leadership myths do you feel are affecting you right now?
2. On a scale of 1 to 10, how would you rate your ability to be in the zone and stay in the zone most of the time?
3. What type of leader do you feel you've been to this point, and what type of leader would you like to be going forward? Use the pairs of opposites outlined in this chapter to rate and inspire yourself; for example, command vs. communicate, individual vs. whole, detract vs. attract, conflict vs. peace, intellect vs. consciousness, achievement vs. awareness, ego vs. love, reactive vs. proactive.
4. What conflicts do you need to resolve within and outside yourself?
5. How is your current attitude toward failure? Do you require a mindset shift about failure? What can you do to bounce back quickly from failures and setbacks?
6. How can you make your leadership more universal, so you're less run by your ego and more run from a state that supports and protects all aspects of your and others' lives?

PART 2

INTERNAL PROTECTION DEVELOPMENT

3) Purification
4) Coherence
5) Leadership State

3 Purification

Purifying Fear of Loss, Stress, Bad Impressions, and Inner Enemies

Purifying these enables smoother more supported progress.

Purification is the process of purifying, removing, dissolving or resolving unwanted negativity, stresses, vices, toxins, incoherence, from a system so you have less resistance, more simplicity and energy.

This is the first step to establishing protection inside and outside of you.

Purifying yourself and your environment allows better things to come in. Progress alone cannot happen without purification. These are messages we consistently remind our clients of because they're so gripped with wanting to progress, not realizing the basis for progressing most effectively is purifying what needs to be purified first. If you want better digestion, it would be wise to first purify the toxins in your system causing bad digestion while shifting to a healthier diet.

The same can also be done with leadership, business, culture and reputation. This chapter goes deep into discussing what has to be purified in yourself and your leadership to activate maximum protected progress.

The Process of Purifying

The process of purifying fear or any stresses, past bad impressions, and inner enemies (vices like greed, anger, lust, jealousy, vanity, and false attachments) is reserved for the most developed leaders in business. Not because we aren't openly sharing this information, simply because leaders who aren't developed either:

1. Have a hard time admitting in the first place they have fear or retain past bad impressions, stresses, and vices.

2. Are unwilling to accept the truth that fear exists in them.

3. Have blind spots preventing them from seeing how fear is affecting them.

Purification is an often overlooked component of achievement, and is an especially important factor for sustained achievement. Purification is the first and most vital component of the Science of Protection. You have to clear away that which impedes and blocks progress to create something new. Leaders get in their own way due to having unresolved stresses, vices and incoherence's that impede them. Purification is the process that allows you to naturally dissolve resistances to getting out of your own way so progress can naturally unfold. We can only get the best from our body when we've removed the deeper stresses that make us feel tense. Regular continual purification is required for optimal progress and the protection of that progress.

A leader with a tired, stressed, fatigued, distracted or overly excited mind isn't going to see the best way to progress, and more than likely make costly mistakes. These incoherence's have to be removed first, then one can more easily have a more coherent orderly settled and clear mind to naturally know the best way forward. Unfortunately, leaders don't take enough time or know how to do this most effectively due to being gripped by the need to always be seen to be taking action. This results in making more costly mistakes than necessary, which then leads to thinking it's okay and normal.

Purifying Fear of Loss

The fear of loss is an overwhelming lump in your throat that can cause you to choke at crucial moments, hold you back, or push you forward at the wrong times, based on the wrong reasons.

Fear has the ability to permeate everything you create and achieve in life and make you stressed. At times, you might not even be aware of this fear, because it moves below the surface, dictating thoughts and action unbeknownst to you.

In general, the fear of loss is losing something that is very important to you and you're very attached to. A predominance of fear causes us to function from our lower brain amygdala, causing fight, flight or freeze reactions, without much use of the higher brain to properly and holistically interpret those impulses to know if the fear is real or not. Most of the time fear is a phantom, a mirage of the mind. It appears to be real yet it is not.

In business, the fear of loss is that feeling of doom and gloom, that if you do not stay in constant motion, you will lose. The fear of loss also tells you that you have to hold onto everything you achieve, which causes unnecessary stress during periods of change and growth. This fear is an overwhelming lump in your throat, holding you back at the wrong times, and then pushing you forward when you should hold steady.

Because of this fear we are afraid to stop the speeding train of the hyper-competitive modern business world. We are afraid to pause, if even for a moment, because we are responding to the fear that is driving us rather than focusing on the big picture. Fear interferes with our coherence, and forces us to underestimate or overestimate the effects of change. You and your business cannot afford the unnecessary risks driven by fear, with this fear being heightened by change.

One of our clients worked so incredibly hard to develop and grow his leadership state that he actually outgrew his leadership position at the helm of a business worth hundreds of millions of dollars. He knew he was ready to move on and embark on a journey that was more fitting of his capacity, but he was afraid. The fear of loss, absent during his ascent to the top, slowly crept into the back of his mind, and was actively interfering with his desire to let go of his prestigious position he knew so well. That voice of fear would say things like, "You'd be crazy to give something like this up" and "Look how far you've come—what if you fail after this?" and "You've already achieved so much, what's the point in moving on?"

Fear oftentimes wears disguises, and in this case the disguise was "rationality," telling him to stay where he was safe and had it made.

Your voice of fear is probably agreeing with these statements right now. We've been taught that the conventional lists of achievements and experiences are worth more than anything else.

We hear people say things all the time about change and letting go to make room for change. The problem with thinking this way is, change can be good or bad, and how do you know when to let go? And which change is good or bad? And how do you know when the voice guiding you is your voice of fear or your inner awareness?

The answer to all of those questions is the same. When you exist in your leadership state, and have developed your inner awareness, you are protected. This protection is your preventative insurance policy. Rather than paying out after the damage is done, protection pays out before the damage is done- by guiding you and expanding your big picture view to see all of the possibilities. When your prefrontal cortex is developed, not only are you capable of the level of coherence that is required of true, high-level leaders, you are also capable of intellectually understanding the path of your success. This is where we see leaders confidently navigating the good change while steering away from the bad change. You just know.

When change is happening, you must awake to that change before it happens, or be left behind. The truth is that we are all afraid, and for good reason. We are inundated with negativity everywhere we look; we see leaders around us fall hard and early in their careers.

What you have to begin to understand, as a true leader, is that this is your choice. You can choose fear or you can choose protection. It's 100% a choice, your choice. Leaders who choose fear, consciously or unconsciously, either don't know that there is something better or, ironically, are afraid to choose something better. This is a perfect example of how deep fear can run, and how damaging its effects are.

Fear creates a victim mentality. When we are afraid, "we can't believe these things happen to us" and "we did everything we could" and we "don't know why this keeps happening to us" and we "can't believe someone else would do this to us."

A developed leader is not a victim of change. A developed leader is a victor of change because they are a product of protection. Fear creates a mental downward cycle which creates an external downward cycle of action. It goes like this: fear, stress, action from fear, putting out fires, fear, stress, action from fear, and putting out more fires.

This cycle is nearly impossible to escape because, in order to break it, you would have to simultaneously eliminate the fear, get ahead of the change, and practice patience. If that sounds like an impossible set of tasks to add to your everyday to do list, that's because it is. Which is exactly why leaders stay trapped in their fear for a long time, and why they so often plateau and die early. It is exactly why only 1% of leaders will ever reach their full capacity and potential.

Collectively, we have to stop letting fear of loss prevent us from reaching our full capacity. We have to strive for something better.

Is the Fear of Loss Driving *You*?

Think back about the story we shared of our client who suffered the stroke. He was so afraid to stop achieving that he tabled his health and forged a destructive path ahead, all in the name of success.

Everyone is well aware of Steve Job's story. The pieces that we seem to acknowledge less are the most telling aspects of his journey. Jobs gave up everything to achieve, to solidify his legacy and set the future on fire. He led and succeeded in his efforts to create amazing, world changing hardware and software, only to have his own humanware become corrupted, diminished, and sadly lost soon after.

When his health came into question, he was so detached from his inner self that the clear path could have been labeled and he still might not have taken it. This devastating loss of life, too early, too fast, is something that could have been prevented. We watch leader after leader take the sacrificial path, and for what? Imagine the good Jobs could still be contributing to the tech world if he were still here.

Fear of loss is often the driver on this sacrificial path, accelerating us toward the cliff, with no intent on braking. When we are detached from our inner self, we are attached to our external achievements. It doesn't have to be this way. Inner fulfillment and outer achievement can coexist in a way that is evolutionary and protected.

> **"Far more money has been lost by investors trying to anticipate corrections, than has been lost in corrections themselves."**
>
> —*Peter Lynch*

What Type of Action Are You Taking?

There are two types of action:

1. There is individual action that helps leaders evolve their physical and material needs.

2. There is evolutionary action that helps leaders evolve their awareness and coherence capacity.

Of these two, the only action that is protected is evolutionary action.

Individual action is where you have to take care of the obstacles confronting you, are viewing (and reacting to) short-term challenges, and act out of regard for the self over the whole. This type of action is often fear-driven and short-sighted.

Evolutionary action is where you have support from your environment and nature takes care of you and your obstacles. This protection allows you to take a longer, broader view of challenges, changes, and potential opportunities. This type of action represents coherence and forward thinking, and always leads to long-term gain, not just for you, for everyone.

Favoring evolutionary action is what enables you to master the fear of loss. In order to favor evolutionary action, you must stabilize your outer world, and the only way to stabilize your outer world is to align with your inner stability. You cannot create protection, nor do you need to. This protection exists everywhere, in everything, even in you. To live in the reality of protection, you must align with that reality.

Fear Is often Mistaken for Courage

Courage is a word leaders seem to love, and often misidentify. We create these unnecessary conflicts from our fear of loss and then, when we go to battle them, we call that courage. That isn't courage. That is one big bundle of fear. It's all fear actually, from beginning to end. And when we face those self-created fears for self-gain, we call that courage. That isn't courage either. It's still fear—from beginning to end.

Courage is the ability to do something in spite of fear, challenges, and risks. In Steve Jobs case, we might say that he was courageous in the face of his illness. We might also say that he was courageous in his journey to share his tech vision with the world.

Courage is being able to honestly identify fear, the root source of it, and to be developed enough to know whether you should pause or take action. It's the ability and skill to trust your heart and mind, and you can really only trust your heart and mind when they are coherently aligned with one another. Courage is not fearing loss and then being forced to act on that fear, creating and then fighting unnecessary battles, all in the name of self-gain or self-preservation. Real courage is going inward to silence to know what is right action and then taking that action, not being attached to action for the sake of being seen to be taking action.

Fear is a sneaky weasel, tricking you into a reality and mindset that is inhibiting your inner growth and holding you hostage to its cyclical actions and consequences. Everything fear creates seems so real, but it isn't. Fear is mostly an illusion. The moment that you stop feeding the fear of loss cycle is the exact same moment that cycle will cease to exist.

The key to this shift is inner development. This is the answer to every disruption, fear of loss cycle, failure, or challenge you face as a leader. When you're able to connect with your deeper, purer, coherent Self, you'll know that every bit of this knowledge is true, and you'll know there's another reality. This deeper reality gives you more inner stability, invincibility, and protection. Inner stability is not created by what we do. We're familiar with the outer stability, in terms of achievement or having enough money to support a comfortable lifestyle. Outer stability is what we achieve. In contrast, inner stability is how grounded and unaffected we are inside by the external changes, challenges, and risks we face.

"Stress is fear."

—Louise Hay

Fear of Loss Also Applies to Acknowledgement

Oprah gave a speech at Harvard, and in that speech, she pointed out something you might find surprising. She said that after every interview she did, no matter how successful or how powerful the interviewee was, they always asked her the same thing: "How did I do?" They needed accolades, to be appreciated and acknowledged, to know that they did okay. This is very telling of how the fear of loss is so embedded into our lives, regardless of how far we go or how much we achieve.

If we go one step further, peel back one more layer, it is apparent that we achieve to be loved, to be appreciated, and to matter. As humans, we fear this loss of achievement because—the Beatles said it best—all we need is love.

The shift to inner development provides the acknowledgement and fulfillment and love that most leaders seek out from achievement. When you start with a full bucket, it will overflow regularly. If your bucket is empty, your time spent filling it takes away from your impact as a leader.

When you aren't stuck in a constant cycle of seeking out accolades, achieving, and fearing loss, you can do and be so much more, and it happens with much less effort.

Wavering between inner and outer realities also impedes on your abilities as a leader.

For many leaders, it isn't one reality or the other driving them—it's both. But it isn't both at the same time; it's a constant shift between the two, which doesn't work either. Because high level leaders often have more inner development than they realize, they find themselves experiencing the leadership state. A state of increased coherence that supports having x-factor agility, courage and protection. Then because it's not stabilized, they end up flipping back into the fear of loss and achievement cycle.

This shift, to a focus on inner development, helps stabilize and enable that leadership state. The more a leader develops their inner self, the more their outer state reflects this development, and the less a leader will find themselves flipping between the two realities.

This integrated leadership state is the Holy Grail when it comes to leadership, business, and high-level performance. This is the best, most efficient, most fulfilling way to lead. Your leadership state enables you to stay true and in tune, so you don't have to compromise your instincts or your values to lead or achieve.

Case Study: Tesla vs. Volkswagen

Elon Musk building out Tesla is a great example of evolutionary versus individual action. Over 10 years ago, Musk shared his master plan for Tesla, identifying exactly why he was taking action, and where he hoped that action would lead his revolutionary brand. Step one of his master plan was to create an expensive, low-volume car. Tesla would then use that money to develop a less expensive, medium volume car, and so on. In Musk's own words:

> **"The reason we had to start off with step one was that it was all I could afford to do with what I made from PayPal. I thought our chances of success were so low that I didn't want to risk anyone's funds in the beginning but my own. The list of successful car company startups is short. As of 2016, the number of American car companies that haven't gone bankrupt is a grand total of two: Ford and Tesla. Starting a car company is idiotic and an electric car company is idiocy squared."**

So Musk, understanding the business landscape, and working in alignment with his beliefs, along with evolutionary action, has just hit the

300,000th production mark on electric cars, and they are only beginning. While Musk was busy playing out his master plan, Volkswagen was busy attempting to interrupt that plan. Their desire to be number one in environmentally friendly vehicles to beat out Tesla, among other competition, created a company culture at Volkswagen that overrode their moral belief systems for the sake of winning. Of course, they only won in the short-term because when the public found out Volkswagen had been cheating on emissions testing, the outrage was as expected. When the dust settled around the scandal, Volkswagen went back to work, determined to undermine Tesla's success, in a more truthful way. With $280+ billion in revenue, Volkswagen has the resources to forge a mighty path ahead, and ironically, by doing so, they are moving everyone closer to Musk's vision of sustainable solar energy. As a by-product of pushing to win, Volkswagen is also helping Tesla and Elon Musk to realize their vision for the future. When action is evolutionary, you have the support of your environment. Sometimes this looks like minimal friction along the way; and sometimes this looks like your competition setting out to beat you, while simultaneously working to help your vision become reality.

In the second quarter of 2018, Tesla surpassed analysts' estimates by producing 5,000 Model 3 vehicles per week, increasing revenue to $4 billion from $2.79 billion in 2017. Their progress seems well protected.

Then at the beginning of 2018, Musk's controversial behavior made investors cautious about the brand's recovery, and he has lost support from some devoted supporters, like Instinet, causing a 2.1 percent stock price decrease in one day in September. Only time will tell whether Musk will be developed enough to protect himself and his company's progress.

Relearning the Benefits of Patience

To be in tune with change requires patience. Sometimes you have to briefly pause and allow the best solutions to appear. If you haven't mastered the fear of loss, this will be seemingly impossible, because the fear will spur action—any action—over patience. Patience through pausing allows you to separate yourself from the gripping fear of a fast-paced life.

This is important because fear causes you to:

» Act irrationally
» Take unnecessary risks
» Make costly mistakes

Pausing helps you transition from the fear of loss to the joy of potential new growth, adopting a more motivated and forward-thinking mindset.

The rapid rate of change in our business economy forces leaders into an endless series of fear of loss cycles, leaving them no room for patience, pausing, or silence. When leaders are faced with uncertainty or challenges, they feel compelled to act immediately, to put out whatever fire may be sparking up, or to make sudden changes. You cannot afford to do this any longer.

Moving forward, this new approach of patience through pausing and silencing the mind will help you purify the noise in your mind, allow you to be more coherent to stabilize your leadership state and compete at a high level, sustainably. In the chapter on coherence we recommend the most validated way to do this.

The reason why pauses and patience through silence is so important is because it heightens discerning power to make the right decision. We've all been involved in business situations where a decision has been made and it turns out to not be the right decision, often leading to derailed progress, or at worst a failed business. Like Juicero, that raised more than $118 million in funding from top prominent VCs like Google Ventures, Kleiner Perkins, Melo7 Tech venture fund … even The Campbell Soup Company threw money at it. Leaders hold the reigns of great responsibility for making the right decisions that ensure and protect a company's progress in the right direction, so it ultimately succeeds.

Our ability to fulfill an outcome, or at least make great progress towards it while maximizing positivity and minimizing negativity and stress along the way, comes down to having good discerning power. This power allows you to make the best decisions that support this happening. You can't fulfill outcomes if your discerning power is not well developed because you can't decide properly. Making an important decision needs to be based on clearly knowing what is right for everyone involved, especially the marketplace being served. We all think there's a choice when in reality there's no choice, there's only the right choice.

The ability to correctly discern and decide comes down to our intellect and intuition, which is simply a more refined aspect of our intellect. This is the responsibility of the sub-thalamus in the brain. The thalamus perceives the possibilities to the degree it is awake and coherent, and the sub-thalamus processes both logic and feeling to discern and decide what is best given the situation.

The key to having great discerning power, to make right decisions, is having a good level of silence in your mind. This creates a more settled coherent alert mind that more clearly feels, sees and knows the right decisions. The most powerful culture is a culture based on silence, not a flat dull silence where no one speaks up, rather a lively dynamic silence that empowers people to powerfully speak up with the right energy, intelligence and insights that gives clear direction to making the best decision. Culturing the most powerful culture based on silence requires deeper knowledge, techniques and technologies that cultures silence in the minds of leaders and those they lead. Something we've spent a combined total of 25 years developing as full-time meditating monks and 20 years implementing with top leaders around the world.

Leaders must have a high level of energy and strength in mind and body because investors are really buying this first and are feeling and testing if you're fickle or not. They want a strong coherent CEO. Being influenced and affected by challenges and resistances means your mind is weak. This is why internal protection development is required.

Remember, there are two types of action, and only one is protected. The only way you are going to have the insight and knowledge to know the difference is through development of coherence. And there are two types of leaders, with only one being protected: the patient, coherent, developed leader.

This ability to pause and transcend the noise, fear, and uncertainty is the first step in your transition from the fear of loss to the joy of growth. By pausing and being patient, you avoid unnecessary risks, you interpret situations better, and you can see more of the bigger picture. Patience through pausing and silencing the mind will help you go beyond fear that a fast-paced life can create.

Case Study: Long-Term Capital Management

With two Nobel Laureates on their startup staff, and star trader John Meriwether as their founder, Long-Term Capital Management started as strong as any hedge fund could start. The firm began with $1 billion in seed capital in 1994, but by 1998, its impending collapse almost took the global market down, along with all of LTCM's pennies. At the very beginning, everyone was banking on the success of this giant, literally, as investors clamored to get in. The price tag to participate was a cool $10 million, and investors were locked in for three years. Under no circumstance could they request information about the investments being made on their behalf. The reputations of its owners kick started a frenzy and the cash flowed into the billions.

As Warren Buffet pointed out after the fact, "To make money they didn't have and didn't need, they risked what they did have and did need. And that's foolish." But they seemed too big to fail. They had their finger on the pulse, and their resources were in the billions, so what went wrong?

Of course, there are plenty of theories about this massive failure, and they may all share in the truth in some way, but one thing we know is for certain: the firm lacked developed leaders who could see far enough into the future to take evolutionary action.

Their belief system in this giant working forever was based on their experience, resources, and desire to achieve, which, as they proved, is not enough. Nor is it a protected route. LTCM's leaders' lack of foresight could have proved devastating for small banks, and sent the financial world spiraling into chaos, all for gains they ended up losing anyway.

When you take action on faulty beliefs, your level of intelligence or experience doesn't matter. When you lack the development to take evolutionary action, your level of intelligence or experience doesn't matter. When you lack the ability to pause, rather than acting from a place of fear, your level of intelligence or experience doesn't matter.

Intelligence and experience are not the sum of a great leader, contrary to popular belief. A developed leadership state, where evolutionary action is clear and fear is not the driver, is the true measure of a leader.

Jeffrey Likers' book The Toyota Way classifies the 14 principles driving the world's greatest manufacturer. Principle number 13 sounds quite familiar: "Make decisions slowly by consensus, thoroughly considering all options; implement decisions rapidly." This ability to pause, a key factor in Toyota's decision-making process, is a cornerstone to sustainable, long-term success.

"Adopt the pace of nature: her secret is patience."

—Ralph Waldo Emerson

Taking a note from Mother Nature, we must learn to pause as well. Don't let the fear of loss drive you into unnecessary and non-evolutionary action. Just like the truths in the previous chapters, the truths in this chapter are not ours; they are the design of the Universe, and designed into the Universe. When we act in accordance with these truths, we fall easily into alignment with evolutionary action, and gain protection as a by-product.

As a true leader, you must choose to lead into the future, rather than from the past.

You will never lead into the future, if you are stuck in a cycle of leading from the past. The only way to break that cycle of leading from the past is to achieve freedom from the stress and conditioning you have experienced. Stress most forcefully strikes us when we are stretched beyond our coherence or capacity. So, the obvious answer or solution to stress is to purify it so you can increase coherence, which we discuss in the next chapter.

Good Stress vs. Bad Stress

Externally, stress is a part of life. Without healthy or good stress there wouldn't be a stimulus to act, to take care of our health, wealth, happiness, relationships, and reputation. The unhealthy, or bad stress occurs when we internally take on the external stress, or allow it to invade our mind, heart, and nervous and immune systems. In this state, it is very difficult to achieve what we want, protect it, and keep it.

Stress Is the Unseen Enemy in Your Life

Another word for stress is incoherence. When internal and or external incoherence/stress is stronger and more powerful than our coherence, we become stressed. When left unchecked, this can lead to incoherent thoughts, feelings, behaviors, actions, crime, or even violence. We often view stress as situational, however stress doesn't live in a little box. It touches every area of our lives.

Workplace violence is on the rise for the fourth consecutive year, according to the latest data from the U.S. Bureau of Labor Statistics. We know, here we are, back to talking about stress…again. But here's the thing: even with our clients, we talk about stress repeatedly, yet we still see plenty of leaders default to acknowledging stress while not doing enough to dissolve it, especially when the impressions from past stress and trauma, or fear, run deep, and end up becoming a victim of stress.

The current average life span of a human being is around 30,000 days. Your ability to dissolve or avoid stress will determine the quality, productivity, and happiness of those days. Your ability to dissolve stress well will also determine how protected you are while achieving and progressing during those days. When you're truly dissolving bad stress, you may even gain the opportunity to live beyond those 30,000 days.

Bad stress creates impressions. Those impressions can mask our decision-making process and cause us to make decisions that are not in full favor of our evolution, achievement, and progress. Simply put, stress will cause you to undermine your own success without you even realizing it.

What Are Bad Impressions?

When you see those two words stuck together, what comes to mind? Probably, upon a first-time meeting, what others think of you or what you think of others. However, the most influential bad impressions are your internal impressions, the ones based on what you think about yourself. These bad impressions are based on past experiences that have negatively influenced you; you have created belief systems around these bad experiences, belief systems which take up space in your subconscious mind.

These faulty belief systems wreak havoc on both the micro and macro levels of your leadership, probably without your even realizing it. Equivalent to shackles bearing the weight of every individual past emotion, thought, or action, these impressions weigh you down. They reinforce your fear of loss, keep you stuck in cycles you hate, and even cause or continue self-destructive behaviors and habits that you are way too intelligent to keep perpetuating.

These bad impressions are like tire tracks. When the roads are clear and everything is fine, they seem to be gone, erased from your subconscious. But the minute it snows, or the road conditions get a little muddy, your tires fall right back into those tracks and travel that already determined path, the one of least resistance. This is the reason self-help fails for many leaders in the long run:

1. The road conditions clear up temporarily, the leader believes they are free from their bad impressions or the negative cycle they were trying to break, and they stop working on their internal development.

2. The impressions (or tire tracks) are deeper than the development the leader is attempting.

In both scenarios listed above, the leader is tricked into believing their development is changing their habits, ridding them of their conditioning, and changing their life. Then suddenly, when the road conditions change, it is too late for that leader to take a deeper look and figure out why they are "on this road again," because they are too busy spinning their tires. When you are in the middle of putting out a fire, it is not the time to question how the fire happened, how big it might become, or why you are there in the first place. You must first focus on putting out the fire and trying your hardest to minimize damage—you ask questions later. When you get stuck, and the tires are spinning, you aren't trying to figure out why. You are trying to get unstuck as quickly as possible with the least amount of damage.

All the while, those impressions have still been in the driver's seat, solidifying your belief system, upon which you base your entire life, business philosophy, and approach to leadership. Chris Griffiths, a Toronto based entrepreneur, describes his bad impressions like this, "I've had seven businesses over the past 20 years and let me tell you, they were not all entrepreneurial fairy tales. In fact, in those two decades, there were months of memories that still tie knots in my stomach." These bad impressions can cripple a leader going forward unless they purify them and turn them into valuable lessons and wisdom as Chris did.

What Role Does Fear Play in Bad Impressions?

Unsurprisingly, one of the biggest reinforcements of bad impressions is fear. Once again, an example of fear causing chaos in your life and disrupting your alignment with your true abilities and purpose as a leader.

Fear, in this case, might not look or even sound like fear as you usually know it. When it comes to bad impressions, fear can take many forms, tricking you into action or inaction that is not evolutionary. When we speak with clients and the word fear comes up, it is generally followed by an unusually long silence. High level leaders have never been the ones to admit or submit to fear. As a leader, you aren't "built that way," so to speak, and that is probably how you have been able to strategize, calculate, and take risks others weren't willing to.

What we want you to know, as you grow into an even more refined leader, is that fear exists within all of us, and the sooner you can recognize this truth, the sooner you can move into fearless territory. That's not to say some fear isn't a healthy response to the world around you, but there is a major difference between the fear that we rely upon to detect danger, and the deceptive fear that tricks us into believing there is danger around every corner, or the fear that makes decisions for us subconsciously, or the fear that prevents us from becoming invincible and fulfilling our potential. This brings to mind the parable of the snake and the string, which goes something like this:

> A man is walking alone in the woods as night falls upon him. In the light of the moon, he can see something just ahead in the middle of his path. As he gets closer to the object, the man realizes there is a poisonous snake blocking his way and he runs off in the opposite direction. The following morning, the man returns to the same path and finds a coiled string on the ground. The man realizes that he mistook the string as a snake, and that his perception had been clouded by fear and rapid judgment.

When we are not in tune with reality, unable to see the bigger picture, paralyzed by fear, or acting out of partial knowledge, we make mistakes. How many times in business have you mistook a string for a snake and acted too quickly? Most of life is just strings, yet we always seem to imagine the snake and take action based on the snake, whether it exists or not. The snake represents our worst stresses, fears, and impressions; the snake is our tendency to assume the worst possible scenario, and then take action based on that perception. The irony is that when you fear the potential snake bite, that fear poisons you, whether you get bit or not.

As *Star Wars* Jedi knight Obi Wan Kenobi says, "Your eyes can deceive you. Don't trust them." But it isn't actually your eyes encouraging the perception. It's your internal coherence (or lack thereof) that is driving your ability to predict, which is influenced by fear, stress, and past experiences.

John Stumpf resigned from Wells Fargo after 34 years of service, having held the CEO position for over 9 years. He resigned after a scandal revealed more than 2 million customer accounts had been opened by Wells Fargo employees without the customers' approval.

In two congressional hearings, Stumpf blamed low-level employees instead of holding himself and other top executives accountable. A further 1.4 million more fake accounts from Stumpf's tenure were publicly revealed in August 2017. Due to a combination of a lack of vigilance and not purifying his own wrong thinking, his tenure ended abruptly.

This is unfortunate, because when leaders shut down the conversation about fear and bad impressions, we often never get to the good part about the process of purification, which is that it's easy. You don't relive your entire life, or reprocess every misstep you believe you took. The process of purification starts with acknowledging something needs to be purified in order to progress in a better way. Then, it's all about identifying what needs to be purified and taking the appropriate actions to go through the process of purification. If you've got bad digestion it's because toxins are interfering with the process of digesting and you need to purify those toxins as the first step to strengthening digestion. If there's bad behavior from team members that behavior needs to be purified and transformed into better behavior. Otherwise, the individuals may need to be asked to leave because they are ruining the functioning of the whole system.

There's a reason awareness is highlighted as being one of the most important skills for a leader: it's effective. Becoming aware of impurities, stresses, or fears allows you to expand your clarity around those issues, and clarity allows you to dissolve what doesn't serve you, such as bad impressions you've retained in your mind.

Here are two examples of CEOs who weren't afraid of purifying what required purifying to create a better environment that inspired, enhanced, and protected progress.

1. Gordon Bethune was CEO of Continental Airlines from 1994 to 2004 and led the revived of the airline. He cited poor management for the company's consistently low customer satisfaction ratings, and then turned the airline into the highest-rated by treating employees and customers better and giving them what they really want and required. This shift had an immediate impact on the company's bottom line, which went from a $600 million loss in 1994 to a $225 million profit in 1995. All this was accomplished by shifting focus to employee satisfaction initiatives, treating staff right, getting to know them, and earning their trust.

2. Alan Mulally led Ford Motor Company from 2006 to 2014. In 2006, Ford lost $12.7 billion. Mulally changed the culture of the company from being cutthroat to being collaborative and efficiency based. Mortgaging $23.5 billion in company assets, he got the cash he needed to improve Ford's vehicle range. In 2014, Ford had net income of nearly $3.2 billion.

Will You Continue Repaying the Same Debt?

This is the exact thing you do when you relive or base future decisions off of past bad impressions. If your stress and fear were business debts, would you pay them over and over and over again? No, of course not. You would pay them once, and move on. There's no need to continue punishing yourself. Refer back to the Failure-Success Blueprint and identify the lesson, and move forward. This is the only way to purify the bad impressions in your life. You have to go deeper, to the level beyond the old level of thinking and acting. This development is not on the level of your intellect. You must transcend the impression and stresses, which means to go beyond them. Going beyond them means bringing your awareness back to pure consciousness or energy at the source of thinking to purify old thinking and inspire new thinking and action. This is why we put consciousness, awareness and fulfillment at the basis of the Science of Protection chart. It's like turning on another level of light, energy, connectivity and coherence in your brain which we'll discuss in the next chapter.

We can know problems exist on a logical level, but not possess a full understanding of how to take care of them. It's not about the punishment; it's about learning the lesson to dissolve bad impressions. It does you absolutely no good paying the debt and not learning from it.

You can fail and not have a clue why, and the why is the most important part. You can fix the problem and still not truly know how or why you're failing. You can pay down the business debt, but if you make the same mistakes, you'll wind up right back in debt.

Yes, you can indeed correct your mistakes and still not learn from them. So then what was the point? If you do not learn from the experience, your subconscious mind will put you in a position to repeat the process until you learn the lesson.

Have You Been Conditioned?

Conditioning, much like bad impressions, creates cycles or conditioned learned responses to previous stimuli that you repeat and perpetuate in your life. Because these cycles are so deeply ingrained, they are nearly impossible to see if you haven't developed yourself enough to recognize what is happening.

We have found it to be persistently true, among leaders around the world, that conditioning is holding them back from true mastery and invincible success. Even leaders who seem to have a lot of energy and capacity fall victim to conditioning and bad impressions, which prevents growth and allows failure.

Your subconscious beliefs will hold you in a pattern of attracting the same experiences until you choose to release those beliefs, judgments, and preconceived notions and stop blocking your own alignment. Your brain recycles experiences until your experiences change. While your conditioning may be the result of current or past environments or events that were once out of your control, you are still responsible for all of it. It might not have been your doing, but it is still your responsibility to free yourself of the impressions.

In fact, the bad impressions, the fears, the successes, the failures, are all your responsibility. We all have conditionings that hold us back from being the people we're meant to be. It could be a conditioning of not realizing the leadership influence we have; or perhaps we are not motivated to achieve because we've conditioned ourselves to believe that it doesn't really matter.

Going back to your brain for a moment, there is an actual physical change related to traumatic occurrences in your life. Your hippocampus, which is designed to help you distinguish between past and present memories, actually shrinks with trauma-based occurrences. Traumatic events in your life can range from small to large, and can look like a lot of different things. This type of change in your brain chemistry proves that, in order to reverse this type of damage, there has to be a more substantial approach taken.

Self-Censorship Is the By-product of Conditioning

As you move into adulthood, you find yourself in fewer situations where those around you are attempting to condition or control you. When this transition happens, you take on that role yourself and begin self-censoring every single thing relating to who you are. This is another process connected to fear and the bad impressions that have settled into your subconscious, and sometimes conscious, mind.

These fears and impressions encourage you to censor who you are, so that society only ever sees or knows the parts you or society deems acceptable. High level leaders are often the most self-censored, because they are continually role playing who they believe they should be in a high stakes game, where "getting into the club" decides how well they will do in business.

Take a look at your thumb on your right hand. If you send the command, your thumb will wiggle, stretch back and forth, tuck in, and so on. Now, imagine living your entire life as if you didn't have that thumb. Of course, it's there, but what if you were pretending it wasn't there? Things might get a bit tricky as you take on daily tasks. Your brain knows the thumb is there, and will attempt to rely on the thumb to effectively get things done. Think about how much you would have to battle, how much effort you would have to apply, to pretend that thumb wasn't there. This is a lot like self-censorship. The parts of you that you are attempting to pretend don't exist are still there. So you use up a lot of energy and effort to not rely on those parts, and to not acknowledge those parts. But that still does not change the fact that they are a part of you.

When you self-censor, it forces you out of alignment with your higher self, your purpose, and your growth. This, often subconscious, behavior also leads to a lack of genuine energy, increased fear of self, and fear of loss, and attracts those types of energies back to you in other forms. And remember, these stresses don't stay in their own separate boxes; they spill over and touch everything, including business, deals, and prospects for long-term success. Finally, they also affect personal relationships.

The strangest thing about self-censorship is that people often participate in this type of behavior because they believe they are protecting themselves from pain or failure. But, as you are learning, real protection already exists in everything, all the time. You don't need to create it. If you feel you have to create protection, by participating in certain behaviors or censorship, this is a great way to gauge whether or not the protection is real.

Just like your thumb, you might believe you are protecting your whole hand by not using it, but you are actually creating more friction and making things more difficult for your other extremities. And you might think you are protecting your thumb by not using it, but you are forcing it out of alignment with its purpose, and creating unnecessary stress throughout the rest of your body.

You Might Not Ever Crash and Burn

For a top performer, like you, crashing and burning is not an option. So you may go on for decades, out of alignment, restless and lacking contentedness, without ever using that thumb. You've been trained to forge on, to be thankful for your success, and to lead by example. You don't get to complain because you are the captain. Who would listen, anyway? Who would even understand? For some, crashing and burning is the worst case scenario. For you, the fact that it isn't even an option should be terrifying. This is why leaders self-destruct or die young, or both.

When you live in a way that is out of alignment with your truth, purpose, and the Universe, by the time it catches up with you, often it is too late to make changes. When you add fear into this equation, paralysis caused by the mindset of "good enough" sets in. It's the idea that, when things are good, we should let them be. But good enough isn't … not for you. You deserve better. You are capable of better. The world needs you to do better.

> **"When I was 20 years old, I launched my first business. I would go in and secure large contracts with apartment complexes and corporate offices, so my cleaning staff could maintain their buildings or do turnover cleanings. The overhead in the business was low, and the pay was great, if my cleaners could maintain a speed of approximately 600 square feet per hour. Anything beyond that would begin eating into my profits, something I couldn't afford to let happen. The first year went well enough for us to continue into year two and year three. But when year four hit, everything seemed to change. The contracts were drying up because companies were bringing this task in-house, and I was forced to lower my prices in order to compete. Eventually I had to close the business, a devastating decision I put off until the last possible moment. Fast-forward two years later: I had another opportunity to try my hand at entrepreneurship. The business was lucrative and after weeks of nonstop deliberation, I turned it down. That business today is a top-rated subscription box service, and was one of the first of its kind to hit the market.**
>
> **"My fear of loss, failure, and bad impressions made the decision for me to pass on a great opportunity, a decision that was made well before I began consciously contemplating the pros and cons. This is how our subconscious mind is influenced by past conditioning, impressions, fear, and stress. Sometimes this works in our favor, and sometimes it does not, if it's being driven by negative experiences."**
>
> *—Sara Burke, co-author*

> **"When there is no enemy within, the enemies outside cannot hurt you."**
>
> —*African proverb*

Inner Enemies Cause Outer Enemies

Certainly, you've heard sayings like "You reap what you sow" and "Your life is a reflection of your thoughts." What these sayings are getting at is the most obvious and most overlooked fact of life, a true law of nature: Through our thoughts and actions, we create our reality. The problem with applying this approach to life is that there seems to be some gray areas. Here's an example:

When an individual comes to us, and they are at their wit's end, we often hear them say, "I've done everything right, I've worked hard, and I've tried to create the reality I wanted to live." If this is true, and that particular leader had worked hard to do everything right and to create the reality they desired to live, how do they still end up on the losing side of leadership?

We tell leaders that all outer conflict begins with inner conflict. This message doesn't always go over well, especially in vulnerable moments, but it is true, and something that needs to be addressed for the betterment of leaders around the world.

The weaknesses in your mind create conflict. We tell leaders this because, from the beginning of our work together, they have to be willing to own up to their weaknesses and grow from them—that is the baseline reality. Our goal with pushing leaders into this uncomfortable territory is very specific. When we get uncomfortable, we instinctively run back to where we are comfortable. For growth to happen, we have to break that cycle, and recognize the discomfort, to begin to understand why we are uncomfortable, so we can let go of those imbalances and impressions.

Those uncomfortable areas are what we call inner enemies, and we see more leaders today driven by inner enemies than we do leaders driven by truth. This must change.

Not even the greatest darkness can withstand the light of truth.

Past occurrences of inner enemies interrupting business, clarity, and the ability of leaders to survive in the fast-paced business economy, in the form of direct quotes:

"We've learned and struggled for a few years here figuring out how to make a decent phone. PC guys are not going to just figure this out. They're not going to just walk in."

—Ed Colligan, CEO of Palm in 2006
after learning that Apple was developing a phone

"Neither RedBox nor Netflix are even on the radar screen in terms of competition."

—Jim Keyes, CEO of Blockbuster in 2008

"It's a little bit like, is the Albanian army going to take over the world? I don't think so."

—Jeffrey Bewkes, CEO of Time Warner
when asked about Netflix in 2010

"It would be a daunting task requiring tens of billions of dollars in capital and years to build sufficient scale and density to replicate existing networks like FedEx."

—Mike Glenn, Executive VP of FedEx in 2016,
when asked how Amazon would compete
with major parcel carriers

If we revisit what we've learned about how a leader's brain works, we now know that our brains are really just fancy predicting machines. Your ability to predict well can be undermined by your inner enemies, and the result, as we can see from the quotations above, is the inability to predict future change.

What are these inner enemies dominating today's leaders?

(We thought you'd never ask...)

Lust, anger, greed, delusion, intoxication, vanity, jealousy, false attachments (things you think you need but don't), and procrastination are all inner enemies that leave you unprotected and prevent you from performing at the top of your leadership game.

Where do these inner enemies come from?

Past experiences, failures, fears, and your ego are in the driver's seat when it comes to inner enemies. These inner enemies lead to:

- **Ignorance:** not knowing or choosing not to know
- **Arrogance:** thinking we know when we really don't
- **Status Quo Inertia:** being bound by what we currently know

One telltale sign that these inner enemies exist in a leader is when we see that leader quickly dismiss and deflect new possibilities to grow, either themselves or their business, even when those possibilities are proven to be effective and create sustainable change. Another sign of inner enemies is when we see a leader intentionally delay development that is needed now and is of real benefit to themselves, business, process and people. When we get so busy in our minds, consumed by our egos, and bound by a fear of loss or self, we lack the healthy curiosity and desire to seek out better possibilities.

Kodak had the opportunity to take the digital photo revolution by storm in the 90s, yet they deflected, dismissed, and eroded their own competitive advantage. Blockbuster had the opportunity to buy Netflix, same outcome.

The deeper reason these inner enemies can halt a leader's achievement and progress is due to a lack of capacity. When you can't feel, see, and know what is going on (the bigger picture and the finer details)—a lack of inner development, in short—it's easy to mistime changes, something we discuss more in the next chapter.

> **"The anxiety I feel is just unreal. I'm taking antacids a handful at a time, and being honest, it takes a few whiskeys for me to fall asleep. I know everything is screwed up, but I just get up every single day and do the exact same thing I did the day before. When a month goes by, I look back and think maybe I should have done something differently, but I don't know what that is. Then, there are some days I think maybe it isn't that**

> **bad, and maybe if I just hold it steady, things will keep moving forward. Thing is though, it doesn't feel right, something isn't right, and it eats at me, day in and day out, even though, on the surface, everything looks okay, I mean, nothing is on fire. I just find myself wondering what the heck is going on and whether or not I'm going crazy. It's like these emotions have created this invisible world I can feel but I can't see, and I am tired of feeling restless, tired but can't sleep, anxious, and angry. If that's what this job calls for, I don't know if I want to do it anymore."**
>
> *—anonymous CEO, 2017*

When you read that statement from one of our clients, do you think he chose any of those feelings consciously and on purpose? Of course not. Nobody would ever choose anger or anxiety over bliss and calm energy, would they?

Inner Conflict Creates Outer Conflict

When our inner enemies are running the show, the conflict they create on the inside finds its way to the outside.

We act based on that conflict and friction, which is really dangerous territory.

> **"I reacted strongly to a deal, in a negative way. I told my partner and our associates that I trusted my gut, or my intuition, whatever you want to call it, and it ended up being a really bad call. I was wrong. I made a very poor business decision relying on this instinct, and that was probably the biggest eye-opener of my career. I guess I had been lucky up to that point because I had been relying on that intuition for a long time and nothing had gone terribly wrong, so I figured I was in pretty good shape to keep doing that. The problem was that a lot had changed in our business, and with our competition, and I just don't know if I had the capacity, at that time, to comprehend all the changes**

and potential opportunities or failures. On top of that, I had gone through some personal hardships, and mentally, I think it affected me and prevented me from doing what was best for our business."

—anonymous CEO, 2017

How many times have you thought, "I don't feel like myself?" Or how many times have you felt like you were waiting for something to change, happen, or take off? That is you, innocently admitting that you are out of alignment with who you truly are on the inside. How often have you wondered why you feel this way? How often have you tried to figure out what feels "off"? How many times have you become distracted by life, and left this open issue to sit until "the next time"? How often do you shove those feelings down, or brush them off because you don't have the time to deal with them? How many times will this happen before that inner conflict makes itself known on the outside...and how will it affect your business?

Why Is Aggressiveness Such A Common Trait?

It's a dog eat dog world, right? Or is this something that we, as leaders, tell ourselves in order to justify conflict and "protect" our inner enemies?

When we see CEOs or high level leaders portrayed in media or TV, they are generally aggressive, willing to do whatever it takes, and ruthless in forging their path forward. CEOs are depicted as sleep deprived, caffeine fueled, intoxicated, and yet still witty, and all without a care in the world. Research reported in the Harvard Business Review (84(9), 55-62) found that 80% of American's don't trust corporate executives and nearly 50% of all managers do not trust their own executives. So either this is real or perceptions are askew due to the media and TV highlighting the stereotype above.

We can confidently tell you, with over two decades of experience at this point, we've never met the CEO outlined above. The CEOs who make their way to us are exhausted, or frustrated, and often times both. If you look around, have you ever met the popularly portrayed type of CEO? Or do you, like us, see leaders in your same shoes, wondering what comes next?

At a screening of The Wolf of Wall Street, the $100 million dollar Scorsese and DiCaprio film detailing the life and crimes of stock broker Jordan Belfort, I found myself wondering why the leaders we depict in film are drowning in greed, corruption, and extreme highs and lows. Could this constant depiction of ruthless and morally devoid leaders be part of the greater problem with leadership? Are CEOs aiming for a status that will eventually cause them to fail?

In the book World Class Brain, researchers Harung and Travis found the top level managers, those who have consistently performed at a high level for a long period of time actually have higher level of moral reasoning than their controls, this is correlated with their higher levels of brain integration, not age, experience, education, training or incentives. Higher moral reasoning means they have expanded awareness to think and act for others and the world as a whole not just themselves.

Going Beyond Mind Games

All of these inner enemies have the effect of consciously, unconsciously, or subconsciously causing mind games within yourself or others. Mind games mean trying to trick or delude ourselves or others perception into accepting something is okay when it's not for the sake of one's competitive advantage. As a result, others will also play mind games with you. The current business landscape is overflowing with mind games. When we are caught up in mind games, we switch from predicting to pretending or faking. Leaders caught in this dynamic waste time, money, and energy.

As a result, nothing impactful really gets accomplished, and this game of pretending can go on for years, or until implosion occurs.

These mind games are due to very subtle problems within the leader stemming from the inner enemies we've mentioned. Mind games weaken a leader's mind, reducing their predicting and performance abilities, and resulting in a lack of simplicity, a lack of truthfulness, and a lack of a sense of unity. From this point, the cycle of lack continues and protection is lost, which means trade, commerce, and communication will be corrupted.

Conquering mind games and the side effects of pretending requires a leader to get real, with themselves and others. This transformation starts with a core level change in brain coherence, as we'll discuss in the next chapter.

The Most Effective Inner Enemy

Your ego has been around the block a few times, and knows all the tricks to control and manipulate your thoughts and behaviors. For this reason, we call the ego the most effective inner enemy. As billionaire and business expert Ray Dalio puts it:

> **"Because our need to be right can be more important than our need to find out what is true, we like to believe our opinions without properly stress-testing them. We especially don't like to look at our mistakes and weaknesses. When our ideas or opinions are questioned, the natural reaction is to be defensive and angry. But that doesn't mean it's the right reaction. This leads to our making inferior decisions, learning less, and falling short of our potentials."**

What Mr. Dalio is referring to is simply a lack of protection, as we let inner enemies influence who we become each day. As he so rightly points out, anger, vanity, and all of the other inner enemies feed your ego, allowing reality to be distorted day in and day out.

Revisiting the Fear of Loss

The very real fear of loss is commonly increased by inner enemies. When there is a problem, we are hardwired to assume the problem has taken root on the outside, and to therefore seek out solutions on the outside. We now know that outer conflicts are the result of inner conflicts, which means there are no external solutions that will correct outer conflicts long-term.

> **"There is no outside, because the outside is always a reflection of the inside."**
>
> *—Paolo D'Angelo, New Mavericks Co-Founder*

This tells us that real success is based on the brain and level of internal development of a leader, because all problems that are purified on the inside will not corrupt a leader's success on the outside. This also tells us that leaders who always seem caught up in conflict or struggle are interfering with their own potential success. All problems leaders face arise from weaknesses within the leader.

Know the Internal Obstacle that Creates the External Obstacle

This is how you really remove and dissolve an obstacle on the outside. Any obstacle outside is an obstacle inside of yourself that you created from past actions.

For example, before we started working with one of our clients they had gotten themselves into a real financial pickle and owed a lot of money to a number of people, some who were even close friends. He wasn't able to meet the obligations he had with them but continued trying to move forward, improving his situation. Not long after, he came across another obstacle where he wasn't able to move forward and exit a project. We reminded him that he hadn't taken care of past obligations and the key to getting through this obstacle was to have the intention of actually meeting those past obligations and purifying the resentment he created by not meeting those past obligations. Not meeting obligations is usually due to the vice of taking on more than you can chew. By removing the internal obstacle that created his external obstacle, he was able to move forward. Growth is always an inside job.

Know that wrong actions of the past create obstacles in the present. When something or someone is idle it means that idleness has been created somewhere in the past.

Cognitive Dissonance in Leadership

> A fox one day spied a beautiful bunch of ripe grapes hanging from a vine trained along the branches of a tree. The grapes seemed ready to burst with juice, and the fox's mouth watered as he gazed longingly at them. The bunch hung from a high branch, and the fox had to jump to reach it. The first time he jumped, the eager fox missed the branch by a long way. So he walked off a short distance, pressed firmly to the ground, and took a running leap at it, only to fall short once more. Again and again the fox tried to get to the ripe fruit, each time in vain. Now he sat down and looked at the grapes in disgust. "What a fool I am," he said. "Here I am wearing myself out to get a bunch of sour grapes that are not worth gaping for." And off he walked very, very scornfully.

This classic tale is from *Aesop's Fables*, is a collection of stories designed to teach moral lessons credited to Aesop, who was a Greek slave and story-teller thought to have lived between 620 and 560 BCE.

The moral lesson, in this particular story about the fox and the sour grapes, has to do with what psychologists would call cognitive dissonance. The fox boldly claims that the grapes were sour to help him cope with the reality he was facing, which was that he couldn't reach the grapes. We do this to ourselves when we justify behavior as not being "that bad," or when we offer extreme comparisons to show that our habit could be worse. An example of this might be a smoker justifying their smoking because they recently received a good doctor's report.

Cognitive dissonance is incredibly common in leadership, especially where leaders feel they must make morally questionable decisions to stay on top (fear of loss). In situations like this, it's common for the leader to justify those actions, or downplay them, so the jump between who they are in that moment, and who they think they are internally, can connect on some sort of common ground. Research also suggests that the impact or effect cognitive dissonance has on an individual has a lot to do with their level of awareness. We laid out two types of leaders in Chapter 2, and if you go back to that chart, it should be easy to identify which one of those leaders would be the most impacted by this separation from reality.

This wraps up the first component of the Science of Protection. Purification gives you a clean slate to allow progress to unfold in a more efficient way due to having less fear, negativity, stress and vices. Purification heightens protection and the ability to progress. Think of it like the Olympic sport of curling, where the players clear the ice the curling ball is traveling so there's less resistance to it having the best chance of reaching its intended goal. Through purification there's less friction and more simplicity and energy which naturally gives you more clarity. Clarity is strengthened and stabilized through coherence which helps you integrate your clarity into the world. We'll be diving deeply into this in the next chapter.

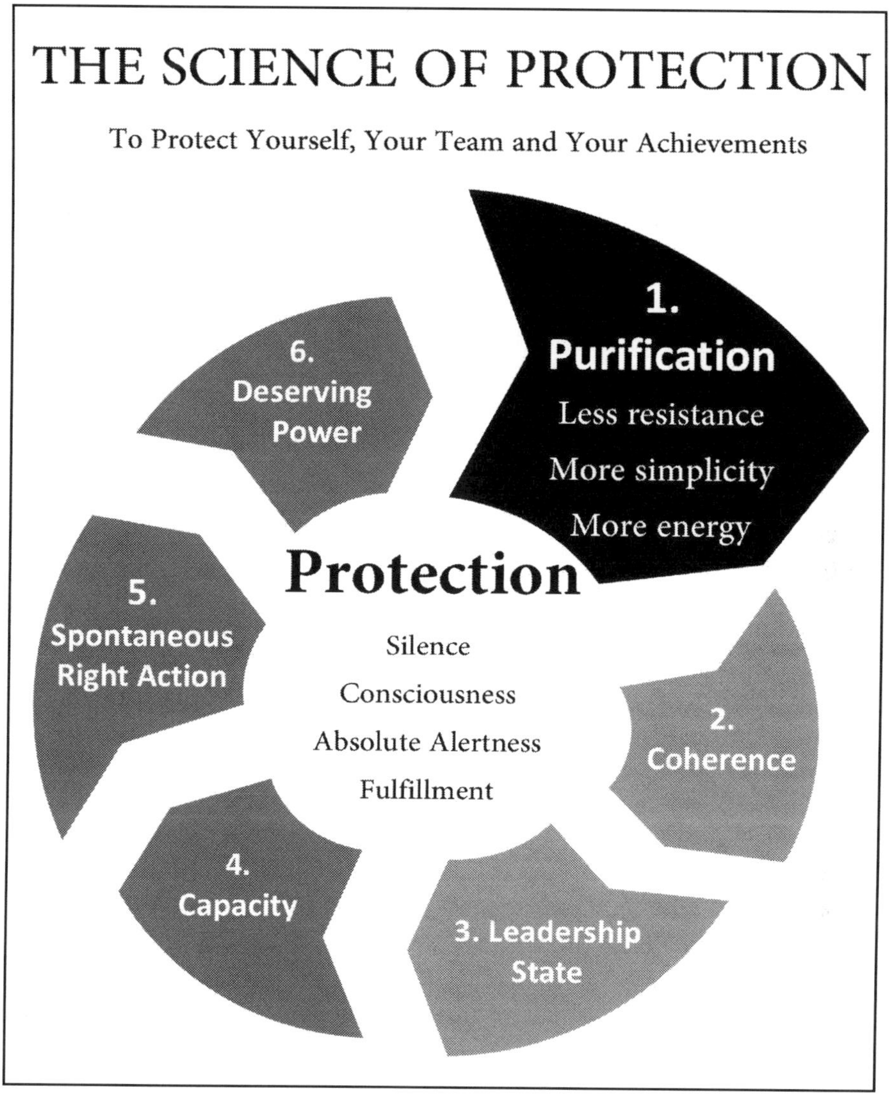
THE SCIENCE OF PROTECTION
To Protect Yourself, Your Team and Your Achievements
1.
Purification
Less resistance
More simplicity
More energy
2.
Coherence
3. Leadership
State
4.
Capacity
5.
Spontaneous
Right Action
6.
Deserving
Power
Protection
Silence
Consciousness
Absolute Alertness
Fulfillment

YOUR TURN

What Requires Purification in Your World?

1. What do you fear losing the most? What stresses and bad impressions are behind this fear?
2. What can you do to purify the stresses and bad impressions so you're freer from fear?
3. Once you've removed the fear, stress, and bad impression, what clarity do you have about the path of least resistance to protected progress?

4 Coherence

The CEO of You

A CEO's greatest challenge is learning how to be free from actions that allowed them to be successful yesterday, lest they be left behind due to their brain's inability to develop new coherence to be in tune with change.

Having purified what needs to be purified, it's time to infuse more coherence so you can avert going back to the negativity, fear, stress and bad impressions of the past. This will allow you to move forward with greater orderliness in bringing all the parts together.

co•her•ence
ˌkō'hirəns/
The quality of forming a unified whole.
Also known as: Integration, Connectivity, Orderliness
For the science of protection coherence means:

Global Alpha Brain Coherence gives clarity to have the right unifying (and protecting) thought at the right time.

Coherence is what creates the wholeness that is greater than the sum of the parts. Coherence integrates, connects and protects the whole and the parts so they're orderly. We're using the word coherence from a neurophysiological perspective where it means harmony; orderliness and synchronicity between different parts of the brain so more of the whole brain is utilized enabling you to feel, see and know more. This is what allows you to have the right unifying (and therefore protecting) thought at the right time.

Understanding how to take care of and develop the CEO of you, your prefrontal cortex, is the most important thing you can/will do as a leader to establish more coherence. Over the years, we've seen plenty of top leaders and performers—sometimes slowly, sometimes abruptly—corrupt their high brain coherence, leading to their own demise. Watching and hearing about top leaders suffer strokes and heart attacks, tarnish their reputations, lose their wealth, and damage their relationships has been difficult. This is especially true because the science and application exists to protect these leaders. Sharing this knowledge, The Science of Protection, allows us to shift the tide, and begin navigating leaders away from self-destructive leadership.

Over the last decade, CEOs aged 30-60, from top companies such as Samsung, Nintendo, Fonterra, Deutsch Bank, Apple, Goldman Sachs, JP Morgan, ESPN, Fox News, GE, Wells Fargo, Theranos, and Tata Motors, have either stepped down from their roles or lost their lives due to health issues, suicide, harassment, fraud, poor performance, or other mysterious, conflicted, and complicated circumstances. This list is expanding rapidly. We would like to welcome a new era of leadership, where protection is the foundation you build your empire upon.

Fittingly, this chapter, titled 'The CEO of You', will explore the prefrontal cortex, and its leading influence on you and the rest of your brain, to simplify the processes taking place. This will allow us to fully explain why the development of the prefrontal cortex, leading to higher coherence, is the secret to your high performance and invincible leadership state. Our goal in writing this book has always been to take ideas on consciousness, coherence, and high-performance from the realm of the unknown and move them into tangible territory. We can do that by understanding how the brain works, and how exactly it applies to you and your future.

Protection through Coherence

Listening to a grown man weep is never easy. Especially a man who has a wife, two young children, has just lost his luxury home and business, is over his head in debt, and is questioning his will to live. In this moment, we have to allow our client the time to let go of and purify his stresses. We listen to Peter's[5] quiet sobbing, as the weight of the world crushes every achievement he's ever gained throughout his business career. The pressure of being on the wrong end of the global financial crisis is starting to take its toll, as he is

5 Client's name changed to protect and respect his privacy.

not sure how to break the downward spiral. Between the sobs and sighs are outbursts of anger, as Peter tells us how unfair all of this is, and how he just wishes it would all go away. A common set of questions in a scenario like this tend to be: "Why me? Why now? What can I do?"

Clearly, a deep overhaul of Peter's mind, emotions, and purpose for continuing in business (and life) is required. It's not just one decision that has caused this near-total collapse. It's a multitude of decisions, stemming from his current leadership state, that have accumulated over time to create this painful experience for Peter.

> **"Success is a lousy teacher. It seduces smart people into thinking they can't lose."**
>
> *—Bill Gates*

In a similar vein, Stan O'Neal's leadership as CEO of Merrill Lynch from 2002 to 2007 lacked protection. He was considered, by many, one of the players responsible for the financial crisis.

O'Neal was a strong leader, known for his confident and ruthless management style. These traits allowed him to create strong profits for Merrill Lynch from 2003 to 2007.

In a Fortune magazine interview, O'Neal said he didn't understand the magnitude of the collateralized debt obligations the firm had on its books. In August 2007, he began looking into the matter and realized the firm was in big trouble. He stepped down in October 2007, but by that time, Merrill Lynch had already lost around $8 billion on mortgage foreclosures and delinquencies.

In short, he didn't have sufficient coherence—the degree to which different parts of the brain are working in synchrony and harmony with each other, to make the best decisions—to be aware of what was really going on. He could not neutralize or avert this danger before it was too late. Unfortunately, O'Neal's lack of protection showed up in several different ways:

- Lacking deserving power
- Incoherence
- Lacking spontaneous right action
- Minimized leadership state
- Too many stresses, not enough purification

Through having inner coherence negativity cannot touch and affect us, our company, nation or even the world, even though it is always there.

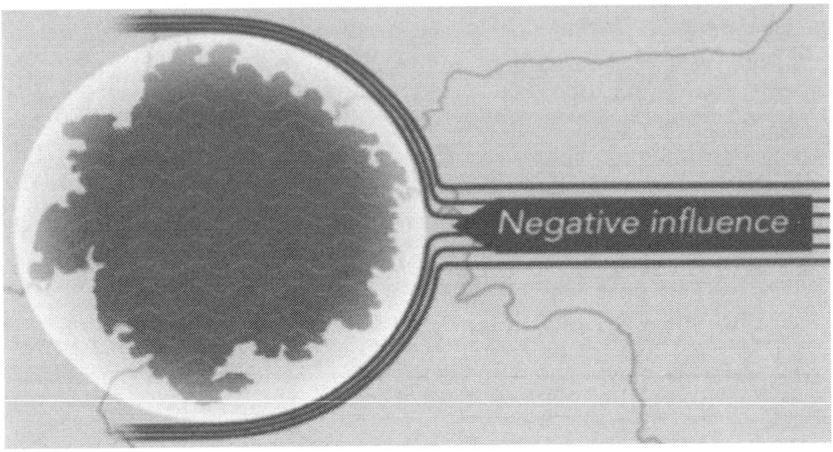

This phenomenon in physics is called the Meissner Effect.

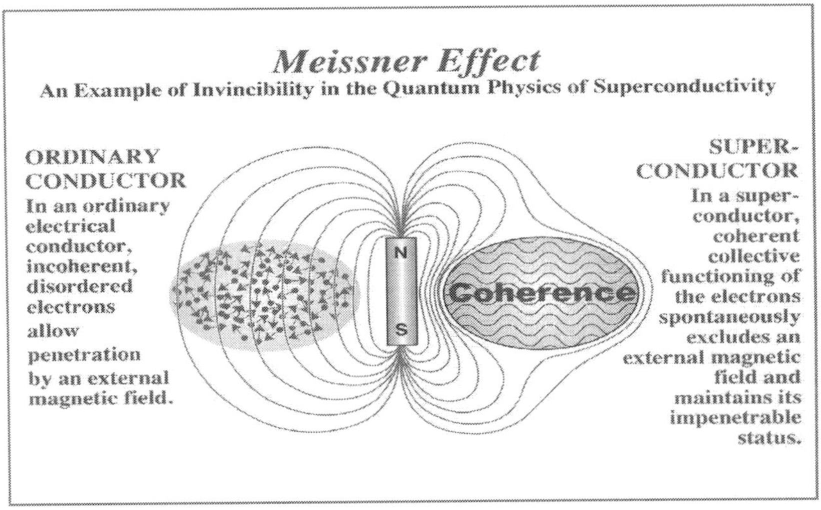

So Where Do We Start?

Much like with our client Peter, there needs to be a starting point, a way to stop the downward spiral and begin the process of rebuilding. We have to get Peter's internal CEO back online and coherent so he can begin making better decisions. Which begs the question, if he is the CEO of his business and life, then what is the CEO of Peter? What is the CEO of you?

The answer is the prefrontal cortex, that part of your brain that makes and executes all of your decisions, goals, motivations, and beliefs about yourself and the world around you. Your prefrontal cortex's integration and coherence with the whole brain is vitally important, if you want to make what we call Evolutionary Decision Making.

Evolutionary Decision Making: Decision making that serves you, everyone and the environment, in both the short- and long-term, and adapts quickly with changing dynamics.

Why is this important for leadership?

Based on research presented by two of the world's top high-performance neuroscientists, Dr. Fred Travis and Dr. Harald Harung, we are developing a deeper understanding of how top performers are able to "get in the zone."

Dr. Travis and Dr. Harung found that after age 25:

- » Education accounts for only 1% of performance levels.
- » Work experience accounts for only 3% of performance levels.
- » Age in adults accounts for a flat 0% of performance levels.

If these traditional factors don't significantly improve performance, which essentially is the by-product of decision making, what does? More coherent integrated brain functioning.

How did you become a leader?

With the help of the statistical data shown above, we can easily say that it is not your education, age, or experience that has landed you right in this moment, right now. So how did you end up here? How did you become a leader?

Dr's. Harung and Travis looked deeply to unearth the secret of world-class performance and their work was successful. They discovered that excellence in any profession or activity depends on the single variable of high mind-brain development.

What Is High Mind-Brain Development?

High mind-brain development is a sequence of fundamental shifts to new realities, in the way our brain functions, as well as the way we look upon ourselves, others, and the world. For success, Travis and Harung found that who we are is far more important than the accumulation of what we do, or the knowledge, skills, and relationships we have.

With higher mind-brain development, our knowledge and skills become more useful. With higher mind-brain development, our relationships become more enriched and enriching. **With higher mind-brain development, our actions become more effective.**

The book by Dr.'s Travis and Harung, *Excellence through Mind-Brain Development*, details inspiring peak experiences in top performers who are able to identify brain functions that are more orderly, restfully alert, and efficient, over average performers. In simple terms, through specific characteristics, they can identify what makes a top performer a top performer. We can now tell you how to get in the zone, but more importantly, how to stay there.

Often, we can look at high-performers and say, "Oh, it was their confidence, their competence, their courage, their ability to connect with people, their ability to connect the dots, their congruence." But what is the fountainhead of all of these qualities? Here is where the research from neuroscience over the past decade allows us, for the first time ever, to look under the hood and objectively say that it is, in fact, high-performers' inner coherence, or neuroplasticity, that elevates their performance. Top executives have been found to have high coherence in the pre-frontal cortex, the CEO of You, your executive center that integrates and decides on all that you perceive. It is the activation and substantial development of their Global Alpha Coherence (GAC), which is a composition of…

» Alpha 1: Relaxed wakefulness, inner directed attention
» Alpha 2: A quiet primed brain that is ready to be used

…that allows a leader to be awake and alert and calm and centered at the same time. Alpha coherence is a composition of both the alert, dynamic brain frequencies of gamma and beta (when we focus on things and process information), and the slow and relaxed delta and theta frequencies (when we sleep, dream and imagine). You can read more detail about this in Dr. Harald Harung and Dr. Fred Travis's book *World Class Brain*.

Global alpha coherence is really the basis for all-encompassing coherence between the heart and mind; the right brain's creative instincts and left brain's logical execution; between lower brain survival instincts and higher brain moral thriving instincts; between your team and their needs; between your clients and their expectations. This coherence has the ability to equalize and add efficacy to everything mentioned in the previous sentence. This is also the coherence between the inner truth of who you are, your "inner why," and the actions that project who you are and fulfill your purpose. **This all-encompassing global alpha coherence is the key catalyst to have the optimal state of mind for protecting your achievement and progress.**

Global Alpha Coherence gives you greater ability to more quickly and efficiently connect the dots between the bigger long-term picture and the finer short-term details and have a high degree of morality. This coherence is all-encompassing across all hemispheres of the brain, heart, and body, merged with what is going on in your greater environment. This is the highly developed leadership state that leaders seek but usually don't achieve because they don't have the knowledge and techniques of how to.

World class athletes, business leaders, and musicians have shown to have a high degree of alpha coherence in their brain functioning, enabling them to feel more, see more, and know more. This allows them to have fewer thoughts than the average person, simply because this coherence filters out the usual flood of low quality "noise" in the mind and allows in more of the right thoughts, at the right time (spontaneous right action).

"The biggest pollution we have is thought pollution." Raamon made this statement to Leonardo DiCaprio, after complimenting him on his *Before the Flood* documentary, because thoughts create products and businesses that pollute. He agreed and responded, "We need to legislate." Which brings up the interesting observation that legislation, like everything else, is based on the quality of people's thoughts, which is based on their level of coherence. The more coherence a leader has, the better, more profound, and equitable legislation will be created, implemented, and lived by.

This development of coherence capacity also gives the ability to live the ZERO Factor more often.

The Zero Factor: The near-zero time gap between having a great winning thought and taking the right action on it; effortless, spontaneous, right-action.

The Zero Factor allows for more or less flawless execution of high-performance thoughts. Here's an experience from a client functioning with high Global Alpha Coherence:

> **"Organizing the biggest deal in our corporate history involved long hours, tight time frames, and multiple**

go/no-go hurdles, which meant multiple possibilities for stress. Despite this, I personally felt like the eye of the storm. All is calm and relaxed and unfolding on the most evolutionary timeline. Interestingly, since our last session, things seem to be falling into place quickly and effortlessly."

—Mark Waller, Former CEO and Chairman,
EBOS Group, New Zealand CEO of the Year 2010 and
New Zealand Business Hall of Fame 2019

As a leader you have a good degree of world class brain function just to be in that role. If you're leading a significant company or are top in your field, you probably already experience these higher states of being, and may just be unaware of the impact this has created in your life thus far.

It's important to understand high performance brain functioning, so you can fully own, develop, and protect your functioning. For you, as a leader, the ultimate goal is to have more of the right thoughts, at the right time, for efficacy of action. This is what will truly protect your achievement, your peoples' achievement, and the progress of everyone.

Bottom line: you need to learn how to not only get in the zone, but stay there without having it corrupted or diminished.

The master key for sustaining the zone and growth is inner silence. A silent and settled mind allows your brain to be more relaxed, coherent, awake and efficient. Silence allows more synchronicity to happen for you because you see more and believe more, therefore you can achieve more. Being steadfast in silence means no resistance or challenge can affect you, because when the mind is small you feel the pain. When the mind is developed and coherent, you still feel pain but aren't affected by it. When caught up by resistances and obstacles- you're stuck. A good leader remains fluid by having a developed pre-frontal cortex.

This kind of development is so simple but it's been made complicated because people want to control and lead through ego. Aligning with the source of intelligence in silence means you gain maximum support and protection to achieve unconsciously. Inner silence and brain coherence provide the agile mindset leaders today desperately need.

This means you're fixed on an outcome, you want to grow as a person and business and you're agile how you'll grow to get the outcome. As our top client says when people ask him how he'll achieve something, "I don't know, but we will".

True Leadership Involves the Ability to:

1. Stabilize your Leadership State.

2. Enhance your Zero Factor.

3. Maximize your Evolutionary Decision Making.

Understanding your brain's performance based on coherence is key to enhancing and stabilizing these three factors.

Understanding Your Brain's Performance

In order to completely understand your brain's performance, and how it ties into protecting your achievement and your people's achievement, it helps to understand the tasks your brain performs regularly. We'll start there, and at the end of this chapter, we'll share why this is so important for fully living your "inner why," which is instrumental in protecting all that you are doing as a leader.

Task #1: Predicting

You have a belief system, and that belief system is based on how you feel about the world. Belief is another word for everything you've predicted. This can range from something as mundane as a belief that when you turn your doorknob to enter your office, it won't fall off, to your belief in the next best product to invest your company's resources in, to what capacity you must produce at to meet predicted demand. If the doorknob fell off, you'd be shocked because you predicted it would turn and open. If the product you invested in takes off, your belief is accurate in predicting the best product. From the doorknob to the best product, most of these predictions lie deep within your subconscious and seldom see the light of day. They are the subconscious matrix of who we are and how we function. Your brain is making these predictions nonstop, reinforcing your beliefs, from the moment you start your day, every single day. But beliefs need to be flexible, in case the next batch of doorknobs function differently, or the market changes dramatically. Imagine the shock and resistance when door pulls or pull handles were first replaced with doorknobs.

How well you *predict* depends on how coherent you are.

Beliefs are connected to perceived consequences: "If I do this, or this happens, what will it lead to?" We are constantly setting up these types of scenarios, attempting to predict the future so each step, both literally and figuratively, leads to advancement and protection.

How well you predict depends on how coherent you are. If you are an incoherent person, you might predict birds falling from the sky all over Manhattan. That doesn't mean it won't happen, it's just a poor prediction. Serial thieves hold a strong belief in stealing. That doesn't make it right, it just means their level of coherence is so diminished that their beliefs and predictions are damaged as well. Many thought the market wouldn't collapse in 2008. Only a few predicted what indeed happened.

- » Why were there only a few coherent enough to believe and predict this?
- » Why were there only a few who were able to position themselves accordingly, not only to protect themselves, and their position, but also to benefit from the destruction?

Our ability to predict accurately is the foundation for high performance and protection, which means coherence (orderliness). This ability is what separates the top performers from the average.

Task #2: Self-Identification

Who are you? When you read that question, the voice you heard, who was that? Who or what is inside of you talking? And how does what's inside become external? Through awareness, we understand that we exist, but existence is only the baseline. As your brain works away at predicting, it is also simultaneously deciding whether or not to take action. From there, every action lends to your self-identification. If you accepted a partnership, that is now part of who you are. You are the partner of XYZ Corporation. If you turn the doorknob and it falls off, you are the CEO without a doorknob. Every time you predict and act, you reinforce, and potentially modify, your belief system as well as your identity. If you predict well, you achieve effortlessly. If you predict poorly, you have to battle to protect your achievements and identity to stay afloat. Everything is more predictable and therefore more protected when you are operating from a place of high brain coherence.

Task #3: Unifying Diversity

> **"It's truly extraordinary that you have this body of impulses, neurons, molecules, and so on, with the power equivalent to all computational power on the planet. Every little piece is different and the diversity is enormous. The diversity in the brain is responsible for all of the other diversity that takes place within you, both mentally and physically. Each brain is a vast storehouse of all possibilities. All of the thoughts that come up are powering information based on what your kidneys need, what your heart needs, how that car reminds you of your first contract. Within you 100-billion, with a 'b' billion, brain cells and trillions of synapses are being unified by your brain. This is the most important function of your brain, to unify diversity. And the unification, the primary design characteristic of the brain, depends to a great extent on the coherence of the prefrontal cortex"**
>
> *–Dr. Alarik Arenander, PhD, director of The Brain Research Institute and president of The Leader's Brain*

If a leader can't unify differences and create agreement, they are bound to have conflict, complexity, and complications. These complications and complexities will undoubtedly corrupt and disrupt achievement and progress. Inner complications and confusions lead to external complications, corruptions, chaos, and confusions.

Task #4: Interfacing

As world-renowned brain expert from the Center for Brain, Consciousness and Cognition, Dr. Fred Travis, PhD, puts it in his book *Your Brain is a River, Not a Rock*:

> **"The brain is not a rock. It's a self-adapting structure. Rather than a rock, it's a river, and its function is to connect us to the outside world. The brain is the interface between the inner and the outer. Your**

> **picture of what will happen or how things look will be decided by what your brain is seeing. Based on trauma, incoherence, or poor predicting abilities, your brain can give you a picture that is incomplete or wrong, and that is how you see the world. Then, when you come up with an idea or make a decision, it's also wrong because it's being influenced by the trauma or the incoherence, and all the other things your river flows around."**

If the brain is not coherent in its ability to interface between our inner self and our outer environment, we have difficulty connecting the dots. In real life, connecting the dots refers to our ability to connect with others, or to connect with the right decisions, or to connect with the right people, or the right action. Interfacing is just another way of showing how things connect and interact with one another.

Task #5: Experiencing

> **"What you are, so is your world. Everything in the Universe is resolved into your own experience."**
>
> —*Maharishi Mahesh Yogi*

The most common way we hear people say this is, "You don't know what you don't know," and that's because you haven't experienced it yet. It's important to remember this: nobody could ever experience the world for you, nor you for them. Every experience you have changes your brain, but your brain doesn't create experiences, it only validates them. Every experience either strengthens or corrupts the neural pathways in your brain, and the more you experience one thing, the stronger those pathways become. This is called neuroplasticity—how the brain molds itself at each moment to your inner and outer experience. All of this activity creates the world you see and experience, which is your reality. You want to give your brain experiences that make your neural pathways more connected and coherent.

Most neural activity is based on past experiences you've already had. As you continue to have more experiences, your brain continues to change, a process that takes place without your realization.

How Does Change Occur in the Brain?

Change can occur in your brain in three specific ways, as described below. These changes are called neuroplasticity and they occur throughout your entire life, whether you are young or old. Research has also found that your brain is highly active, even in moments of silence, based on fMRI and neuroimaging results, proving there really isn't a complete "shut off"" time where your brain stops changing. This constant state of change, as previously mentioned, is rapidly inspired by your thoughts, behaviors, environment, development, and experiences.

Change Type #1: Chemical

According to Dr. Lara Boyd, PhD from the University of British Columbia, chemical change is the increase of chemical signaling between neurons to create actions or reactions. This type of change does not represent learning, as it is of brief duration.

So, for example, if you spent a single day learning better sales techniques, or how to negotiate better, or how to run faster, and you returned a week later, there's a good chance you may have forgotten plenty of what you learned the week before.

Achievement also falls into this category of short-term change in the brain, as it is not permanent, as many believe. The explosion of feel-good chemicals released when we achieve is a short-term event. Unfortunately, it often pushes leaders into a place where they crave that same feeling, so their leadership approach becomes an iteration of all the cycles we talk about in this book, desperately seeking that rush and temporary euphoria of achievement.

Another example might be if you took a single piano or music lesson. You would certainly react to the information you were hearing, but you might not retain any of what you've learned. This is why people go back for more than one lesson.

Change Type #2: Structural

In order to create structural (physical) change in the brain, your behaviors must be repetitive. This allows your neurons to create new evolutionary pathways or strengthen existing evolutionary pathways, which in turn is what will allow you to effectively change your default settings.

This is why the saying "practice makes perfect" is actually true. It isn't so much about the specific act or habit you are performing; it's more about what is taking place internally. As you practice, you are actually changing the structure of your brain by allowing your neurons to secure those new default settings, therefore creating and strengthening new neural pathways.

Unlike chemical changes, structural changes in the brain represent possible long-term change, and also take longer to occur. These structural changes are the foundation for new skills you learn or knowledge you practice to retain. In order for those pathways to be created by the neurons working hard below the surface, you have to practice, or repeat, behaviors or skills. This allows the structural change to begin taking place, for long-term learning, growth, or memory. Sadly, most people stop doing things while this change is occurring, because the changes or results cannot be seen or felt immediately.

We can use sleep as an effective example here. Fifty years of sleep research has found that 7-8 hours of sleep is what is required for optimal brain function. Anything less or more than the recommended 7-8 hours is considered a sleep abnormality. One night of too little sleep is going to have a slight structural and chemical change on the brain. This slight structural or chemical change will have slight effects on your ability to predict or make accurate decisions the following day.

We've all been there, where we've burned the midnight oil and felt "off" the next day because of it. If we go several nights with too little sleep, the structural and chemical changes begin to accumulate, creating potentially long-term effects on your brain.

These larger changes will lead you down a path of more inaccurate predicting and less precise decision making, two grave side effects that will cause loss of time, money, ROI, key talent, shareholder value, opportunity, and, most importantly, your health and reputation. It hardly seems fair. Leaders who dive into the busy business marketplace, and participate in all of the activities that "thriving leaders" participate in—keeping long hours, eating junk food, drinking every evening—eventually fall victim to those same activities.

We cannot reiterate this point enough: you do not have to abuse/corrupt/destroy/ruin yourself to achieve. You do not have to sacrifice your health, wealth, or happiness to achieve success as a leader. That way of life is outdated and dangerous, and no matter how "big" or successful you are, you will never be immune to the effects of poor lifestyle decisions. Your life is worth more. As a leader, you owe your people more, and you owe yourself more. It's of great concern to us that we see leaders practicing these extremes way more than we see leaders practicing balance. We either see leaders settling for mediocrity or leaders constantly risking it all for small payoffs, fleeting fulfillment, and non-evolutionary action. This level of mediocrity is so much less than your capacity, and you must realize this to move forward.

Change Type #3: Functional

Lastly, we are going to discuss functional change in the brain. Your brain can alter its functionality, something we find to be astounding. This ability to change paints an even clearer picture of the awesome power and capabilities built into your brain. The more you use specific areas of your brain, the easier it becomes to use those areas of your brain.

These types of changes support learning, and most importantly, remembering. The more you are able to develop your mind and yourself, the more you are able to remember, and the more you are able to remember, the easier it will become for you to tap into the infinite knowledge within you. Bottom line: you can use neuroplasticity as a means to develop yourself.

This is really incredible because, based on these facts about your brain and its function, we can validate our theory. The most important thing you can do to become a better leader is to develop yourself and increase coherence across your brain. By accessing your global alpha coherent state, you achieve more and more inner development, you create default settings that are designed to keep you growing and developing—you initiate a cycle of success that truly unleashes your potential. This cycle of success works when you're increasing and stabilizing your GAC- Global Alpha Coherence (where both silence and alertness co-exist), which we've already identified as the secret of top performers.

Companies don't fail because of action or even lack of action; rather they fail because of the lack of their leaders' internal silence to identify and support more effective action. Favoring evolutionary progress is silence and dynamism together, which enables businesses to experience right-thought/right-action scenarios more often.

Leaders can get so attached and identified to developing things on the outside that they neglect developing themselves on the inside. This is where trouble strikes their personal health, wealth, happiness, and relationships, and affects the prospects and potential of their companies. When leaders exist in a constant state of vulnerability and stimulation, they are unprotected. When the inner development of coherence capacity has not kept up with the growth on the outside, that leader will start to experience instability. Now, vulnerability is a valuable thing when it results in purification, because it creates new energy which leads to clarity of understanding. Heightened clarity of understanding means you have greater coherence to be in the leadership state and more capacity to handle any obstacles or opportunities. Coherence and capacity are the foundation for enhancing your powers of comprehension, foresight, competence, confidence, connectedness with self and others, and congruence.

The change occurring on the inside will be the source for the change happening on the outside. **Perception drives reality, and development decides perception. Development comes from greater coherence, which allows for better predicting capabilities, leading to an enhanced protection capacity.**

Built-In Brain Protection

While we're talking about your brain, it's important that we also point out the ways in which you have been designed to protect your all-important brain. The brain is protected by the skull, meninges, cerebrospinal fluid, and the blood-brain barrier.

So while we are presenting a case for protection you can develop, it's also important to point out the protection written into your genetic code, a reminder which fortifies our overarching concept of The Science of Protection. We want to show you that protection is inherent to you and a part of you in every way, but due to being caught in the grips of our world's exponential rate of change, we may be unknowingly corrupting our built-in protections.

Your brain has built-in systems for protection because without those systems, the brain would become easily damaged or injured, thereby prohibiting you from fully living or possibly even surviving. Without those systems your brain would be incredibly vulnerable, at the mercy of its environment.

Taking on too much responsibility for achievement and progress can be disastrous for your brain health if you're not dissolving the stresses you accumulate along the way. Remember, stress occurs when we don't have enough capacity to handle everything on our plate. An example of this comes to mind: we encouraged one of our clients, for years, to do something about his health. The effect that the stress of running a multi-billion-dollar business, day in and day out, was visible on him. Unfortunately, he did not heed our advice and ended up having a stroke. The stress of perpetually driving progress slowly accumulated over the years, and eventually caught up with him. The systems for protecting his brain were weakened, and eventually were left with no other option but to initiate a stroke to help restore a more natural and balanced level of functioning.

Structuring the Brain Occurs in Two Steps

If you've only heard about a strawberry, you may have an intellectual understanding of what a strawberry tastes like. If you've actually tasted the strawberry, you have the experience and the understanding. Experience is primary to complete understanding. This is how life works. As we have experiences, we develop deeper more complete understanding of those experiences. Watching a roller coaster race over the tracks, looping and barreling down the steepest slopes you've ever seen, still isn't quite the same as being in one of the cars, along for the ride. Experience comes first, and then the brain validates and integrates the experience through understanding.

This simple cycle of input and output is constantly creating the state of you—whether it's for the better, the worse, or has no net effect one way or the other—with each decision and experience.

State Your In + Intellectual Understanding + Decision
+ Experience = Complete Understanding

How Do Experiences Happen?

Everything begins with the state you're in. This is the foundation for every single experience, and to create the right and most enriching experience, your state must be stable, coherent, and protected. We will further discuss this leadership state of coherence and protection in the next chapter.

Now that we've explained the functionality and processes of the brain, we want to go one step earlier in the process. We want to identify the foundation for the tasks your brain is completing. Before you ever act, or strengthen any of the neural pathways in your brain, there is a state of existence deciding everything.

These explanations are, of course, a simplification of the complex processes taking place every second of your life, to show how prefrontal cortex brain functioning is the CEO of you, and to demonstrate how you can stabilize these processes for maximum results by existing in a state that encourages growth, rather than inhibiting it.

To avoid sounding like a sci-fi novel, we won't use the words *mind* and *control* in the same sentence, but this knowledge is part of your next level shift.

Put All of Your Training to Work

Plenty of self-help material, coaches, and consultants talk about the inner world, but haven't personally experienced that level of development. Therefore they cannot teach this deeper level of inner development. So they will talk about the inner world and then default, unknowingly, back to the outer world for examples. They talk about the roller coaster, but they've never experienced the thrill.

We had one client who spent more than $100,000 over the course of a decade on development programs with a very well-known self-improvement organization. After working with us for one year, he said he felt more developed than he ever had. Oddly, he had invested about 90% less time and money into his interactions with us, which is a nod to the knowledge we are sharing in this book. The other programs he participated in were only scratching the surface of development, mainly focusing on the level of intellectual change. The time he spent with them was topical, and never led him to the deeper coherent source of thinking and feeling.

These attempts at explaining to you how to "hack your brain" are tremendous, and we applaud these efforts, but they are not realistic. If you think you can control all of the synapses, **and** unify the enormous diversity of your being, **and** control thoughts before they bubble to the surface in a fraction of a second, **and** constantly stabilize the connections, **and** do all of this on every level, while everything is occurring so rapidly—well, that is equivalent to insanity.

While these coaches and consultants might use the language of inner development, these tricks and shortcuts never work. They only ever create external superficial change, rather than a durable, internal, structural change.

If you want lasting change, you have to transcend what is on the surface, so those affirmations work on a deeper level. You must transcend not only the constant streams of thoughts and diverse necessities, but also the very processes of the brain, in order to access the part where you can change the state you exist in. This is something we'll explore further in the next chapter on Leadership State.

These top coaches and consultants have a broader perspective, so they can see more, but seeing something and teaching something are two different things entirely. So they might be telling you what they see, but they can't tell you how to develop it—and they don't even realize it. They work hard to come up with action-oriented habits and 10-step programs, but you always end up where you were before you began. The knowledge is valuable on a surface level, but it will always remain intellectual knowledge, not developmental change.

Training programs have as much value as *your* brain has coherence. Coaches and consultants can only offer as much efficacy as *their* brains have coherence.

So, coherence is fundamental, and you need a bucket that doesn't leak before spending time and money trying to fill it. This is one of the many reasons so many leaders never experience deeper awareness and protection. Your experience may have some value in protecting you as you achieve, but that is not enough. Do not let yourself be one of the many disillusioned leaders who believe their time and experience is all they need to keep soaring to the top.

Why do you think so many millionaires, and even billionaires, are being minted in their twenties and thirties now? They certainly don't have as much experience in business or life as someone in their forties, fifties, or sixties. So we can safely say it isn't their experience level that is primary to their massive success. The credit goes to their elevated level of awareness, which allows them to see and feel more. This opens up possibilities for evolutionary and positively disruptive action.

You can exhaust all of the resources around you, intellectually learning everything you possibly can about how to be a better leader or decision maker, but you likely won't see lasting change from this because learning doesn't actually change your brain itself in a meaningful way when it comes to leadership. More is required. And by more, we are referring to coherence.

Upgrading Your Executive Brain

Everything in this book illuminates the obscured foundation for all of the training you've ever received. The knowledge in these pages is the missing piece of your development puzzle, and the most important piece, by far. Sometimes, we take steps forward only to go backward. In the case of protection, you are taking steps back to your foundation, to begin taking giant leaps forward.

The more you develop your prefrontal cortex, the more coherence you have, the higher your mind-brain development, the better leader you become, the better life gets, the more you effortlessly achieve, the more you experience the Zero Factor (where the time between the right thought and right action is near zero), the more fulfilled you are, the more bliss you experience, the more you can live out your purpose, and, ultimately, the more you can affect the world by doing what's right for everyone, including yourself.

A high-powered engine needs oil to run. It doesn't matter how much power the engine has, without oil the power amounts to nothing and the engine will eventually break down and cease functioning. The time you spend developing your prefrontal cortex is the time you spend oiling your high-powered engine, your brain, so it can do great things.

Living in disorder creates disorder in every area of your life, just as living in coherence creates coherence in every area of your life. You live in coherence by developing your prefrontal cortex. This is your control panel, and as a leader, it needs coherence to be orderly and function at a high level. When your prefrontal cortex is confused, stressed, and fatigued, your value system, ability to make sound decisions, sense of self, belief systems, morals, creativity, intelligence, ability to predict, decision-making, and self-control are all reduced. All of these systems begin in the brain, and more specifically, within the CEO of you, your prefrontal cortex.

ONLY Coherence Breaks the Incoherence Cycle

When you take time each day to infuse more coherence into the CEO of you, you are less likely to get stuck in cycles or ruts. Coherence literally breaks the incoherent cycles in your life. If you become stressed and attempt to hyper-focus on breaking the cycle, you may end up only repeating the cycle because stress essentially shuts your brain down. For the same reasons we can create new, stronger pathways by practicing positive and growth-accelerating behaviors, we can also get stuck in ruts, or cycles we have relived several times over.

Wherever you are in your growth as a leader, right now, can be made better through more coherence in your brain. This is a fact. If you want to experience stabilized, long-term, high performance, to become a true leader, having protection through coherence is the answer. Gaining the ability to understand and reach higher levels of brain functionality is a key indicator of a true leader.

Developing your inner self will leave you with the realization that you are in control of you, even on profound levels that perhaps once seemed unattainable. This new way of leadership is one that allows you to identify with the parts of yourself that drive and motivate you to action, your brain being at the center of your path to high performance leadership. We promised not to say mind and control in the same sentence, so we will call it protection. Achieving and maintaining Global Alpha Coherence, and the truths that uphold this new Science of Protection, are the beginning of a new era in leadership, business, and all arenas of high-level performance.

Adaptability, Change, and You

Our business landscape is experiencing such rapid change, all the time, if we were to graph this change, the line would curve straight up on the paper. This change isn't only in one area either. Everything is changing all the time, exponentially. Yet the curve for human adaptability is still almost flat. According to Dr. Harung, this is why the brain is the new technology everyone wants to discover.

A well-known observation made by Intel co-founder Gordon Moore, known as Moore's Law, states that the number of transistors on a chip doubles roughly every two years, while the costs are halved. That means that computers are doubling processing speed and thereby increasing their potential at a rapid pace. This hardware development, which has led to a corresponding explosion in software development, has left us in a position where we, as human beings, need to begin developing our own humanware to keep up.

Our obsessive attachment to our outer development has outpaced our inner growth. Now we have to go back to inner development in order to support and protect the outer development. Remember, inner development is the foundation for outer development.

This isn't only true for development. We are being outpaced by the change of everything we have created. We are not successfully predicting, and for this reason businesses are struggling and failing at a rapid pace. With so much change, so quickly, it seems nearly impossible for businesses and leaders today to see what is coming down the pipeline. Add to this the fact that today's leaders are operating with limited capacity due to a lack of inner coherence and development, and predicting the amount of change to come is near impossible. You only have to read the title and first 30 pages of Thomas Friedman's Thank You for Being Late: An Optimist's Guide to Thriving in the Age of Accelerations to catch a glimpse of our current pace of change, and what that predicted acceleration rate will look like in the future.

When you see a business struggling, it isn't because of a bad PR move or poor quarterly projections. Those are merely symptoms providing a warning flag. Leaders impair their own progress by continuing and contributing to this age of ignorance we are currently experiencing. We are going so fast without more fully developing our inner intelligence and wisdom to guide us. The key to this intelligence, the secret to transcending rapid change and potential crash-and-burn failure, is coherence that gives protection. Protection is important because once you've lost something, the chances of you getting it back are slim, and you then have to live with that. The captain always goes down with the ship. When you take care of and develop the captain, or CEO of you, you're much less likely to find yourself sinking in the first place.

Speaking of the Captain, Back to Your Prefrontal Cortex

We have previously mentioned that the prefrontal cortex functions as your executive control center in life. On average, we know that it takes your prefrontal cortex around 25 years to develop into its mature form. The problem we see now is that the most valuable development time is often wasted, which contributes to the age of ignorance we currently live in.

Most everything we participate in fights the potential of our growing brain, causing damage rather than encouraging growth. Think about what we've created:

» We are a society who brags about a lack of sleep as if it's something to be proud of.
» We encourage our youth to start early in high impact sports.
» We wear stress around like a badge of honor.
» We take chemicals, drugs, and drink drinks to wake us up and help us sleep.

Then we repeat this over and over and over again, through generations of people. We overcommit to the wrong things while we leave no time for the right things. Everything embedded in our society—from personal habits to social conventions to the way our workdays are structured—is not designed to develop our prefrontal cortex. And as described earlier, when our prefrontal cortex is underdeveloped, we lack potential, capacity, and protection.

This cycle has been going on for so long that everyone simply follows suit, assuming if all of this were wrong, everyone wouldn't be voluntarily participating. So we continue flat lining in our adaptability, as we cram our lives full of too many of the wrong experiences, and not enough of the right experiences.

This explains why we often see leaders busy putting out fires. This level of adaptability is purely reactive, and without expanding our potential or capacity on this front, this will remain true. You can buy more water to help put out more fires, but what prevents the fires from starting in the first place? You can create firewalls to try and keep the fire in one area, but there's still fire, and eventually it will spread. You can take action once the fire starts, but until you increase your potential to protect yourself, and avoid the fire altogether, *nothing will change.*

The Highest Value of the Amygdala Is not Fight or Flight or Freeze

Here's the thing; the amygdala really gets a bad and oversimplified reputation, even being called "the fear center." But the amygdala performs a much more complex set of functions than merely activating our flight or fight responses. The amygdala is a roughly almond-shaped mass of gray matter inside each cerebral hemisphere of the brain; it is involved with experiencing and processing emotional impulses. A more appropriate overview would be to say the amygdala is the area of the brain that is part of the process for controlling how we respond to, and more importantly foresee, stimuli. Fear is only a symptom, and the amygdala isn't there to be the slave of fear. Its capacity is so much greater. At its highest levels of development, the amygdala provides valuable functionality in the forms of proactivity, preventative protection, and vigilance (in addition to its basic roles of responding to fear and activating flight or fight responses).

In order for this to be the reality of how your amygdala functions, it must be coherent and integrated with your prefrontal cortex. To properly assess situations, to maintain proactivity rather than reactivity, to get ahead of the rapid change currently driving our business market, you must develop this higher level of functioning.

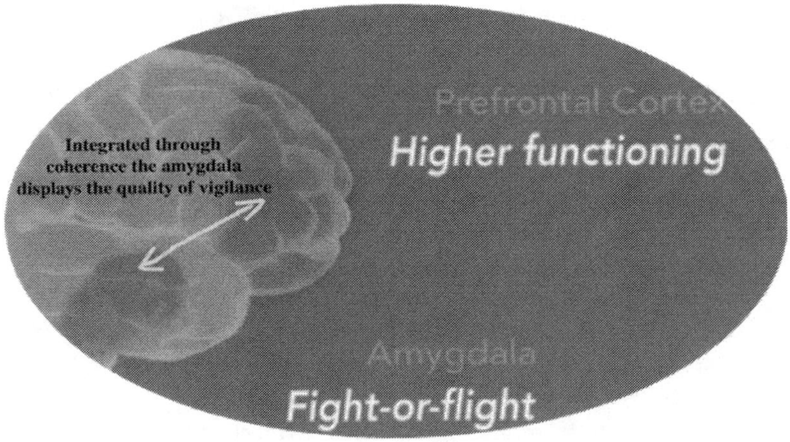

All of the qualities of a developed prefrontal cortex ultimately result in the amygdala performing its highest function of protection. A developed prefrontal cortex provides:

» Maximum Coherence (foundation)
» Maximum Predicting
» Maximum Interfacing
» Maximum Evaluation
» Maximum Response
» Maximum Recording

Rather than always reacting and creating fear for the amygdala to deal with, you can develop your prefrontal cortex to stabilize your responses, and anticipate processes. A developed prefrontal cortex gives stability and vigilance to your amygdala, allowing it to anticipate and respond better. This will help you become more in-tune with change, rather than feeling like a victim of change, all with the goal of protecting yourself, your team, what you achieve and become an enlightened leader.

Here's a real world example of prefrontal cortex–amygdala "team's" ability to avert danger and problems before they arise, something we commonly refer to as your sixth sense. Hubert Joly became Best Buy's CEO in August 2012, despite critics saying he was unqualified for the job. Many predicted the retailer would follow in the failed footsteps of Circuit City, but Joly had other ideas. His "Renew Blue" program helped Best Buy reverse declining sales, improve customer satisfaction, and increase profitability by growing online sales and cutting costs. Best Buy reported Q2 2018 results that exceeded expectations, and diluted earnings per share increased by 28 percent from a year ago. Just as we can clearly see the lack of protection in situations where leaders and businesses fail, here we get to see the opposite, where a business leader anticipated risks and dangers and proactively counteracted them.

We know you do not want to unnecessarily suffer or fail. So why does it happen? The answer is simple: brain development. Developing your brain to a higher level is the root-cause antidote, your insurance policy, to ensure that whatever you are conceiving, believing, and achieving is less likely to be corrupted, diminished, or lost.

Everything is changing around you all the time. In fact, we experience so much change; we almost become blind to it, and passively permit ourselves to be pushed back and forth by it. We simply don't have the capacity to sense all of the change, both micro and macro, that surrounds us, so we oftentimes tune it out, until we are forced to revisit that change at a later day—usually right after something goes wrong. But what if you could be in tune with that change, rather than fearfully hiding from it and tuning it out?

Go back to the examples in the beginning of this book and consider how many giants, in the history of business, have been forced into a state of reactivity, and consequently fell from their perch at the top because of their inability to have vision and stay ahead of the change or at least be in tune with it.

In order for the relationship between your prefrontal cortex and amygdala to achieve this elevated state of coherence, stability, and vigilance, you have to give your brain more of the right experiences and less of the wrong experiences. You have to stop putting bad things in and naively assuming you are above their lasting and deep impressions. As a leader, you require an even more developed prefrontal cortex to better predict what change is on the horizon and stay ahead of it.

You have 100 billion brain cells either working in your favor or working against you, depending on what you're feeding them. With this much activity constantly taking place, it is easy to see how mistakes are made, especially in business, and how quickly we can get off track. The only method to improve your capacity to see the hidden variables in everything is to increase the coherence, or orderliness, of your brain.

Your brain is the humanware that has and will, through neuroplasticity, continue to make even better hardware (neural connections) and software (decisions and insights), as we continue to develop and utilize more of these 100 billion neurons by increasing coherence. A comprehensive and grounded ability to see the big picture is a by-product of development.

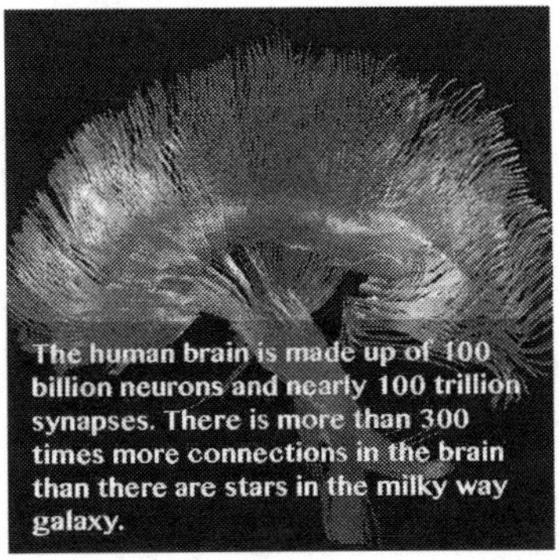
The human brain is made up of 100 billion neurons and nearly 100 trillion synapses. There is more than 300 times more connections in the brain than there are stars in the milky way galaxy.

Unfortunately, our research has shown that many leaders struggle with really seeing the big picture. Imagine your business as your ship, with you the captain, unprotected, in a vast sea full of potential dangers. You must navigate your ship through rough waters, avoiding other ships, pirates, running ashore, or sinking. That's quite a tall order for anyone, but then imagine we asked you to do this every day in a blindfold.

We constantly see leaders who lack development and coherence, and are therefore poor at predicting future change. This leads to deficient long-term decision making that negatively impacts the future of their business and employees—all because they are basing their decisions on only half the picture. Compounding the problem is that these leaders fully believe they are looking at the whole picture. Their ego tricks them into believing they have/know/see it all, and then they fail. As history has shown us, the crash isn't pretty, and few ever fully recover.

The reason we see this so often is because, as Dr. Fred Travis puts it, your brain is a river, not a rock, and your brain is being influenced by each experience of fear, trauma, or failure. You don't realize this influence because much of it happens subconsciously. Each moment of influence helps to create the world you see, which in turn informs how you perceive situations. You have no idea, as you perceive, that your river is flowing around all of these influences. These negative impressions can definitely make your brain seem more rock-like, as it normalizes a state of existence that is rigid and fear-based. This gives you a fragmented view of the world, and cements those neural pathways for future activation in your brain.

> **"90% of doctors' visits are for stress-related health complaints."**
>
> *–National Library of Medicine, Study on Stress*

> **"55% of Americans feel stressed, 45% worried, 22% angry."**
>
> *–Gallup World Poll 2018*

> **"The US is the 7th most stressed country in the world."**
>
> *- Forbes Statista*

Your Brain on Stress

Part of the shift into true leadership territory involves realizing the ways in which we inhibit our own growth. Stress sits at the top of this list. As leaders, one of the most destructive things we do is hold onto stress. This isn't always intentional, because sometimes we think we've let go of stress—but it is usually still boiling below the surface, causing damage to our organs, interrupting our cognitive processes, and diminishing our ability to be settled.

Stress creates negativity, setbacks, brain fog, pointless losses, errors in judgment, avoidable accidents, blind spots, illnesses, burnout, and even injury or death. Stress forms in layers, some personal, some professional, but each layer covers every aspect of your life. It's not realistic to assume that your professional stress stays at work and your personal stress stays at home.

A study completed by the researchers at the Ruhr- Universität Bochum found that chronic stress can change your brain's chemical, functional, and structural make-up (the three types of change discussed earlier), even down to the level of your DNA. In addition, chronic stress suppresses your immune system, leaving you unprotected and vulnerable to numerous health problems, creating perfect environments for viruses and cancers to make a home for themselves.

We know that you know just how terrible and heavy stress actually is. The reason we are talking about stress, again, is because many leaders are unwilling to give it up. For many leaders, giving up stress means relinquishing control—something they flatly refuse to do. A common reason for this is that plenty of leaders self-identify with their deep levels of stress. The stress is a part of who they feel they are, and letting go of that stress makes them feel like less of a leader. This can be compared to the idea of modern busyness.

> **"Doing nothing is better than being busy doing nothing."**
>
> —*Lao Tzu*

Busyness vs. Business

It's a very common mindset of people in business to believe that the busier they are, the more important they are. We have to get rid of this idea that we always have to be "on" or "grinding" or "hustling" to be successful. **Being aligned is the new hustle. Being coherent is the new grind.**

This idea of doing things the way they've always been done, for the sake of non-change, brings to mind an old parable.

A young boy is fishing with his father just off the river bank. As the sun begins to set, they take their catch of the day and head back to their modest home near the edge of their village. The young boy watches carefully as his father removes both the head and tail of their catch before placing the fish in the pan to cook. "Father," the young boy asks, "why do you cut off the head and tail?" The father thinks for a moment and replies, "This is the way we have always done it my son. Your grandfather taught me." Curious, after their meal, the young boy travels across their village to his grandfather's home. "Grandfather," the young boy asks, "why do you cut off the head and tail of the fish before cooking it?" After considering the question for a moment, the grandfather giggles and leads the young boy into the kitchen. He opens his cupboard and pulls out his only pan, very small and narrow in shape. "Well," the grandfather says with a smile on his face, "that's the only way I can get the fish to fit into the pan."

As the parable aptly illustrates, we can't always see how our actions are often based on past experiences which no longer apply. We are so immersed in maintaining the external balance, that we don't realize how our big picture goals are based on a very small picture that relies on the ways of the past to stay alive.

In the minds of some leaders, stress is the same. The more fires they have to put out, the higher their rank, the more important they are, the more they are needed. This becomes a cycle that leaders feed on to remain in a state of relevancy. Plenty of leaders get stuck in meaningless busyness, which interferes with real business.

Your ability to deal with stress doesn't make you more of a leader. It simply means you haven't developed yourself enough to escape this cycle.

Stress isn't the real problem. Stress is only a by-product of not investing the time to expand your brain's coherence. As a result, you end up defaulting to handling and managing the stress you needlessly generate. You will never get rid of stress by just trying to "cope" with it. Stress is a symptom.

The solution to the symptom is to treat the cause, which is a lack of coherence. More coherence, which gives you a more settled and alert mind, will purify and wash the stress from your mind, brain, and nervous and immune systems. Purifying your mind takes away the ability of stress to leave a seed impression for disease to grow. As you develop a more robust, coherent, and supple mind, brain, and body, you will find that stress cannot easily leave an impression on you any longer. That's not to say you will no longer be able to identify or recognize stress. What changes is the effect stress has in your life.

The result of purified stress: Brain development leads to the ability to neutralize stress altogether by having higher coherence to make decisions that are free from negative consequences.

Someone who is always caught up in doing things, rather than taking time to reflect, connect, and develop their coherence, is a busy fool. Always doing for the sake of doing is equal to wasted time and busyness, which causes even more stress; wasting resources, time, and energy. The cycle needs to be broken. Coherence breaks the cycle. Author Ben Hardy wrote in Medium that:

> **"In 2005, the National Science Foundation published an article showing that the average person has between 12,000 and 60,000 thoughts per day. Of those, 80% are negative and 95% are exactly the same repetitive thoughts as the day before."**

It makes sense that a more coherent brain, functioning at a higher level, is much more efficient at consistently generating positive, productive thoughts. A low-performing brain is less coherent, and therefore regularly experiences fragmented, stressed, and distracted thoughts.

If you've experienced trauma of any kind, this stress cycle may be all you know. To escape this cycle requires you to rewire your brain, to change the pathways those neurons have been traveling for a long time, and to develop and strengthen new pathways for new default settings.

> **"The mind is like water. When it's turbulent, it's difficult to see. When it's calm, everything becomes clear."**
>
> *—Prasad Mahes*

The Real Goal in Non-Doing While You're Doing

Paolo and Raamon having been both competitive athletes for 10 years each and full-time meditating monks for 25 years combined learned that non-doing is the real goal, not doing. This means being established in the silent non-doing coherence and then perform in a more effective, accurate and supportive way. Because when you have that silent coherence it pervades everything inside and outside you. When you don't then errors, injuries, mistakes and accidents creep in more easily. We'll talk about this at the end of the next chapter on Leadership State which completes the internal protection development part of the Science of Protection.

Coherence Brings About Protection

In order for this method to be effective, there must be coherence. Another word for coherence is orderliness, which is what the brain really (*really*) wants, so it can build up its functionality to become a powerful ally.

In nature, we see that coherence is how the environment protects itself to survive. While completing research for her doctoral thesis, ecologist Suzanne Simard made an astounding discovery. Simard found that trees have a secret life, which takes place below the ground. Trees talk to one another, communicate their needs, and even send nutrients by way of a complex network in the soil. This secret life of trees provides us one example, of many, of how coherence in nature is necessary to survival.

We've all witnessed birds flocking together, synchronizing their movements as they soar, sometimes at speeds over 60 miles per hour. In a flash, the entire flock of birds can shift, morph, or create an opening to avoid predators. They also change direction and/or altitude to swoop for food.

Schools of fish have exhibited similar behaviors of coherent functioning, remaining in constant orderly motion. You can imagine if those fish were drunk or under the influence of some substance, or perhaps lacking sleep, injured, traumatized, or stressed, the school probably couldn't execute such orderly movements. They might have trouble keeping up or anticipating the next movement for survival.

Protection is based on your mind being coherent

Logic can be dangerous when used as the sole source of deciding as it comes from the small mind. Logic wants proof and is calculated. Protection comes from the coherent big mind or higher brain that sees more of the whole picture. The goal is to avert the danger not just be aware of it when it can be too late. A coherent mind is what naturally protects you. Also, really believing and having faith is because your mind is coherent. When you're not coherent you'll doubt and corrupt your believing and faith.

The infinite organizing power of nature and the universe, which is upholding everything that allows planets not to smash into each other going around the sun, is an example of perfect coherence. This is what we want to align our mind with. When we do this, we realize everything already exists and is created starting from within. We simply grasp what to create when we're coherent.

A company with good leaders can fail when they haven't been developing more coherent minds from the inside out. The bottom line is this: when we're not coherent we're not protected and we lose money, time, opportunities… fill in the blank.

We don't progress when the mind is incoherent. When each individual becomes more coherent there is an amplifier effect as seen below:

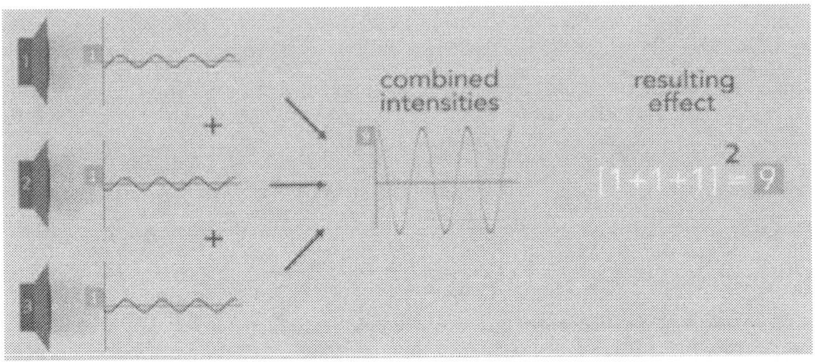

More coherent people naturally create a more coherent protected world:

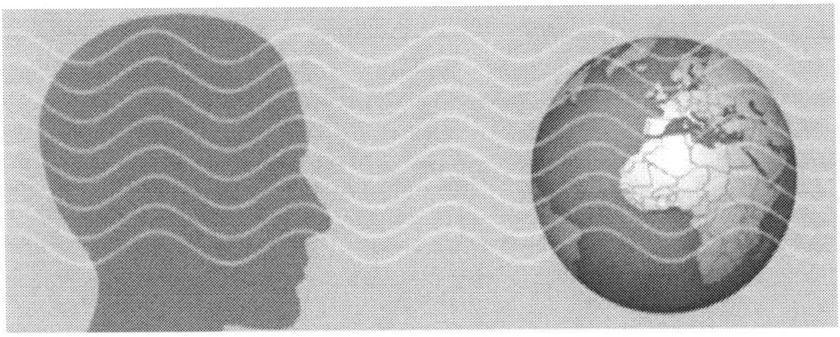

Leading Yourself Out of Ignorance, Arrogance and Incoherence

A true leader first leads themselves out of their own ignorance, arrogance, and incoherence by developing GAC-Global Alpha Coherence. Whether you realize it or not, you have a powerful influence on your environment, and this influence is based on how your brain is functioning. If you are functioning at a high level, you will have a higher vibrational energy, and your effect on those around you will be greater.

Coherence allows you to take full advantage of the complex power of your brain. It's the internal development of the whole brain that influences outcomes. If you focus on developing the inside first, coherence makes it easier to:

- » let go of stress
- » achieve
- » make decisions
- » have clarity
- » love your people
- » be a great leader
- » achieve sustainably

Life becomes easier when you focus on developing the inside first. When you develop the inside, the outside will develop as a by-product. Just as watering the roots under a tree allows the whole tree to grow, your inner development will do the same for you.

**For the cup of water to overflow,
it has to be full on the inside first.**

As a leader, you either have 100% coherence between your creative instincts and your logical execution, or you have less than 100% coherence. You either have 100% coherence between your team and the needs of your clients, or you have less than 100%. You either have 100% coherence when predicting, acting, and experiencing, or you have less than 100% coherence.

The more coherence you generate inside, the more coherence and support you experience outside. This increased coherence naturally generates a threshold of positive energy, clarity, creativity, and power. This power shows up in your life, and in your role as a leader. Coherence allows you to inspire more spontaneous support for what you want to see happen, while neutralizing what you don't want to see happen.

For most leaders today, leadership is a conscious and sub-conscious experience. They can report what is going on consciously and feel what is going on sub-consciously, to whatever degree they have developed their sub-conscious. What is missing from this modern approach to leadership is the source of the conscious and sub-conscious which is consciousness. Conscious and sub-conscious pertain to individual awareness whereas consciousness is all-pervading awareness of self and everything in the environment.

We have become obsessed with finding cures, without ever learning about the cause. Understanding the source of your development; the source of the world you see, the source of the change we are experiencing, is paramount to ascending into greater levels in leadership. We need to stop focusing on the symptoms and go back to the root cause of this lack of protection and stability in business and leadership.

Using the sun as an analogy, we can say that the sun shines everywhere the same, but reflects everywhere differently. The reflectors are the brain and the body. The reflections are our experiences and our individual personalities. Modern science has completed study after study showing if you do something to the brain, you change the conscious experience.

Decisions and changes shouldn't be made based on influences on the outside. Leaders should make decisions by learning to go to the source of their intelligence and leadership, rather than always working to handle the symptoms.

Leadership of the future will require this coherence, which is necessary for protection. Existing in this zone, this leadership state is the only way to get ahead of the exponential and rapid change we will continue to see. For the first time in history, we can use science and the functions of the human brain to explain the need for coherence in a leader's brain, and also how to achieve this state of heightened connectivity.

As the world begins to wake up with greater depth, breadth and quality of consciousness, our business landscape will follow suit. This is no longer a fad approach to "hacking leadership" or "hacking the brain." This is the new leadership state you must exist in, if you expect to get what you want, protect it, and keep it.

This unified agreement puts you in the position to lead while:

» Minimizing loss of time, money, energy, ROI, key talent, shareholder value, health, and reputation
» Diminishing fear and fear-based decision-making
» Preventing and reducing costly failure and mistakes that slow achievement and progress
» Ensuring that you are going to gain what you expect in the long run
» Giving you the ability to continue to achieve and progress amidst exponential change and challenges
» Preventing you from being hijacked by your ego, or someone else's
» Preventing you from falling out of alignment with your "inner why" and purpose

» Allowing you to overcome inertia in yourself and others faster. Inertia can show itself in the form of ignorance, arrogance, stress, vices, illusions, delusions, impressions, resentments, and incoherence.

Just as we have taken the most complex organ in your body and simplified it, coherence will do the same in your life. Coherence is the bridge from over complication to simplification in every aspect of your business and life.

Creating a unified agreement with the CEO of you is the foundation of achieving your leadership goals. This unified experience will leave you feeling at ease in your leadership abilities. For the first time in your life, you will know, without a doubt, that you are taking the most impactful path in leadership. You will be immersed in confidence of your purpose, a feeling that is almost indescribable. You will experience deep fulfillment that will be more profound than all of your achievements combined.

Every single bit of personal development training you've had to date has likely promised to stabilize your leadership or help you find your purpose. Did they deliver? Now, you finally have the missing piece, the answers to your questions, and the foundation for anywhere you want to go in leadership and in life. The Science of Protection provides you the knowledge to implement time and field-tested techniques, technologies, and programs to upgrade the CEO of you.

Your battles and your triumphs have led you right here, to this moment. And you must choose. Are you ready to fulfill your inner why? Are you ready to step into your true power as a leader? Are you ready to develop, protect, enhance, and fully switch on the CEO of you?

So that's the understanding of how you can be the most coherent you and help others understand the same. The benefit of this high alpha coherence is more clarity to pick up on the right unifying, protecting and progressive thought at the right time. Now you're ready to be in the leadership state which is next.

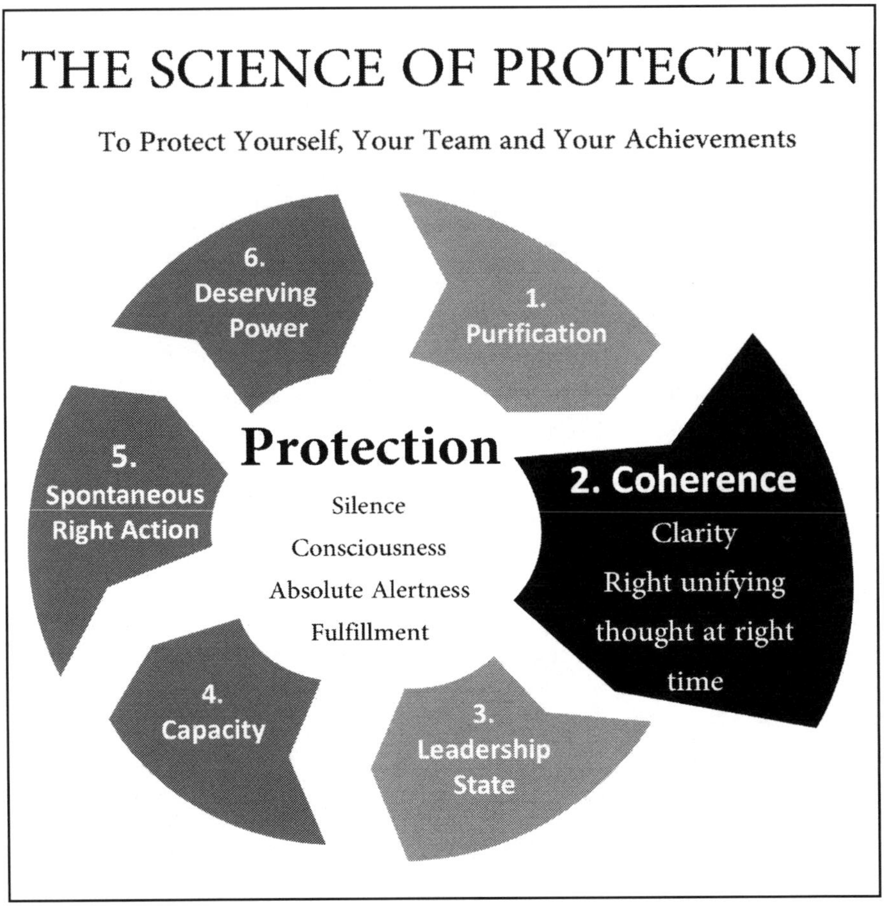

YOUR TURN

Being the Most Coherent You

1. Where are you most coherent in your leadership right now? Where are you least coherent?
2. What can you do to enhance and protect the CEO of you, your prefrontal cortex?
3. Go to YouTube and type "Fred Travis transcendental meditation" into the search box to learn more about how this simple effortless mental technique helps develop the most coherent CEO of You.

5 The Leadership State

The Awake Truthful Creative Mind

Where there is complete wakefulness (absolute alertness), there is victory and protection. Victory, fulfillment of what you want, comes from a pure, truthful, integrated, self-referral state of mind and leadership.

High performers are pioneers, providing us a glimpse into the possibilities of the future and helping us as we begin to understand that our state of consciousness is who we are, and the foundation of what we do.

In the previous chapter we brought out the value of coherence, the ability to have a Global Alpha Coherent brain to have optimal clarity, which means having the right unifying, protecting and progressive thought at the right time. This is what activates, supports and sustains the next component in the Science of Protection which is being in the leadership state.

The Leadership State is having an awake truthful creative state of mind to proactively avert danger and see the best possibilities.

The first part of this chapter is a very in-depth continuation of chapter three. Through new, exciting research, we will explain the leadership state, and how to stabilize this state for maximum performance.

Plenty of us know about "the zone," but few understand how to experience this high performance on a sustained and continuous basis, to maintain achievement, progress, and inner fulfillment. We touched briefly on the leadership state in previous chapters, so let's take a more in-depth look at this consciousness-based shift.

Only 1% of leaders will live up to their potential.

In plain terms, we do not perform at our highest level as consistently as we could for three reasons:

1. We do not cultivate and protect our inner leadership state.

2. We do not expand our capacity of coherence to stabilize this leadership state.

3. We aren't provided the most effective tools or knowledge for this level of growth.

Launched in 2009, The Human Connectome Project has proven to be the best documented long-term study, thus far, recording the effects of coherence, or incoherence, in the brain, in relation to function and behavior. This project uses brain imaging to build a network map of the neural pathways that underlie the brain functioning and behavior of hundreds of participants in controlled studies.

This joint effort of universities around the world has shown us how increases and decreases in connectivity directly relate to performance, diseases, and mental disorders. For example, scans of people diagnosed with ADHD showed altered connectivity, while scan of people with depression showed atypical increases and decreases in connectivity.

Connectivity is another word for coherence, which describes how much the brain is working together in synchronicity (aka unifying diversity), or not.

If the brain images showed us disruption in connectivity, we would call that cognitive decline, which is representative of diseases such as dementia or Alzheimer's. In the past, this might not have meant much to you. I could tell you that Mr. Smith was experiencing cognitive decline and you might think, "Alright, well what's to be done about it and what does that really look like?" Now we can use these brain scans to see that cognitive decline, poor decision-making, poor memory, anxiety, disease, and every other state you experience in relation to your brain comes down to coherence.

When looking at behaviors, individuals whose brain scans indicated less connectivity, or coherence, experienced higher instances of substance abuse and emotional negativity, in addition to a host of less obvious effects, such as a smaller vocabulary.

In contrast, individuals with higher connectivity, or coherence, showed more instances of satisfaction in life, higher income, and an increased vocabulary.

For the first time in history, we can see, in brain activity, the importance of inner development leading to increased coherence, and ultimately protection:

- Of our health and mental capacity.
- From mental disease and decline.

In business, there are other things leaders need protection from or for, as costly mistakes lead to loss of time, money, energy, ROI, key talent, opportunity, and sustainability. From the standpoint of brain function, the only sustainable way to prevent these costly mistakes is mind-brain integration and development, allowing decision-makers, like yourself, to exist in the leadership state, protect what you've built, and keep it.

Not to keep bragging on the brain, but just from the standpoint of pure functionality, its capabilities are truly marvelous. In the Universe, there are over 100 billion galaxies, yet there are more signal waves in your brain than there are elementary particles in the Universe.

> **"We've been given the whole body, but we only use the little finger. Brain function is a reflection of the huge potential of our brain."**
>
> —*Harald Harung, PhD*

What Is the Leadership State?

If you mentally jump back to chapter two, you might recall we talked briefly about being "in the zone," which we refer to as the leadership state. For plenty of leaders, perhaps even yourself, the content in this book is new, so we will explore the concept of the leadership state further to ensure your complete understanding of what is now required for leadership. The leadership state is an inner state of wakefulness and knowingness of the great organizing power that is working through yourself and everyone. Therefore, it is also a state of highest humility, gratitude, appreciation and encouragement. Leaders have these high emotional intelligence qualities because in the leadership state there's a heightened coherence between their lower brain impulses and their higher brain's ability to correctly interpret them. This disarms a leaders ego thinking it's all about them and makes everyone feel a valuable member of their team aka the leader everyone loves.

This leadership state is where your full potential for high-performance exists. If you take nothing else away from this book, let it be this: If you can learn to stabilize and effortlessly exist in the zone, or in the leadership state, where you have a fully awake truthful creative mindset, you will achieve true fulfillment and bliss. You will no longer worry about failure, stress, or the continuous flow of moving pieces and parts. You won't need to. Your alignment and coherence will clear away inner and outer noise, so you maintain an elevated leadership state, allowing you to lead yourself and others effortlessly forward. **This is true leadership, and this is where leadership is protected.**

- Your experience does not determine your performance or success. The state you're in does.
- Your experiences aren't who you are. Your level of consciousness is.
- The state you exist in is who you are.
- This state then discerns, decides and chooses your experiences.
- We always look to our experience to say, this is who I am, without ever acknowledging or accessing the foundation of those experiences.
- At the very foundation of everything you do, the starting point for every decision you make, is your state of existence.

If you can learn to expand, enhance, and stabilize that leadership state, you will achieve a level of coherent leadership state reserved for the most developed leaders. Consider the quote about being the awareness behind the emotions, not just the emotions. This is the same idea. Go beyond the external pieces of who you are, beyond the paint, beyond the walls, and even the roof; focus on the beams, the framing, the footers, and the foundation.

What Does Invincibility Mean?

> **"We would like to be so bold as to infer that this invincible leadership state is the one thing that simultaneously activates all of the secrets and great qualities of leadership. Invincibility is the roots that nourish the trunk, branches, leaves, and fruits of great leadership."**
>
> *—Raamon Newman, co-founder/CEO of New Mavericks*

Analogies and parables are very effective in revealing the truths we often overlook, but so are real-life stories of high-level performance and protection in action. The following CEOs demonstrated a high degree of invincibility in their tenures as the primary influencers on their respective companies' performances:

1. **Meg Whitman**, considered one of the top CEOs of all time, was president and CEO of eBay from 1998–2008. During that time, she led the company from 30 employees, 500,000 registered users, and $4.7 million in revenue to more than 15,000 employees, hundreds of millions of registered users worldwide, and almost $7.7 billion in revenue.

2. **Lee Iacocca** joined Chrysler in 1978, when the company was failing. In the first year as CEO, he got the government to bail out the company with $1.5 billion in federally backed loans. He then proceeded to save the company by launching a series of groundbreaking automobiles, including the mid-sized K-car line and the automobile market's first minivans. The success of these vehicles, along with a variety of cost-saving measures he instituted, allowed Chrysler to pay back the $1.5 billion in loans seven years early and save 600,000 jobs.

3. **Douglas Conant** was CEO of Campbell's Soup from 2001 to 2011. He started when the company's stock price was plummeting fast. Conant discovered the company had a toxic culture, so he resolved to improve employee engagement. He walked 10,000 steps per day to engage and interact with as many employees as he could, and wrote up to 20 notes per day to staff to acknowledge and appreciate their successes. Through his leadership, Campbell's organically boosted its sales and earnings enough to outperform both the SandP Food Group and the SandP 500 in 2009.

When reading about these amazing feats of success there are so many things we can point to and say it was this and that which allowed these leaders to do this. But when we zoom out we have to conclude they had some level of protection and invincibility that allowed them to overcome the complexities, challenges, stress and obstacles to create the progress they did. Before you think invincibility is pie in the sky Super Man and Wonder

Woman comic story stuff. Here's the definition and understanding of what invincibility really means:

- *Vincible* means "able to be conquered and overcome."
- *Invincible* means "not able to be conquered or overcome."
- The only difference between vincible and invincible is the word "in."

Invincibility does not exist outside our self on the level of our body, senses and objects of your senses, because these are subject to constant change. Invincibility does not even exist on the level of our mind, intellect and ego as these are also always changing and evolving. Invincibility only exists in the field of non-change, consciousness or pure being and silence that is beyond the relative aspects of ourselves. Invincibility is a state of being, not doing, where you are your most coherent, orderly, fulfilled self, fully in tune with evolutionary change with zero resistance to what needs to unfold for you. The effectiveness of your actions reflects this. To achieve invincibility is to go within, to align with this invincible level of yourself, which then supports maximum alignment externally.

> **"As a former full-time meditating monk (for 10 years), I realized that this field and state of invincibility is beyond our mind, intellect, ego, and even our five senses. It's an intimate connection and alignment with the field of non-change, non-action, lively dynamic coherent silence and joy at the source of thinking. We call this the field of consciousness or that pure potentiality of nature's intelligence within, that nourishes, informs and supports our DNA to make our heart beat, skin reproduce, and food digest without us having to tell it to. That's what I wanted to tap into and that's what we help leaders tap into. It's an entire field of intelligence existing within us, and all we have to do is acknowledge and remember it by experiencing it regularly. It's becoming more and more integrated and familiar with this source intelligence so eventually, as we see with our clients, it becomes a constant state to lead from. They're established in their highest leadership state"**
>
> *–Raamon Newman, Co-Founder/CEO of New Mavericks*

This leadership state - where your thoughts, feelings and actions are absolutely synced - is where high performance happens. This is true invincibility, in a superhero sense, where you exist beyond the noise, chaos, and stress that is our current business economy. When you're fully established in this state, you are protected. When you aren't, you lack protection and become more vulnerable to negative events that are unnecessary, could have been prevented, and provide no value or lesson to you. Remember, not all failure is necessary.

If we look at athletes who have experienced "the zone," the characteristics they use to describe this experience are the same characteristics used to describe experiences of higher consciousness. They describe feelings of being invincible, untouchable, floating, experiencing bliss, having no resistance—this is what happens when we experience increased coherence as a result of higher levels of brain connectivity.

Let's go back to our client, Mark Waller, as discussed in Chapter 3. His reference to being "the eye of the storm" is a common explanation of experiencing the leadership state. We watched this man go from a state of resistance and stress to superfluid growth of his leadership capacity. These transformations are why we do what we do, our "inner why." The moment we help leaders understand that they have nothing to lose, and everything to gain, is the same moment progress begins. In that moment, the energy shifts, and you can feel the beginnings of a new leader emerging.

It took time and resistance for Mark to get into his more evolved leadership state, something he now freely admits. At the calendar end of our first year working together, he was awarded CEO of the year in New Zealand. Soon after, he decided his progress was stable enough, and he wanted to take a break from our work together. We made an amicable split and left him with one question: "Why did you win this award?" This was a question he could have interpreted a number of ways.

The surface reason he won seemed obvious. He had done a great job at building his company to over $1.3 billion in revenues. Much of this happened through key mergers and acquisitions, which is not an easy feat. *(For reference, Harvard Business Review collated research shows us that 70-90% of mergers and acquisitions fail.)*

About five months after our amicable break, we checked back with Mark, something we do with all of our clients. The first thing he said to us was that his deals weren't working as well as he had hoped, and he wasn't sure why. We asked if he had a chance to answer the question we left him with several months prior. He admitted he hadn't given it much thought, and we had a discussion around the question itself. We revealed to Mark that recognition or an award of such high honor is a pivot point. In those moments, it becomes less about you and more about working on a higher purpose that involves not just you, but also those around you. That purpose is to grow into a more invincible leadership state and help others do the same, a message plenty of leaders need to hear at the time of their most profound achievements and challenging pivots.

Ten years later, we worked with Mark till his retirement end of 2019, that culminated in him being inducted into the New Zealand Business Hall of Fame, and have continued to work with his successors. Mark is an exceptional leader in his own right, one of the best in the world at what he does. He describes the support, insights, and knowledge he gained as invaluable, though we know it is the knowledge and growth he has developed on his own that is the real champion here. Mark went on to do the biggest merger and acquisition in his company's history, a multi-billion dollar deal. At the beginning of this deal, major shareholders weren't supportive, they didn't get Mark and his vision, but as Mark focused on developing more of his invincible leadership state (rather than attempting to win them over), the less resistance he was met with, and at the end of it all, his team made the deal happen with full support.

The results below speak for themselves. Mark lead and helped his company achieve more between 2010 and 2017 than in the previous 25 years utilizing this protection-based support. He knew how to achieve and we simply helped him protect himself, his team and his achievement, in a very competitive, tight margin industry.

	2010	**2017**	**Increase**
Group Revenue	$1.3 billion	$7.6 billion	484%
Group Profits	$25 million	$133 million	432%
Share Price	$5.87	$17.50	198%

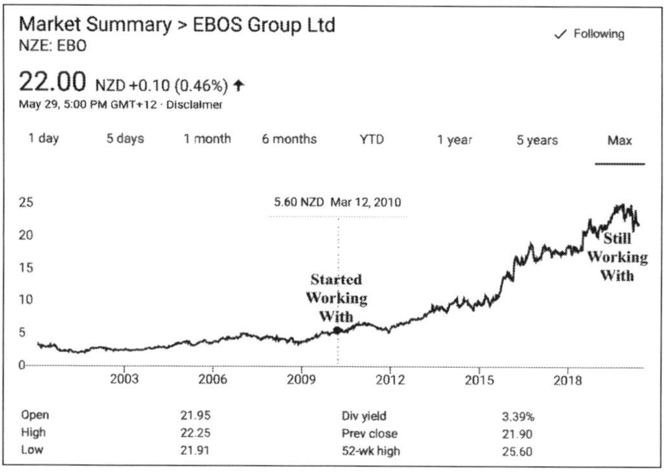

See endorsement in Appendix 1, as well as two other client case studies in Appendix 2 and 3.

Experiencing Superhero Invincibility

In every Batman movie we've ever seen, there's a certain scene where Batman is really in dire straits. He seems to have lost his car, he's been beaten to a bloody pulp, and it appears there is no way out for the superhero, who is seemingly lurching towards his ultimate demise. Yet, somehow, Batman finds a conveniently located weapon, finds the strength to get up, fights the good fight, wins, finds his car, rescues the girl, races back home, and manages to show up fashionably late to his own black-tie event in a custom suit, sporting perfect hair.

This isn't usually how things go down for the everyday leader. When a leader gets knocked down, they become consumed with surviving so they go into reactive mode. At this point, their view of the bigger picture becomes so fragmented, they almost always end up contributing to their own demise, rather than locating a conveniently placed weapon and fighting their way out.

One of our current clients found himself in a similar situation. His story will change how you think about superhero invincibility and even true leadership.

> "About six months ago, I was working on a new commercial development project, something I have spent the past decade of my life doing. Our project was moving right along, and then it was as if I

ran directly into a concrete wall. Suddenly, everything was going wrong, things you couldn't prepare for, things that were absolutely unexpected, and they were happening one right after the other. Not exaggerating at all, everything was going wrong.

In the moment, I felt the best use of my time would be to stall my other projects until I could figure out how to turn things around. This drastic measure was necessary because I knew if I couldn't turn this around, I was done. I had investors who put their faith in me, and workers to pay, and my reputation to defend, and a young family to take care of, and I was on the verge of losing everything.

I talked to my legal contacts, and they all told me that there was no way out aside from cutting my losses and walking away. But somewhere inside of me, I knew starting over was not the right option. When I reached out to Paolo and Raamon and explained what was going on, we decided to shift our focus to the bigger picture, rather than just what was happening in this moment. The idea was if we could take a broader perspective, and create more coherence around potential outcomes, we could save my future.

It sounds funny putting it all on paper, because we were attempting to shift the course of one of the biggest disasters I have ever been a part of, without any real basis for doing that, other than consciousness and development. In the world of business, everything is rational and fact-based, so this approach doesn't sound appealing at all. As a leader, I've been trained to say, "Okay, what can I do right now to fix this?" But this was too big, and I knew there was nothing I could do to change the situation, aside from walking away, which just wasn't an option in my mind.

I knew if I walked away, not only would my reputation be damaged and my business shot, but everyone else would lose too, and that didn't seem fair. Not to mention, the karmic effects of that catching up with me down the road. I had experienced similar failure in the past and I knew I had to break this cycle.

Raamon and Paolo encouraged me to look at the larger truth, that to break this cycle, I needed more coherence, and I trusted in that, mainly because at the time, it was really my only option. I set the fear aside, I tried to remain upbeat, I ignored the calls to walk away, and we went to work behind the scenes.

What happened next is almost unbelievable. If this whole thing hadn't happened to me, I would think you were stretching truths at the very best. It was like, on Tuesday everything was finished and I had failed and lost everything, and by Wednesday everything was back to normal. There was too much happening for me to call it all coincidence or chance. But if it wasn't coincidence, that means there was some sort of invincible connection occurring between events and our thoughts. Or it's magic. What else is there? What else do we know about our Universe that explains this level of turnaround? What deeper knowledge do we rely on, in business, to explain these situations? Well, we don't. Because things don't usually play out like this. In fact, failure is an acceptable option. Walking away, counting losses, and screwing everyone else along the way is the normal and recommended response. This is the legally acceptable solution that businesses take every day. For me, it took having everything on the line, for me to look at this and say, I am willing to try anything. Even at this point, in my mind, the best-case scenario was that somebody would have to lose, and I thought it would be me, but at least I had protected the others who believed in and invested in me.

From there, I realized that this approach with consciousness was actually the easier path. Everything else was a guessing game. I talked to consultants who were stumped, and coaches who had zero solutions. The coherence and consciousness were already there, I didn't have to go and try to find it. It wasn't like with habits, where I had to put that intention there and try to follow it. I learned that consciousness is more tangible than anything else we can find on the outside. You don't have to try and find it, it's effortless and it's always there. That's invincibility. You aren't trying to make things happen. It's just there, and the more you contact it, the more you know it's there and the more protection you have."

(In order to protect the identity of our clients, like this one, specific details and names have been left out.)

Our client's experience above is demonstrative of the corrective powers of the Science of Protection. He purified what needed to be purified, gained a new level of coherence and orderliness to be a new leadership state to inspire and find a way to correct a situation that all his peers said walking away was his only option. This is what can happen and the protection you can have when you do the inner work to get more attuned to enlivening that field of invincibility and your leadership state deep within.

This Doesn't Work When You Are Operating from Ego

It's important that we make a strong distinction here. We like to believe, from the level of our ego, that we can control outcomes, but ultimately, we can only influence outcomes to a certain degree. If we could completely control outcomes, we would all lead magical lives 100% of the time. The action is important, but the action from the level of consciousness activates being in this x-factor leadership state is what is required to get an outcome of the highest quality on a constant basis.

Everybody performs action. We all act. It is the action from the level of consciousness, beyond the mind, intellect, and ego, which creates the transformation we experienced with our client and the transformation we all want to experience. Without being more fully established in consciousness, action is just not as powerful. It would be similar to throwing darts while you're falling asleep, the chances of hitting the bulls-eye is next to zero. But with higher consciousness, which allows you to be in a leadership state to have greater precision and accuracy, you will hit the bulls-eye much more frequently.

> **"I realized that no business knowledge or strategies could turn this around for me, and that a higher state of existence was required. It was the only way."**
>
> —*Anonymous client*

It only sounds impossible because you haven't experienced this higher leadership state. It only sounds like magic because you haven't tapped into this next level of expanded capacity. It only sounds crazy because you're not completely connected to your inner truth.

Leadership is not what we think. Leadership has been buried under the guise of numbers, spreadsheets, and quarterly projections. Those are all by-products. Those aren't leadership, and while that may have been enough 20 or even 10 years ago, today only relying on action isn't enough. Protection is the new requirement.

The greatest monarchs and dictators of the world have only been recorded to have achieved partial success in life; it was not possible for them to make the full use of their surroundings because they did not develop themselves on the deeper levels of life.

As a leader, you are the creator of your own economy, the writer of the script, and the regulator of the rules. The Universe is an innocent reflector of where you are and your capacity. If your potential is limited, the Universe will reflect that. If you are existing in your leadership state, the Universe will also reflect that.

Batman shows up at exactly the right time to save Gotham City and the girl. He doesn't just randomly show up, hoping to be in the right place at the right time. He's the Batman, he knows. Your superhero status and invincibility is in your hands. It's not about miracles, or magic, or good luck; it's about consciousness, coherence, your leadership state, and protection.

Just like the story we shared about our client, when you are on the chopping block, you rarely get to come back as he did, with everything perfectly restored and with nobody losing. This level of superhero invincibility is the perfect example of the leadership state. This is the state where good defeats evil. This is the state where good defeats the vices that cause loss of focus, delays, and poor decisions. This is the state where, what seems like magic, gets to happen in real life.

This is something every CEO and leader around the globe needs to hear. If you are in a position of power, it is time for you to step into that role and become the truly developed superhero you are meant to be. And the only way you can do this is by developing the CEO of you, to increase coherence, and to live in your invincible leadership state.

What you do, how much you make, none of this is enough anymore. You have to go deeper now, to the place that exists before you ever take action, before you develop a thought or an idea. You have to stabilize that place, so your ideas and thoughts are whole and evolutionary, and your actions are protected.

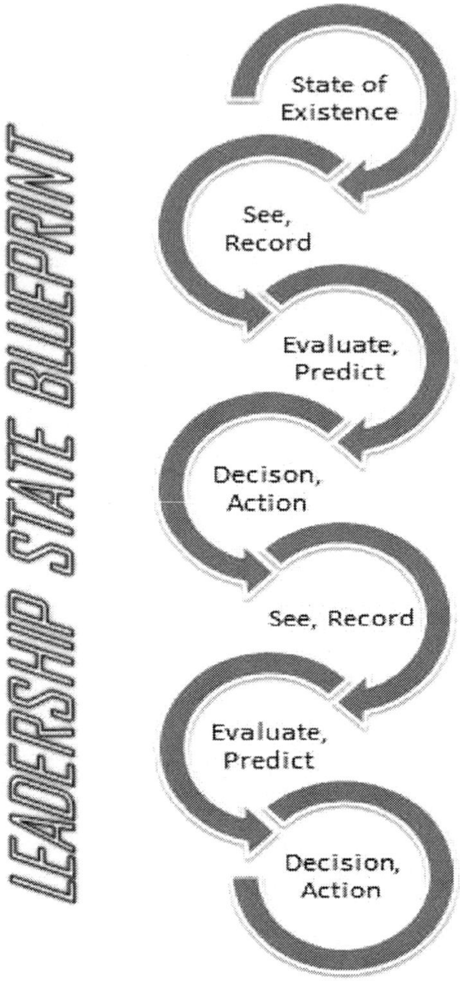

Our client experienced inner victory, by way of his leadership state, which allowed external victory over everything that was happening to him and his business.

At the very foundation of everything you do, is your state of existence. It is not your actions or experiences deciding your development, as we are often taught.

Understanding this process allows us to also understand how important it is to develop your leadership state, if you want to see more, evaluate better, and predict easily. If you are evaluating better and predicting better, you will consequently take the right actions because you are seeing and recording the most accurate reality.

"It's a Learning Experience"

What you take away from situations or experiences is different based on your interpretation, which is also based on the state you exist in, and the coherence in your brain. Whether or not you are actually learning valuable lessons, breaking cycles, or growing from said experiences depends solely on your state of existence, and the coherence in your brain.

If you have more coherence, you have more of this superhero invincibility we all want. Real invincibility isn't building a fortress around yourself, mentally, emotionally, physically, or materially. Batman doesn't hide away in his bat cave. Invincibility also isn't about always being right, or controlling everything, or having everything your way. These are all examples of superficial invincibility, where you think your actions are protecting you, when they are actually causing harm.

Real superhero invincibility is being open and aligned with what allows you to be more coherent both inside and outside, to experience that unified agreement between your inner and outer "why."

There are many states and realities we can experience in this world, but there are really only two categories these states/realities fall into:

- Coherent
- Incoherent

You're either contributing coherence to the world or you're contributing incoherence. The more coherent you are, the more easily you exist in your leadership state. From here, you are making better decisions, you are taking a broader perspective, you are functioning at a higher level, and it's requiring less effort.

It's not that you won't feel the effects of great accomplishment and excitement, or great disappointment and difficult challenges when you're in a coherent state—you'll actually feel them more fully. It's just that when you're experiencing an elevated level of being, you won't be overshadowed by, tainted by, or attached to them so much, if at all. You will know that those things exist only in the field of change, while you yourself are firmly established in that most fulfilling and invincible field of non-change. It's the coolest of cool states.

This is Warren Buffet territory, where you are so established in who you are that everything becomes much more fluid. In the leadership state everything seems so effortless that everybody will wonder what your secret x-factor superpower is, why it's allowing you to reach higher heights and not fall from them, and how others around you can also experience the same through being in this state.

We can compare this to being more connected to the silent still depths of the ocean, rather than the ever-changing waves on the surface. In this state, you perceive, pick up on, and act on the most powerful truths and evolutionary thoughts at their pure source, which most powerfully serve you, everyone else, and the environment.

This is real leadership. Everything else is not. **When all areas of the brain collaborate, performance is world class. This state is rare, but it needn't be. We, as leaders, should be developing more coherence, and existing more in our invincible leadership state. The capacity to do so exists within us; we have but to unleash it.**

This leadership state allows you to cultivate an invincible state of positivity, making you capable of dealing with anything life throws at you, and acting in accordance with what is best for everyone involved, yourself included.

> **"You are in control of your destiny, your success, and your life. It's rather amazing that we are tasked with creating who we are, and because of that, we get the opportunity of enjoying the outcome as well. That old saying, 'you reap what you sow' is your truth. You will get everything you create and nothing you don't. That is the so-called secret to life everyone is trying to sell you. Every second will be what you make it; nothing more, nothing less."**
>
> *—Paolo D'Angelo, co-founder of New Mavericks*

What Is Moral Decision Making?

Coherence gives way to a more ethical thought process in which you inherently know what is right and most truthful. This leads to higher levels of morally sound reasoning and decision making, protecting you from negative influences.

One of the more surprising findings in research on high performance and brain function is the existence of what we like to call moral development and decision making. Research shows us that high morals are directly related to high performance, which we know is directly related to coherence and development. This tells us that when you have a developed prefrontal cortex, you inherently know what is right, and make morally sound decisions based on that knowledge.

A morally sound foundation, preceding action in your life, is its own extremely effective form of protection, helping you to avoid unnecessary future stress and failure, which is usually a result of poor decision making.

Back to Self-Help

Many of the bits of wisdom across the ages have served their purpose by presenting the knowledge necessary for their time. Positive thinking books, for example, have served us well in recent decades. We can say now, without any doubt that the truths in this book will finally allow you to live all of the other principles you've ever learned. Everything you've retained from *Think and Grow Rich*, *The Alchemist*, or *The 7 Habits of Highly Effective People* is able to settle in on a deeper level when you have stabilized your leadership state.

We've finally gone to the core essence of what it takes to BE positive without having to THINK about being positive. These books may have satisfied your intellect, but we want you to think of our book as something that expands your capacity so that past intellectual knowledge can now integrate on a deeper and more powerful level within you.

Conquering Your Mind Is the Shortcut

Controlling the mind can be like trying to train a cage of wild monkeys to all sit still and be quiet at the same time. You might get one or two of them to cooperate, but while you are focused on those few, the others will undoubtedly be up to something, trying to pull the others away. What we're saying with this is that no one has conquered anything until they've conquered their own mind.

You cannot apply knowledge completely until you are at a place where you are developed and can act based on the broader perspective of Universal alignment. And you cannot take a shortcut to this place, nor should you want to, when the natural path to freedom is much less chaotic and truly much simpler. Remember, it's watering the roots that is most effective versus just trying to water the leaves.

The look, feel, and taste of this leadership state is something everyone has tasted, even if briefly, and so learning to stabilize this state is the next step in your development. Try to imagine a moment in your leadership journey where you felt 100% at ease with a decision you made. That feeling of *knowing* that everything is aligned and unfolding as it should is another way leaders describe the experience of being in their leadership state. The goal is to get to a place where your leadership state is not a brief experience, but a persistent reality.

Case Study: Jeff Bezos

Jeff Bezos, founder and CEO of Amazon, has become the world's richest man. He has achieved this primarily because he's able to function from an invincible leadership state. Here's what we know about Mr. Bezos' journey:

- He had a great vision to set up and master the acquisition and distribution of almost any product in the world via the internet.
- He brought to bear consistent, precise focus to enliven and refine his vision and business systems.
- He is deeply established in his invincible leadership state.
- Nothing has overshadowed him in achieving his mission. He even admits he was not completely clear, certain, and confident when he started out nearly 25 years ago, yet he still persisted.
- He has overcome just about every kind of inertia in himself and others, to move his company forward in a way no other company has.
- His success is truly larger than life.

All of these points indicate, at least on the surface, that Mr. Bezos is deeply established in his invincible leadership state. Unclear, uncertain, and unconfident thoughts and feelings don't matter when you're in this invincible leadership state, because these are superficial, changeable mental and emotional influences. Bezos simply stayed true to his invincible state of being, and the impulse and vision coming through him from this state of being—his "inner why."

As a result, his company has yet to be corrupted, challenged, or diminished. Rather, it has been protected, and has flourished into what we experience today every time we visit Amazon.com. The funny thing is that Mr. Bezos may not even be consciously aware that he's experiencing this invincible leadership state. He might not even know how he got there. Here is where a deeper knowledge and systematic regular experiencing of the invincible state of being is required for any leader to fully cultivate and stabilize it, and to enjoy the fruits of their own leadership state.

You can't fully appreciate the taste of the strawberry until you've tasted it for yourself. This is equivalent to owning a chunk of gold and believing it's just a rock. When you don't understand the real value of something, you don't take care of it, or develop it, or appreciate it, like you would if you really knew what you had. Being blind to your leadership state, and without protection, puts you in a position to never fully access the capacity and the abundance in that state.

> **"Everything you can imagine is real."**
>
> *—Pablo Picasso*

The Best Way to Cultivate Your Invincible Leadership State

Continuing to go through life's ups and downs will cultivate your invincible leadership state, but this is the slow path. A faster, more effortless, and more enjoyable way is to use the innate nature of the mind to transcend outer and inner noise and experience the greatest charm, and dare we say bliss and joy, of lively inner silence. Not dull, flat silence, but lively restful silence, which is the source of greater coherent energy—the energy that dissolves inner noise, stresses, incoherence, and vices so you're naturally more in tune with the right thought and feeling at the right time. This is the mental approach that is most easily fulfilled by learning how to let go and transcend the field of change and allow the mind to gravitate to the state it most enjoys, being settled while we act. There are many ways to transcend, however if you want the most direct simple effortless systematic and reliable way to transcend learn an automatic self-transcending meditation.

Transcendental Meditation, TM.org, is one such validated technique of this kind. If you find a simpler effortless systematic and reliable way to have the most settled mind you can possibly have please let us know because we've yet to discover one that does this effectively as TM with the same broad and depth of benefits. This is why many top leaders and performers have adopted this simple technique. TM is not about managing or being mindful of the never-ending array of thoughts and feelings to manage stress, fear and anxiety. It is about going beyond thinking to pure awareness, the silent coherent orderly source of thoughts, where all good life supporting energy, clarity, creativity and thoughts comes from.

TM produces a physiological state of restful alertness that is the opposite of stress. Research indicates that meditators have higher levels of circulating white blood cells that fight viruses. TM meditators have markedly reduced hospitalization in all categories of disease, with 73% lower rates for the category of Nose, Throat, and Lungs diseases, diseases caused by viruses and bacteria, such as common colds, sinus infections, sore throat, bronchitis and pneumonia. Longitudinal studies show that the reduction in health care utilization relative to non-meditating controls only begins after they learn TM. The TM group decreased by an average of 14% per year relative to controls, reaching a 70% reduction after 5 years.

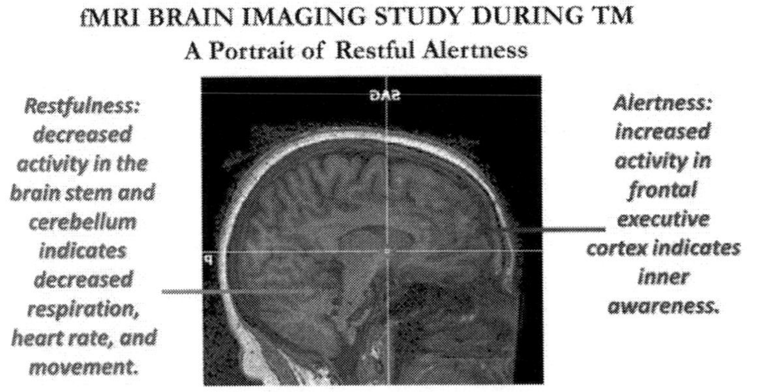

Reference. Mahone, Michelle C., Travis, Fred , Gevirtz, Richard, & Hubbard, David (2018). fMRI during Transcendental Meditation practice. *Brain and Cognition*, Epub 2018 Mar 2.

There is also a supplemental emotional affirmation that supports being in an invincible leadership state. Simply affirm to yourself, "I feel not disturbed" or "I feel invincible or unshakable" and let go. The reason why you can affirm this, without a shadow of a doubt, is because everything is changeable on the surface of life, and everything is steady and silent within the deepest part of ourselves. Also, everything is ultimately a blessing in disguise. These blessings are here to help us evolve, grow, become stronger, overcome inertia, and expand our coherence capacity through deepening our connection to silence. Words of affirmation without silence and coherence behind them are easily blown away by the changing surface winds of the mind and are ineffective. Being in the leadership state allows us to be more protected as we progress. However, in order for this to be true, we have to also perceive, acknowledge, appreciate, and welcome challenges, because life does have its ups and downs. As leaders we have to be beyond the ups and downs, highs and lows by being established in equanimity, the leadership state, to see the dangers, to avert them, and to see the opportunities and capitalize on them. We call this a "challenge-friendly mindset," and encourage leaders to accept challenges while not being affected by them. To have the ability to observe the threats, lessons and opportunities; rather than getting tangled up and absorbed in the problems the challenge brings.

Okay, so you understand that leadership is a state which you exist in, a state that you must develop for coherence and protection. You understand that this development lends itself to your capacity and ability to experience peak performance. We've also discussed your moral development, which leaves us to discuss the single-most important part of this chapter: acknowledging you and everyone around you are all still a work in progress.

Sure, everything else we've talked about is really important. But, if you can't get to all of that other stuff because you will never admit you need to develop, none of it matters. And this is the biggest problem plaguing so many leaders right now.

We see it every single day: a leader on the verge of failure, unwilling to reverse course or admit they need help; or a leader ready and willing to sacrifice everything because they just can't acknowledge they made a wrong turn; or, even worse, a leader only tapping into a small portion of their potential.

We get it. You are tough. The car has to be barreling down the hill with no doors before you are willing to admit that this might not have been the best path. You have a strong personality. You are smart. You have achieved plenty. At this point in your life, it isn't easy to ask for help. So we'll make it really easy for you and change the conversation.

It's No Longer Self-help. It's Self-Mastery.

You're no longer trying to achieve. If you're here, you've proven your ability to achieve. You are developing invincibility and protection. This is a new level. It's not about whether or not you want help. It's about whether or not you want to be the best you can be. It's not about failure. It's about growth. It's not about learning the hard way anymore. It's about learning the smart way. It's not about fighting to be on top. It's about ascending more effortlessly.

So often, in leadership, struggling becomes a way of life. Stress becomes a way of life. Failure and missteps become a way of life. And we get so far down this path, that we forget how good life can be. We forget that we could be incredibly happy, experiencing bliss and stability, and performing at the top of our capacity rather than the bottom.

Our client, who told his story earlier in this chapter, is a capable business man. He is skilled and intelligent. He is resourceful, a strong communicator, and he maintains a positive attitude. Yet, he still lacked protection, which tells us everything we need to know. There are more layers to unfold and you have to keep unfolding these layers to protect your achievements and find invincible success.

Once we were able to move him into his leadership state, he was operating from his most fully awake and truthful mindset. He was proactively and creatively averting danger and enhancing progress, enabling him to move from resistance to the successful completion of his big merger/acquisition vision over the course of a few weeks. The way he was subjectively observing the situation became more fluid; less bound by his situation, and expanded his capacity to understand how others related to him and his vision.

Where you are right now, in your success and in your achievements, is something to be incredibly proud of. Your very ability to reach this height in achievement is an indicator that you are also capable of expanding into new leadership territory. This tells us that you are ready, capable of more. The fact that you are reading this book means you are open to further development, to self-mastery.

When we peel back the custom suits, the wealth, the degrees, the trophies, the habits, the workshops, the speeches...when we peel back all of the layers and get to the source, that is where real magic happens.

> **"Freedom is when you know who you are and are not restrained by anyone or anything."**
>
> —*Herman Siu*

Beneath these layers is a superhero, gifted with invincibility, and the ability to both protect and be protected, just waiting to be brought to the surface. It isn't about asking for help. It's about stepping into your power and invincibility. It's about stepping into your role as a leader and owning it. It's not about self-help; it's about the next step, self-mastery. It's about changing the world, and it starts with you. This is not just another new chapter in the story of you as a leader. This is a whole new reality, and this is what is now required. This isn't just the next big approach—this is the real truth of leadership that you must wake up to.

This truth cannot be realized from the outside. It must be felt on the inside, realized from consciousness. Only then can you bring it out to the world because truth from this level will always triumph in the end, even if non-truth appears to be prevailing. Until then, you have no foundation and your fulfillment will be fleeting.

Stop Selling Yourself Short. Step into Your Real Power.

Intellectual knowledge does not elevate your consciousness; it only elevates your understanding of what's possible. Nor does it increase your coherence or stabilize your leadership state.

Right now you are raw untapped potential, untapped power, undefined purpose, misaligned motivation, and underutilized capacity. It is time for you to expand, to live your full potential as an invincible leader and step into your leadership state.

There you have it, now you know what leadership really is. It's a fully awake, yet relaxed, truthful creative state of mind to proactively avert danger and enhance progress.

This completes the internal protection development part of the Science of Protection. By activating these three internal protection development steps of purification, coherence and leadership state you'll find that you'll be more connected to consciousness, the silent observing witness within you, that contains both infinite silence and infinite dynamism. This is the foundation of protection, invincibility, fulfillment and peace.

When you've sufficiently activated these steps, you'll have more observing power. You'll observe more fully and clearly the big picture and the finite details making up every element of that picture. Understanding these mechanics of silence and dynamism will allow you to relax while remaining alert, to ultimately gain mastery over achieving and protecting what you achieve.

When the mind is settled and alert you feel more and are more in tune with what is required. Having a high level of internal protection development allows you to validate your decision making on both a mental intellectual level and a feeling level. You can validate anything from any angle this way because having lively silence makes you more awake. This gives you a clear discerning intellect and a wakeful truthful feeling, which is the state you want to be in to make business decisions.

Leading Progress without Directly Doing

Leaders have to own up that they are responsible for the whole and all the parts. A leader must be responsible when they delegate, meaning they're overseeing everything because they already see the mechanics even though they're not directly doing. The only way you can do this is by acting from the source of protection, the dynamic silence of consciousness.

Delegating means you see the process and outcome already because the leader creates the impulse of what they want to see unfold to every point. The more silence and energy this impulse has the more powerful effect it will create.

A great leader is someone who takes the whole responsibility for the whole story, which then makes the parts work much better. Everyone's role has to be connected to the source impulse of the leader; therefore, a leader has to be in the purest most coherent leadership state possible because people can only reflect the quality of a leader's state of consciousness.

This is why this book is so unique in the leadership development space because we're not here to give you all the specific usable, practical and actionable leadership advice we know. We're supporting you to act while being based and established in non-action; that internal pure, silent, peaceful, coherent leadership state within, so you know from within your own awareness what advice is useful and what is not. This is when you're really protected when acting as a leader.

Now you're ready to integrate this internal protection development externally by first knowing and enhancing your capacity to handle any situation as we move into the first external step of Capacity in the next chapter.

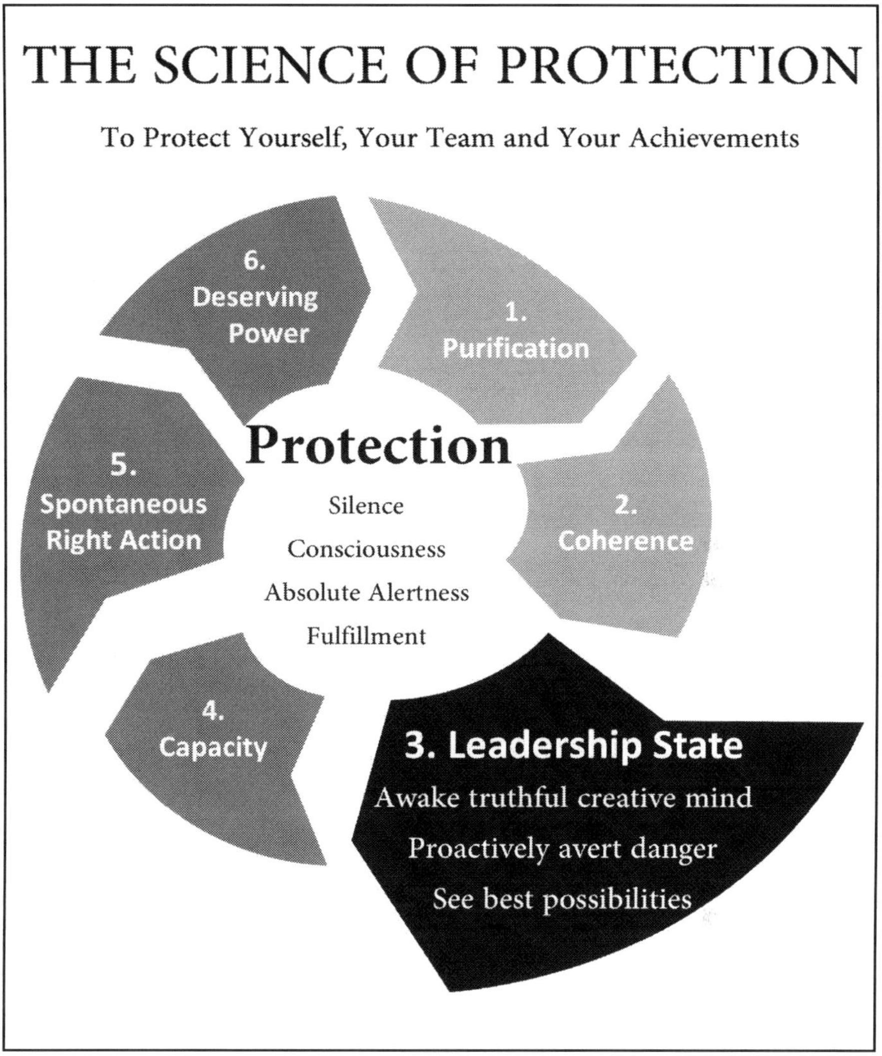
THE SCIENCE OF PROTECTION
To Protect Yourself, Your Team and Your Achievements
6. Deserving Power
1. Purification
Protection
Silence
Consciousness
Absolute Alertness
Fulfillment
5. Spontaneous Right Action
2. Coherence
4. Capacity
3. Leadership State
Awake truthful creative mind
Proactively avert danger
See best possibilities

YOUR TURN

Action Steps to Get into Your Leadership State

Here is an activity you can use to get to your Leadership State and gain higher protection. Ask yourself the following questions in relation to a current problem you are confronting or stress you are dealing with:

Simplicity: What and how can you make things more simple right now, what can you do to make the complex simple?

Unified: What differences need to be unified in yourself and or environment so they're more harmoniously connected? How can these differences co-exist to create something even greater and fulfill everyone?

Truthfulness: What is the greater truth that is good for everyone? What truth inspires a new creative way of seeing and doing things?

PART 3

EXTERNAL PROTECTION INTEGRATION

6) Capacity
7) Spontaneous Right Action
8) Deserving Power

6 Capacity

Expanded Awareness and Focus to Handle Anything

Trillions of seconds and here you are in this one.

Capacity, the degree to which you have developed, expanded, and are utilizing your full intelligence, awareness and focus to handle any obstacle and opportunity.

Capacity is having expanded, heightened awareness and focus to handle anything. Being in the leadership state is a prerequisite for having great capacity. Then it's about optimally utilizing your capacity externally on a conscious level where you're not under or overwhelming yourself so you get the best out of yourself, others and your resources.

In this accelerated age more than ever we have to develop and expand our spiritual, mental, emotional and physical capacity. Not only must we cope with rapid change but also have the capacity to actually enjoy and be at peace amidst all the change, thereby not ruining our health and quality of life. Who really wants to go through their working life and into old age with a bunch of chronic diseases due to all the accumulated stress of their working days? Obviously, no one, so developing capacity spiritually, mentally, emotionally and physically is the key to avert this.

Timing can be tricky. Positivity quotes tell us to trust our timing, 'your time is now,' and simultaneously that timing is everything—something we must explore to understand.

A beggar is on the side of the road and a millionaire passes by him. The millionaire requests that his driver stop so he can get out and speak with the beggar. The driver does as he asks, and the millionaire approaches the beggar, who is the poorest of poor, with only the clothing on his back. The beggar speaks to the millionaire as he approaches and says, "Give me something." This aggressive approach catches the millionaire off guard, so he quickly says back to the beggar, "What do you want?" Feeling as if it might be his lucky day, the beggar's lips turn up into a crooked smile. After pausing for a moment, and looking rather pleased with himself, the beggar excitedly says, "Five dollars!" Somewhat surprised at the small request, the millionaire tells the beggar that he is rich and suggests that the beggar ask for more. The beggar, really feeling lucky at this point, pauses for another moment, and then tells the millionaire he would like ten dollars. Again, the millionaire looks surprised, and begins to wonder if the beggar is playing some sort of trick on him, so this time he is very firm in his tone, and once again tells the beggar to ask for more. The beggar does not have the capacity to imagine more. His mindset is so poor, and his life is so poor, that in this moment, he assumes the millionaire must be playing a trick on him, and he turns and walks away.

—adapted from a parable told by Maharishi Mahesh Yogi

Your Capacity Determines Your Possibilities

The timing of when things happen and unfold in our lives works hand-in-hand with our capacity. The more capacity we have the better possibilities are given to us. The saying's, "nature only gives you what you're ready for" and "luck happens when preparation meets opportunity" affirm this notion. You can only do, be, give, and have based on the capacity you have.

- How can you have it all? Capacity
- How can you keep it all? Protection.

In Chapter 3, we discussed the Zero Factor, and how important effortless right thought-right action is to your leadership success.

The ZERO Factor: When the time gap between having a great winning thought and taking the right action on it is near zero; effortless, spontaneous, right-action.

The Zero Factor allows for more flawless execution of high-performance thoughts, which by default, leaves less room for the wrong thoughts and the wrong actions. This ability to live in the Zero Factor state is the tangible expression of protection taking form in your life.

When growing plants, a farmer never over-waters freshly planted seeds to rush the growth process because the farmer knows that the seed will grow at its own pace, in its own time. The farmer also doesn't attempt to change the biology of the bean to become an herb seed. The purpose of the seed is designed into the seed. In terms of business, a stable leadership state will allow you to set the pace that is right for yourself and your team. This stability will help to create an environment that is naturally supported, which in turn will allow your team members to expand their capacity at the rate that is the most conducive to success.

Expanding into Openness

The reason so many leaders get their timing wrong is because they are closed off to the idea of alignment over control. Even when the leader is not the one truly in control, to let go of that idea challenges their ego, and getting to this point is difficult. Establishing trust is also difficult, especially when the topic isn't analytical. Plenty of leaders mistake their success as being evidence of their own mastery, and believe the work to develop themselves is already done. So when we ask them how things are going, they will rattle off numbers, talk about quarterly projections, and annual goals. Taking our clients beyond these external factors into the abstract is, by far, the most difficult thing we do.

But these same leaders are asking, "How can my life be better? How can I have everything I've set out to achieve without having a heart attack at 45 because I've sacrificed everything? How can I have it all?"

Get Real with Your Capacity

Howard Schultz is credited with creating the world's largest coffee business. He bought Starbucks in 1987, and now the coffee chain has over 28,000 stores worldwide. He stepped down as CEO in 2000 and returned in 2008 when Starbucks lost half its value in 2007, forcing him to close underperforming stores and cut a thousand jobs to get things back on track. This "getting real with your capacity" moment worked as Starbucks earned $22.4 billion in net revenues in 2017, and its market cap is approximately $84 billion as of September 2018. Schultz had the capacity to realign his company's capacity with where it needed to be to be efficient. He had the heightened awareness of the bigger picture and the focus to know what to change, adjust and tweak to utilize the company's resources most efficiently based on the situation at hand. He was in tune with the four steps of the capacity self-assessment below, both his and the company's.

In order to know where you are with your own capacity, you have to first get real with where you are. This requires being real with your capacity self-assessment based on these four steps:

- **Self-honesty:** Ask yourself if you have the capacity to handle what you've taken on or want to take on, or do you need to develop yourself or a skillset first?
- **Self-respect:** Are you respecting the capacity you have right now or are you in a "whatever it takes" state of mind?
- **Self-belief:** Do you believe in the capacity you have or do you doubt yourself?
- **Self-trust:** Do you trust your capacity to handle and take on what you need to take on each day?

The bottom line and reasoning for these questions is this: if you want your self-confidence, competence, leadership state, and influence to be more powerful and effective, you must expand your capacity. Your capacity determines how much expanded awareness you have and how focused you are at the same time. It's the combination of both qualities that determines how adept you are at timing your decisions and actions, and how protected you are from feeling stressed or overwhelmed.

If you put a spoonful of salt in a glass, the water might be barely drinkable. The same amount in a lake would go unnoticed. The point to this analogy is that you are not the salt, you are the container, and the more you expand your capacity, the less you taste the salt. When you have the capacity of the lake, the problem/pain/salt has little to no negative effect on you.

Your leadership state, which creates alignment with protection, is nothing other than being in a settled yet alert state which allows you to have more capacity—more capacity to grow, expand, influence, and decide. Another way to think about capacity is to understand that when your capacity is small and confined, you experience the problem, whatever that problem may be. When your capacity is expanded, the exact same problem becomes small. The key to life and business is having the capacity to give and serve with a settled mind. It isn't achievement, it isn't experience, and it isn't any of the things you are acquiring outside of yourself. Those external objectives should always be step two, the second part of the growth process, not the first. This is why we see so many leaders lose so much after achieving great things. It isn't about luck or being "good", it's about being settled, coherent, and protected.

A Stronger Mind Gives More Capacity to Attract Bigger Projects

To take bigger risks that create better rewards, you require even more energy and strength in your mind. When the mind has energy and coherence, it has strength and so does the body. We focus, learn and do things better when the mind is coherent, energized and strong. Achieving is a side benefit and by-product of a strong, coherent focused mind. You utilize greater capacity of your mind when your mind becomes stronger. Owning the fort of your mind you own the treasures of clarity and creativity that can help you mitigate risk and optimize reward.

Making your mind stronger means you can manage bigger projects. You can even say through more capacity you'll attract bigger better projects that don't collapse. So, if you want to attract bigger and better projects develop a stronger mind to have more capacity to do so.

Capacity Determines How Protected Your Progress Will Be

A study, completed over a time span of 14 years at West Point Academy, recorded 10,000 cadets career goals, and then tracked. Those cadets, who cited intrinsic goals experienced higher levels of achievement in the military and earned commissions as officers, extended their service well beyond the minimum. They gained promotions into higher ranks earlier than their peers, and had a higher overall degree of satisfaction with their service.

Those cadets who cited extrinsic goals were found to be less likely to have the outcomes mentioned above.

This study confirms that leaders who are more motivated and focused on intrinsic goals, such as developing excellence as a leader and communicator, outperform those motivated by extrinsic goals, such as earning promotions and status. In other words, those leaders who focus on developing their inner capacity outperform those focused on outer accomplishment. These inner goals, and the thoughts and internal conversations that go along with them, are planting seeds of protection at the very foundation of their careers. You will reap what you sow, for better or for worse, just like the cadets at West Point.

Back to Belief Systems

The reality you see now is a vast unfolding of all of your past thoughts, feelings, conversations, goals, and beliefs. These are the seeds you have planted, day in and day out, now sprouted before your eyes. They've taken root in your life, and have become very real and tangible. This is why right thought-right action serves to protect you the most. Capacity is the basis that determines the timing to achieve any and everything.

Let us offer one final piece of inspiration. Possibly one of the greatest examples of protected leadership achievement and progress in a high stakes, high pressure arena is the success of Ray Dalio's Bridgewater Associates, one of the most successful hedge funds ever. Many consider Dalio to be the top hedge fund investor of all time. Being a hedge fund manager is all about protection first, in order to make gains second.

Bridgewater Associates was founded in 1975 and has produced more net gains in absolute U.S. dollars than any other hedge fund, even more so than the legendary George Soros' investment vehicles.

When you read his book Principles, you understand, or at least get an insight into, the rigor with which he develops his and his team's capacity. Their expanded capacity enables them to focus on the right investments at the right time and make huge consistent gains.

Lack of Capacity and Protection

With all of the concepts and information in this book (it's a lot, we know), it's important to stop where we are and briefly discuss exactly what it looks like when a leader is lacking capacity and protection:

- Inability to provide accurate or appropriate feedback to teams and/or employees.
- Inability to engage, listen, and interact with teams and/or employees.
- Inability to set clear goals and follow through.
- Poor processes for training and retaining employees and/or teams.
- Inconsistent leadership type.
- Inability to connect with teams and/or employees.
- Inability to attract top talent.
- Poor finances.
- Unstable business culture.
- Excessive conflict management.
- Unstable numbers through economic cycles.
- Poor agility.
- Poor predicting.
- Poor emotional environment.
- Poor projections for future growth.
- Inability to lay out long-term plans and goals.
- Poor application of past and/or current professional development tools and programs.

If you are experiencing these characteristics of lack, this is your moment to pivot. Otherwise, at an unknown time in the future, you will lose what you've built, simply because you were not able to protect it. Take the Science of Protection and use it to expand your capacity of awareness to protect yourself, your team, what you achieve, and become an enlightened leader.

Great leaders have great capacity to handle any situation and this is why understanding this component is so important for protection and protected progress to be your reality. In the next chapter we'll integrate this into action, not just massive action which can wear you out and reduce your useful life, but more spontaneous right action that is in tune with what is required.

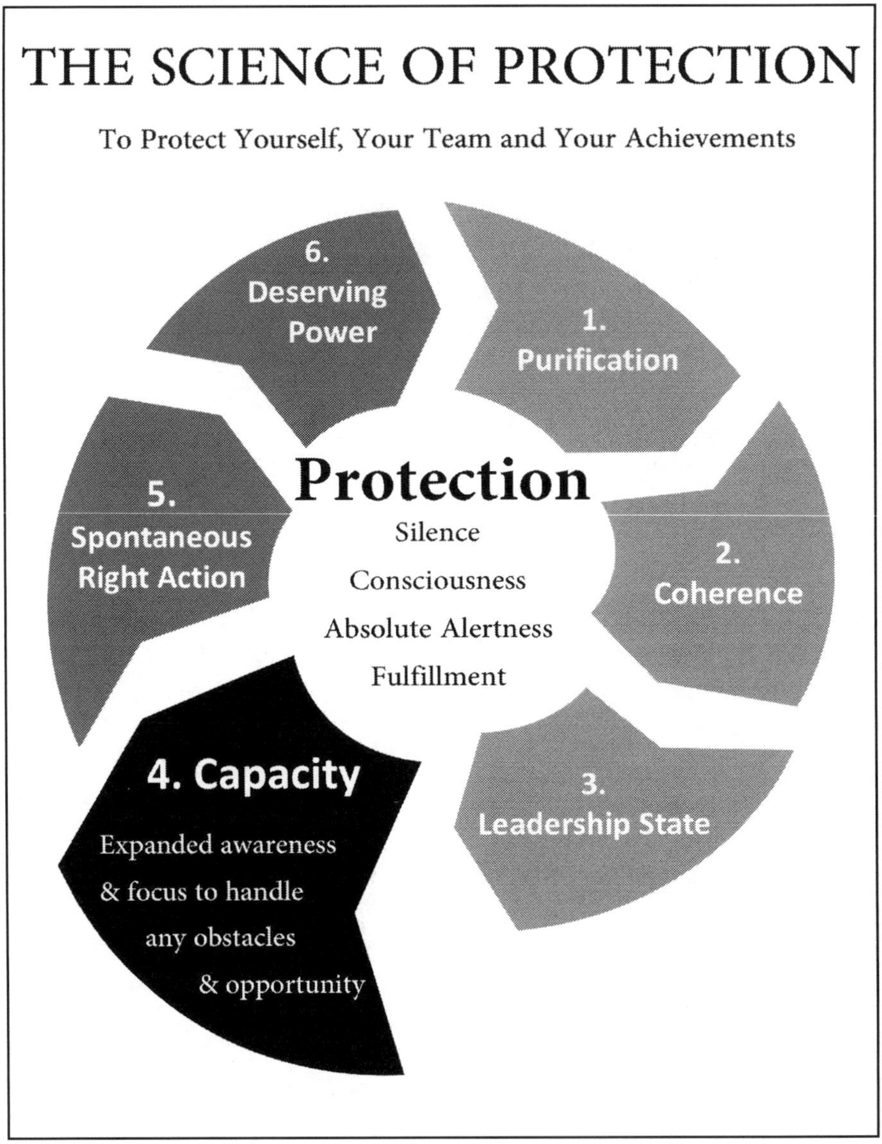
THE SCIENCE OF PROTECTION
To Protect Yourself, Your Team and Your Achievements
6. Deserving Power
1. Purification
5. Spontaneous Right Action
Protection
Silence
Consciousness
Absolute Alertness
Fulfillment
2. Coherence
3. Leadership State
4. Capacity
Expanded awareness
& focus to handle
any obstacles
& opportunity

YOUR TURN

Knowing and Growing Your Capacity

1. What must you protect for your progress to be protected progress? Write down all the critical elements to your progress, both subjective and objective.
2. Take your capacity pulse. Do you feel you are under- or over-utilizing the capacity you have? How can you utilize, expand, or adapt your capacity to handle the demands you face?
3. What do you need to be more aware of that you're not currently? What do you need to focus on to ensure you properly handle what you're facing?

7 Spontaneous Right Action

Timely Evolutionary Action to Achieve Victory Before War

"Every battle is won before it is fought."
—Sun Tzu, Chinese military strategist and philosopher

As you read in the previous chapter, capacity gives you more awareness and focus, the by-product of this is more ability for spontaneous right action.

Spontaneous right action is timely evolutionary action in tune with what is required.

Even if it appears you are doing well, that doesn't necessarily mean you are doing what is required to protect progress. Take former Compaq CEO Eckhard Pfeiffer. Pfeiffer, from all external viewpoints, was succeeding. He grew the company from $3.3 billion in 1991 to $14.8 billion by 1996. But Compaq's board wasn't pleased with his performance. Pfeiffer resigned in 1999, having left behind a legacy of being too heavily focused on growing the business and neglecting its customer base. Compaq never recovered and was sold to Hewlett-Packard in 2002.

Pfeiffer overly focused on short-term gain, probably because he thought that was the top priority of the board and shareholders, plus it makes him look good in the short run. However not doing what is right for the long term is what really kills a company and a leader. Unfortunately, Pfeiffer may have been scape goat for his board and shareholders because their motivations also influence the way he led the company. When you focus on doing what is right for the sake of long term progress you protect your and everyone's interests. Focusing mainly on short term gain you become vulnerable and unprotected in the long run.

As far back as we go in history, we see leaders being dragged (or dragging others) into wars that have raged on for centuries. We are neither historians nor generals, therefore will not identify the meaningful battles over the meaningless, but we can use this as a lesson in our own leadership journeys.

We understand, realistically, that sometimes fights, conflicts, arguments, and confrontations help to bring unresolved issues to the surface. In business, you should embrace these opportunities as a way to transform the incoherence in the situation. However, your optimal goal should be to develop enough coherence capacity to perceive potential issues, bring them to the table, and resolve them before they become more difficult confrontations.

In the development world, there are entire teams of coaches and consultants who go in and either teach companies how to "manage conflict" or provide conflict resolution services. The amount of time and money that goes into solving problems that could have been prevented is unacceptable. Think about all the time you put into trying to figure things out, something leaders pride themselves on. Think about how much more energy you would have if you spent less time "figuring" and more time knowing. Think about how much more bliss you would have in your life if you spent more time in victory and less time in war.

The Real Cost of Conflict in Business

Numerous reports have attempted to break down the monetary cost attached to conflict management and resolution. But let's look deeper than the hundreds of billions of dollars being thrown at putting out fires. Let's talk about the non-monetary costs:

1. **Elevated Stress:** We've already covered stress in earlier chapters, but we should point out that conflict substantially adds to the stress every person involved is already experiencing. This is something you, as a leader in charge of diffusing your people's stress, must be mindful of. Even if the conflict is only on the leader's "plate," the people who come in contact with him during his time of elevated stress will also suffer the negative effects of that conflict. Further, the decisions made during that state of elevated stress will directly affect the business, the leader, and its people. Such conflicts, and the stress related to them, typically compound and reach explosive levels before ever being addressed and resolved.

2. **Unnecessary Risk:** Workplaces and leaders that allow dysfunctional environments to exist put themselves at risk, unnecessarily, for extreme situations to occur. Like hatred, greed, lust and jealousy in the workplace that leads to conflict, stand offs and possibly even harassment, violence and suicide as people can't cope. The rise we are currently witnessing in these types of events proves the need for a more naturally occuring form of protection—now.

3. **Poor Decision Making:** The trickledown effect that takes place when there is conflict in a business environment touches everything. Remember, thoughts and actions are a product of the state you are in (your leadership state). The same is true for your people. If they are in a state of elevated stress or conflict, their decision making will be one of the first things to suffer. Their decisions will reflect the state they are in and the stress they are carrying. Marianne Williamson put this best when she said, "Everything we do is infused with the energy with which we do it. If we're frantic, life will be frantic. If we're peaceful, life will be peaceful."

From there, the downhill ride only gains speed as it races towards defeat. But this is only one layer of potential damage and conflict. There are deeper layers that can prevent you from performing at the high level required for you to be successful. In fact, we see this quite often with leaders, who struggle with internal conflicts and lack protection.

Feeling a lack of anything—be it attention, money, health, happiness, or love—creates internal conflict that interferes with your abilities as a leader.

What Does War Do to the Mind of a Leader?

When leaders find themselves in the position of constantly battling, their self-confidence is reduced, their leadership state is destabilized, their cognitive abilities are weakened, their emotions are overwhelmed, and they will, without a doubt, fall out of alignment. When a leader is misaligned with their own purpose, they are forced to take action they don't necessarily agree with, morally. From here, energy is reduced, resources are depleted, options start diminishing, and further poor decisions are made. It is a vicious cycle. Just like in war, the initial battle may create an economic boom, but eventually this will taper off and the downhill descent will begin. Before you find yourself in the bunker, exhausted, fraught with worry, trying to figure out how you are going to get yourself and everyone else through one more day on the front lines, consider this: you never have to be there in the first place.

There's an interview floating around where, during an episode of *In Depth*, Graham Bensinger asks tennis great John McEnroe about his success. When they get to the point in the interview where McEnroe is trying to explain why he felt he lost his edge, his wife, and his spot at the top, McEnroe changes his tone. "I was going to come back and be a better player. That was the plan. The plan wasn't to come back and be a worse player." But no matter what he can say about the plans he made, McEnroe admits he has no idea what went wrong or why. He was pushing himself to stay on top, but it didn't work. So if perseverance isn't the answer, and effort isn't the answer, and experience certainly isn't the answer, we can only assume he was lacking inner development. McEnroe found himself battling to keep the things he wanted, and in the end, victory did not belong to him because protection didn't either.

The truth about success is that it isn't what you've been told or even what you think. Truly sustainable success is not going to battle every day and winning at all cost, or an endless struggle to remain relevant. True success is playing the long game, and taking the broad view, while aligning with the protection you need to be a leader. Even Tony Robbins agrees that, "In order to achieve and progress to another level, massive action is required." The problem with that is knowing which massive action to take. So many leaders get it wrong, and then find themselves in the middle of a war, fighting for survival.

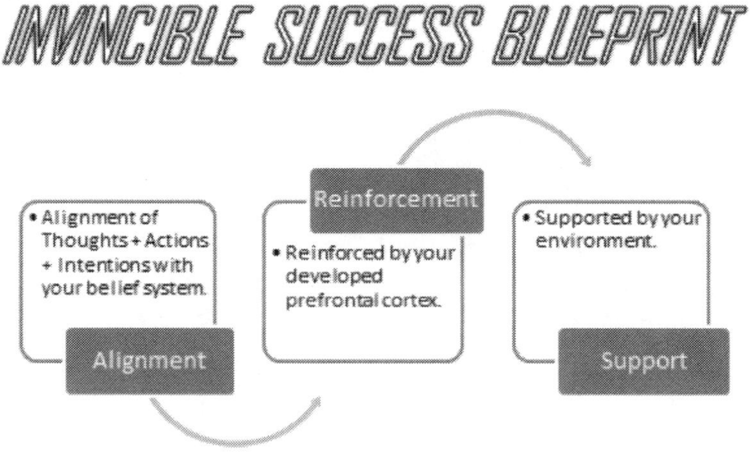

Leading to win = Short-term change in the brain
Leading to grow = Long-term change in the brain

If you go back to Chapter 4 and revisit the changes that take place in your brain as you develop yourself, you can apply that knowledge to your approach as a leader. So if you're solely functioning based on impulses from your amygdala without clear interpretation from a coherent awake pre-frontal cortex then you'll probably takes lots of massive action with great passion but it won't necessarily be spontaneous right action that serves you and everyone long term. This is why you want to protect the coherence of your pre-frontal cortex and not allow it to get tired, stressed or fatigued. When you play to win, you make short-term moves for short-term successes. In this short-sighted approach, you will go to war unnecessarily to win the short-term battles.

Winning can look like a lot of different things, and often the best opportunity to win sits within the long view. It is in this long, broad view, which you can see and know more about where your evolutionary action can take you on your leadership journey. You can enact actions that will fulfill more long-term change. You've learned that this type of action is evolutionary, and therefore supported by your environment. This level of foresight is a requirement to success and the path to protection, aka: victory before war. These are the hard lines in your Science of Protection, the nonnegotiable elements.

As we said earlier there are two types of action leaders take proactive evolutionary action or reactive selfish action. Applying the knowledge we learned about the brain in Chapter 3 and 4, we can see that evolutionary action is protected, long term, and reinforced by a coherent prefrontal cortex. Evolutionary action is therefore nothing more complex than intuitive, spontaneous right action in tune with what is required to achieve victory before war.

It is incredibly difficult to take spontaneous right evolutionary action when your goals are not aligned or your focus is only on developing your habits and sales numbers. Those goals serve the very small, short-term change we've discussed. This shortsighted approach is putting companies out of business regularly, because they are going to war unnecessarily for those measly small wins.

Fear of loss pushes business leaders to remain out of alignment, instead focusing their efforts on attempting to win small battles along the way. With this approach, you will always be:

- Going to war, or
- Preparing for war

This is why a victory-before-war mentality is so important. It doesn't matter if you crush your goals this quarter if this time next year you'll be out of business. Yet, this is the game of risk businesses are playing every single day. This is the most common approach we see to business growth right now. Leaders are willing to take their restless and weary teams into battle as often as they need to in order for those numbers to climb.

There's a better way to win. You don't have to do battle to achieve. You can achieve Victory Before War.

Think About This:

- In war, you have to make sacrifices to win.
- In war, you have to make compromises to win.

If you want victory before war, timely or spontaneous right evolutionary action is required. If your actions are compromised because they don't match your belief system, your achievements will not be sustainable.

An undeveloped leader cannot continuously take timely spontaneous right evolutionary action. You must be established in your leadership state first. This is your baseline, your foundation, your path to Victory Before War. Without inner development, you cannot sustain the alignment necessary for this higher level of consistent, true leadership.

To gain the ultimate competitive advantage in war, you must establish yourself enough to avoid battle altogether. We want to help you move into your unique territory, where you have developed your leadership state to such a level that it cannot be diminished, corrupted, or lost. In this new state, as we previously discussed, your perspective takes place from the top of the mountain, not from the cliffs as you attempt to climb to the top.

> **"We are trying to remove the veil from the last quarter-century to show leaders that they can avoid the war and the wasted resources, and the unnecessary small battles they believe will guarantee them the final victory.**

Because, what we know to be true now is that war has no winners, and the only true victors are the ones watching from atop the mountain."

—Paolo D'Angelo, New Mavericks co-founder

What does war in business look like? What do leaders routinely deal with that pushes them into battle unnecessarily? Here are but a few of the possibilities:

- Bad contracts you have to work out
- Destructive executives
- Deceptive employees
- Clients who aren't the right fit
- Business deals that end up hurting your bottom line in the long run
- Lenders who commit to funding a project and end up bailing before the project is complete
- Partners who leave you vulnerable unnecessarily
- Failure to innovate and take timely right evolutionary action
- Competitors coming into the same niche as you sparking a price and value war

Elon Musk isn't dragging Tesla and his employees into war for competition or innovation. He is atop the mountain, gazing into the future, executing right spontaneous evolutionary action, and operating from a well stabilized leadership state from the view point of influencing the future. In the present, he and the company have their short-term challenges to overcome but compared to the competition they're in a league of their own, and the progress looks well protected and assured so long as he and his leaders are activating all steps of the Science of Protection.

This success cycle also stabilizes the environment Musk has created at Tesla, and we see this in action through the revolutionary ideas they consistently bring to life. A lot of people do not understand or share in Musk's visions for the future, but that doesn't stop them from investing in his foresight. Developed leaders draw support for ideas that seem inconceivable to some because their energy, alignment, and coherence are deeply attractive. This combination of development characteristics is the "it factor" or the "x factor." It's the thing everyone wants, is intrigued by, and has no idea how to get.

It is important to note that being at the top of the mountain does not promise invincibility, capacity, or success. You reach the top of the mountain with what you bring. The only invincibility at the top is the invincibility you bring to the top, it's been developed and earned.

Business History Will Continue to Repeat Itself

One of the least surprising, yet still widely talked about, recent big box failures is Toys R Us. Their inability to look into the future, take the broader view, and innovate killed any chance they had. They were forced into a war with Amazon, and by then it was already too late. A map doesn't help when you're already lost in the thicket.

Businesses and leaders are forced into war or choosing to go to battle for one of three reasons:

- Underdeveloped Pre-frontal Cortex, the CEO of You.
- Fear of loss
- Inability to align

Case Study: Nokia

In 2006, Nokia was selling half a billion phones per year, and enjoyed a net worth of about $100 billion dollars. Also, in 2006, Steve Jobs was working away at the Apple headquarters in Cupertino, California, to develop the very first iPhone. After its amazingly successful release the following year, Nokia saw incredible losses. While Steve Jobs assumed an innovative perch at the top of the mountain, Nokia was forced into war for customer territory they easily owned just months before. By 2009, Nokia's net worth had dropped to $21 billion, a mere fraction of their once high valuation, and by 2012 their net worth had dropped to an astoundingly low $5.5 billion. Nokia may have learned from these failures, as they are now attempting to reclaim their market value. But with a current-day valuation of around $30 billion, it seems hard to imagine this company was once the powerhouse that it was.

While Apple rose, Nokia fell. Nokia proved their development didn't match their market share because at the pivotal moment, they didn't have the capacity required, it was not enough, and they lost big time.

ELEVATED FORESIGHT BLUEPRINT

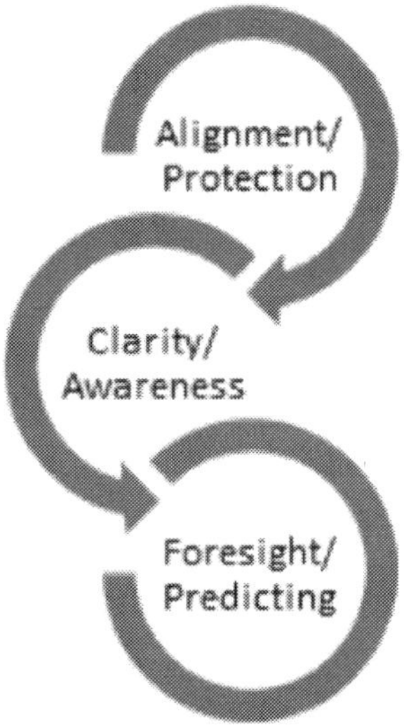

Clarity Is a By-product of Alignment

The reason high level leaders have such accurate foresight relates directly to elevated clarity, a result of the alignment we have been talking about over the last few chapters.

Protection is the resting foundation for everything. If you wish for more clarity, and elevated foresight, protection is the answer. If you wish to achieve Victory Before War, you must seek alignment and protection first. Everything else will follow.

NO VISION

Where there is alignment, there is victory. This applies to everything a leader faces, day in and day out.

NO VICTORY

As a high-performance leader, you must realize that constant war and aggression and hatred is not who you really are. These are just programs. Your mind is the computer, easily infected with viruses, and your task is to disinfect these programs to set yourself free and achieve victory before war.

Jonathan Schwartz was CEO of Sun Microsystems from 2006 to 2010. Sun Microsystems lost $2.2 billion in its last year of fiscal independence before being acquired by Oracle. Oracle's then-CEO, Larry Ellison, blamed the company's downfall on Schwartz, accusing him of ignoring problems as they escalated, making poor strategic decisions, and spending too much time on his blog. If Ellison is right, then this is a case of not averting danger before it arises, and consequently not achieving victory before war.

Let's go back to this question from the beginning of the book: How do leaders develop vision?

Victory requires a vision for the future. Could you ever imagine a general (or CEO) preparing for war by simply saying, "Let's just get there and see how it goes"? No. There's always a plan, a vision of the desired path and potential outcomes.

Anne Mulcahy, CEO of Xerox from 2001 to 2009, demonstrated vision and planning power to avert her company from the danger of bankruptcy. Through her focus on innovation, she helped the company swiftly increase company profits.

Xerox had lost $273 million in 2000, and when she took over in 2001, Xerox had more than $17 billion in debt and was nearing Chapter 11 bankruptcy. She initiated a series of cost-cutting measures and refocused the company on research and development, enabling Xerox to generate $91 million in net income in 2003 and $859 million the next year.

We've established that victory requires a plan for the future. But what if the leader doesn't yet control this vision? What is the force that accelerates a leader's conceptualization of their vision, and clarifies their path to victory?

Vision develops and reveals itself—unfolds, you might say—as a leader's foundation stabilizes, and when a leader is protected. With this information at the front of your mind, let's look at another question: What is the point of developing a vision that is neither protected nor evolutionary?

Vision and victory (before war) are by-products of a developed leader, period. Which means any vision without protection at the foundation is at the mercy of every ebb and flow in the markets, economy, and nature, as well as in the individual leader.

High performers are connected to the future. This connection allows them to pivot, change course, align with change, and take evolutionary, timely, spontaneous right action in tune with what is required to achieve victory before war. Because what is the point of getting what you want, if you can't protect it and keep it?

Least Resistance Leadership

Often times, in leadership, we say things to justify taking the path of least resistance:

- "Let's take the high road."
- "We need to make rational decisions."
- "We should be using common sense."
- "Let's focus on the task at hand."

In reality, these are nothing more than excuses for inaction. During a recent conversation with a client, the topic was a particular scenario that was causing distress within a certain team of executives. Our client was explaining how, when the situation first arose, she decided to let it dissolve on its own. She felt by not giving energy or resources to the conflict—an approach she called "taking the high road"—she would set a precedent of expectation for potential future conflicts. Of course, from the other side of the spectrum, this high road looked a lot like inaction, and was received as such. By the time she brought this conflict among her team members to our attention, things were pretty ugly, and her corporate bosses had brought in an HR attorney to figure out the best escape route.

More often than not, taking the high road is translation for postponement. The neglect of conflicts, in leadership, breeds more neglect, along with denial, confrontation, and potential legal issues.

There are two types of Least Resistance Leadership:

- Taking the path of least resistance.
- Creating the path of least resistance.

Type #1 is the action or inaction taken by our client in the story above. Type #2 is the only Least Resistance Leadership option that has protection as a foundation.

A leader can create the path of least resistance by:

- Dissolving bad impressions and stresses.
- Minimizing the impact of potential failures.
- Increasing leadership capacity.
- Taking timely, right evolutionary action.
- Stabilizing their leadership state.

Leadership is a natural state for you. You can't have invincible success without strong leadership. You also don't need permission to be the leader you are capable of being. You are the source of your own inertia, but you must have the awareness first that allows your reality to change.

> **"Start playing the unspoken, hidden game that allows winners to keep winning while everyone else, even smart, talented people, get stuck and don't even know why."**
>
> *—Ramit Sethi, bestselling author and entrepreneur*

On a very broad spectrum, the Universe is always in a stabilized leadership state. It is constantly in motion, dictating before every moment what must happen next for there to be the perfect balance required for your existence. Leadership also requires a similar constant foresight. A leader must anticipate rather than react, and know rather than guess. Bad impressions, fear of loss, lack of development, lack of protection, these are the things holding you back from accelerating into your invincible success flow.

We are entering a new age of leadership. It is not about spreadsheets and numbers. It is now about optimizing the capacity of the individual leader. Everything else is a by-product.

Habit formation and intellectual training have been the center of professional development for the past few decades. In this odd and backward way, we've confused cause and effect for far too long.

Cause: Low capacity, low awareness
Effect: Low production, low results

Versus

Cause: Stabilized Leadership State
Effect: High production, evolutionary results

> **"Leadership changes everything. There isn't an innovation, customer, partner, ROI, breakthrough, or stock price change that isn't animated by leadership. Leadership is the cause. We get caught up in the effects without realizing that we have to be the change in the cause that we want to see in the effect."**
>
> —*Kevin Cashman, bestselling author and CEO expert*

As more and more leaders awaken to the power within, the new center of professional development will involve concepts such as inner development, protection, and invincibility. Aligning with true leadership is how we will change the way we do business and, more importantly, how we will change the world.

In order to be ahead of this change, rather than left in its wake, you must begin this transformation. You must shift your focus from outer development to inner development. This is the only path to invincibility. This is the only path to alignment. This is the only path to the foresight that will be required of future leaders. This is the path to the cause, rather than all of the effects. This is the only path that will unite and employ all of the outer development you've pursued. As we see our business economy outpace the development of people, it will be up to leaders like you to act as a guide into this new and exciting territory. This is the beginning of a new business era.

On July 20, 1969, Neil Armstrong made history. He was the first human to walk on the moon.

In 1775, American frontiersmen Daniel Boone blazed his wilderness trail through the Cumberland Gap in the Appalachian Mountains, from North Carolina and Tennessee, then into Kentucky. Upon arrival, he founded the village of Boonesborough, Kentucky, one of the first American settlements west of the Appalachians.

In Australia, in the 1850s, Daniel Henry Deniehy, republican patriot, dedicated his life to achieving a genuine people's democracy, making land available to the ordinary citizen and delivering what he deemed the truth the people of his country needed to hear.

In France in the 1400s, there was Joan of Arc. In India, in the 1500s, we read about Mirabai. In the 1600s, we read about the works of the great mathematician, scientist, and philosopher, Galileo Galilei.

Fast forward to today, we pay tribute to visionaries such as Nikola Tesla, Henry Ford, and, more recently, Stephen Hawking and Steve Jobs. We recognize in them an incredible foresight, along with the characteristics of invincibility in the Elon Musks and Jeff Bezos of the world

We can promise you this: no amount of mimicking their habits or advice will take you to their level. Only when you are developed enough to stabilize your leadership state, minimize your bad impressions, and release your fear, will you reach your own measure of invincible success.

> **"In order to establish order, disorder has to be shaken; and for shaking to remain under control, we who are at the basis...have to be unreachable by the surface turmoil. In that integrated state, the fast-moving chaos and change will pass away in a steady manner...**
>
> **Our awareness is the basis for all of these transformations. More than ever before, time demands we remain completely ourselves.**
>
> —*Maharishi Mahesh Yogi*

Throughout the history of humanity, we see example after example, in every corner of the Earth, of leaders having enough foresight to forge new paths in directions others couldn't even fathom. And whether we agree with history or not, we cannot disagree on the fact that extraordinary human beings have gone before us.

These leaders cemented their place in history by seeing a vision others could not. In this new age of leadership and business, if you wish to forge new paths, you must first develop your foresight and protection. We are leaving our history of fighting for what we believe is our seat at the table. Today, and in the future, your foresight must lead you into territory where you are capable of achieving victory before war.

This is what spontaneous right action is about and today's fast-changing digital age requires more of it than ever because too many mistakes quickly leads to a company's demise. The example of Juicero shared earlier is an example of spontaneous wrong action that lost $120 million of investors' money.

If you want protection as you progress you must take more spontaneous right action not just massive action for the sake of massive action. It's efficiency of action that ensures you, your team and company are protected for the long haul. Next, we go into how more spontaneous right action leads to more deserving power and how this protects and supports you in getting what you want and keeping it.

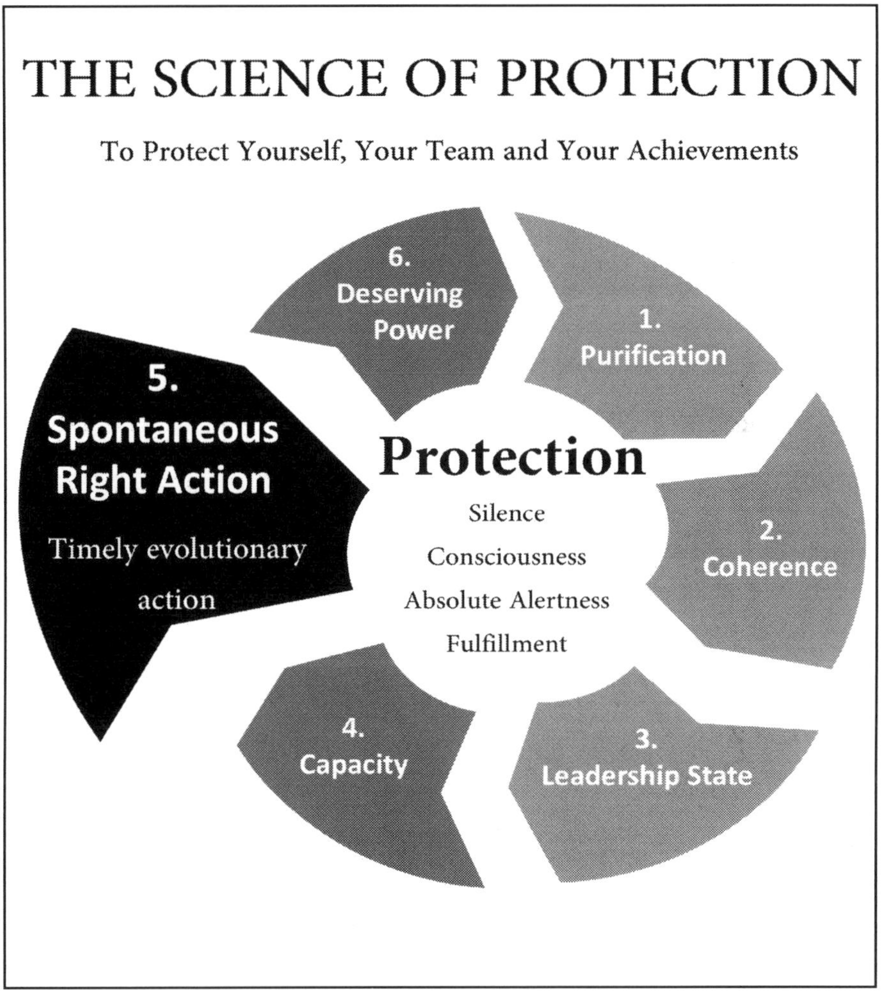

YOUR TURN

Tuning into Your Spontaneous Right Action

1. What are the potential conflicts and battles that could come up on your path to achieving what you want?
2. What is the cause of these potential conflicts?
3. What timely right action can you take to avert the conflict before it arises?

8 Deserving Power

Having Good Merit and Support to Avert Problems Before They Arise to Get, Protect and Sustain What You Want

*"We don't always get what we want,
we do always get what we deserve and believe we deserve."*

This is going to be the shortest chapter in the book because when you've activated the previous five steps of the Science of Protection, you'll have more deserving power, good merit and support, to avert problems before they arise thereby protecting yourself, your team and your achievements and become an enlightened leader.

Firstly, deserving power is one word not two, it's not to be deserving of power. It's you have the power of deserving or the power to deserve. It's not that one is deserving of power, position or status or not.

Deserving power is derived from having done the work of developing and giving of yourself so you have a threshold of positive energy, good merit and support to avert problems and see opportunities before they arise, enabling you to get, protect and sustain what you want.

Spontaneous right action is what gives good merit and builds deserving power. Non-righteous unethical immoral actions create demerit and detracts from deserving power. So deserving power is something you earn, attain and gain and also something you can corrupt, diminish and lose.

Having sufficient deserving power backed by self-belief and skill in action makes breakthrough results inevitable as this inspires support from people in your environment. It means one has earned the right to deserve to fulfill an outcome and you and that achievement are protected in the process and afterwards.

The opposite is being undeserving, like someone who has been unethical or corrupt in the way they're doing things. These people have reduced their power of deserving therefore have reduced their support for getting what they want. If they do get what they want the negative consequences inevitably catch up with them and they lose what they got or suffer in some other way, usually it's the opposite and equal way. Usually life has inherent intelligence of creating equilibrium and justice again. This is deserving power in terms of action and reaction.

We could also call it good merit, good fortune or grace as Tony Robbins calls it. Grace is a by-product of doing good things that enhances and protects yourself, others and environment. It increases your deservingness to have grace or support from nature/life to fulfill what you want. Deserving power is like a good merit bank account that you can draw on anytime to help fulfill an outcome, assuming it has a positive balance of merit and deserving and not a negative balance or debt.

If we do have a negative balance or debt of deserving power then this is when we have to go back to the first component, purification to clear away the negative balance and debt and build up more deserving power. This is why sometimes we may be taking massive action and not getting much fruits from it because we're correcting and purifying something so our progress is more supported.

This chapter will enhance your understanding of what this deserving power really is, how it can appreciate and depreciate and why it is ultimately something you want to help appreciate so you have maximum support to get what you want and protect and keep it.

If you want better results, you require better deserving power. If you've developed and aligned yourself with the five previous steps of the Science of Protection you'll have earned more good merit to have more deserving power to avert and neutralize negativity and enhance and protect positive progress and results.

The first three internal protection development steps of the Science of Protection, purification, coherence and leadership state, help you have more capacity to handle any situation. With more capacity you have better observing power (power of attention and focus) to have better discerning power to make better decisions. This results in more spontaneous right actions which generates more deserving power for more assured and protected achievement and progress.

Building and Using Your Deserving Power

Building up deserving power fundamentally comes from having good thoughts, feelings, and actions that serve your and others' progress. We don't get what we want, we get what we deserve backed by what we believe we deserve. Building deserving is based on how well we first observe what is really going on, then accurately discern, then decide upon, and then act.

Observe → Discern (think, feel, believe) → Decide →
Act (give) → Deserve → Desire → Act → Fulfill

The more spontaneous you are at this sequence of events, the more deserving power you accumulate to be more supported and protected every step of your journey. The basis for desiring and fulfilling higher and higher things in life is based on the power of deserving and good merit one has accumulated. No good desiring if you haven't earned the right and don't know and believe you deserve. Always deserve first then desire.

An elevated power of observation, observing power is the basis of having more deserving power, is mainly a direct result of having more inner lively silence or coherence which gives you better thoughts, feelings, belief, purpose and actions that builds deserving power. Measurement theory states an object is transformed or influenced through the process of observation. Therefore, the degree to which you influence something depends on the quality and quantity of your observing power and attention.

We utilize our deserving power when we desire and act to fulfill that desire. If we fulfill it then we know we must have had the deserving and believing power to do that. If we desire, act and don't fulfill, we know the deserving and believing power was not enough to fulfill the desire.

Protecting Your Deserving Power

A few words of caution about using your deserving power so you protect it. Deserving power is the most precious thing to have if we want to continue to be protected and supported to progress. The goal is to always use your deserving power for evolutionary desires and purposes that help evolve you, those around you and the environment. We are very aware that elite leaders are elite and stay elite because they're consistently enhancing and protecting their deserving power because they:

1. Choose to develop themselves as people first so they can better connect and harmonize with others.

2. Never think they're fully developed, because they know as soon as they think they're complete and have complete wisdom they're asking for trouble and on the verge of falling.

3. Continually culture a calm mind, composed emotions and good physical energy. In other words, they use their mind, emotions and energy wisely not frivolously.

Frivolously wasting our deserving power on frivolous desires, usually because we are afflicted by fear of loss, stress, bad impressions and inner enemies, means we have to go back to step 1 of purification so we can avert doing this and protect our deserving power.

Case Point: High Flying CEOs Who Didn't Protect Deserving Power

It's one thing to lead a fast-growing company it's another to make it a business that progresses in a sustainable protected way. The former CEO of Uber, Travis Kalanick, and now the former CEO of WeWork (America's largest fastest growing private company), Adam Neumann, encountered a drying up of deserving power and protected progress as leaders when they both stepped down prior to their company's doing IPOs due to the increased scrutiny from investors around their personal behavior, actions, spending and skill as leaders. Below are some excerpts from a New York Times article on 24th September 2019, just after Adam Neumann stepped down.

> **Now, with his resignation as chief executive, Mr. Neumann joins an ignominious club that includes Travis Kalanick, who was ousted as the chief of Uber before he could take it public.**
>
> **In a statement, Mr. Neumann said the scrutiny of his personal life and management was hurting the company. "Since the announcement of our I.P.O., too much of the focus has been placed on me,"**
>
> **"Investors saw through Lyft, and they saw through Uber as well," said Matt Stoller, a fellow at the Open Markets Institute, a Washington think tank. "This one has simply been rejected. Investors are saying, 'We're not going to tolerate this nonsense anymore.'"**

> **"The fundamental question here is: Does it help to be a really strong and at times abrasive personality to be innovative?" said Walter Isaacson, a professor of history at Tulane University who knows Mr. Neumann.**
>
> **"The answer is it doesn't always help, and at times it goes too far."**

Deserving Power Creates High Energy Frequency Leadership

In the beginning of this book we talked briefly about Tesla, energy, and how energy doesn't only rule the world, it is the world. Animals, plants, and water are all made up of atoms, which produce, emit, and receive energy. Each of these operates at a specific frequency. The same is true for your cells, your organs, and even your emotions. Everything has its own unique electro-magnetic field. Nikola Tesla said, "If you could eliminate certain outside frequencies that interfered with our bodies, we would have greater resistance toward disease."

One of the pioneering researchers of frequency in the human body, Bruce Taino, built a frequency monitor in the 1990s and stated that the average frequency of a healthy human body resonates between 62 and 72 Hz. He also pointed out that as the frequency drops due to physiological or environmental factors, a person's immune system becomes compromised and creates space for disease. Those leading the field of biophysics into the future recognize that the molecules in our bodies are controlled by these frequencies.

Frequency Resonance

We also know that when two frequencies are brought together, the lower will always rise up to meet the higher. This is something we call resonance, and also applies to biological systems. The reason we are pointing this out is simple: your frequency determines your leadership ability, and your leadership ability determines your deserving power to have success. Tuning in to these internal truths and aligning with the Universal force of protection are the most powerful ways you can truly avert problems before they arise.

Frequency Gives Direction to Purpose and Action

You can have a purpose and take action, but not have the right direction. Direction allows the purpose and action to align. Direction is the frequency of your energy that allows your purpose and action to become aligned. No good having purpose and taking action but your frequency is doubt, neediness, desperation and fear. You don't have full control over everything; you do have full control over your frequency. We don't create energy or atoms, they already exist. We manifest and achieve our purpose through having the right energy frequency when we act. The frequency you must have when taking action to fulfill your purpose is a positive abundant courageous believing in yourself frequency.

Finding Your Higher Frequency

Based on the principle of resonance, when one object vibrates at the resonant frequency of another forcing it to vibrate with greater amplitude you can increase your frequency.

By increasing the speed at which the energy field of your body vibrates, through higher frequency emotions (love, gratitude, bliss), you can eliminate inner enemies. Vibrating at this higher frequency creates more awareness for you, which also purifies stresses and past traumas. A higher vibrational frequency also allows you to move past the level of development that is action and reaction, the lowest level of awareness, and into a more stable territory that provides you with more accurate predicting abilities and proactive compassion to protect the progress of yourself and those you lead.

Again, we see how true it is that you create your own reality—and through deserving power you have inherent protection, allowing you to maintain and keep what you've created, as long as it is life supporting to you, others and your environment.

> **"Oftentimes, man forgets the Source of his power and becomes drunk with power, so to speak. In other words, he misuses the law and selfishly takes advantage of his fellow man. We find that many times men in high places become conceited, opinionated, and arrogant. This is all due to ignorance of the law.**
>
> **"The law is that power, security, and riches are not to be obtained externally. They must come from the treasure-house of consciousness. If you remain in tune with the infinite, you discover that you are always drinking the wine of life, love, joy, and happiness. To the spiritually-minded man, God (I AM) is the eternal**

now and his good is present at every moment of time and point of space."

—*David Allen, The Power of I AM*

The excerpt above is one example of hundreds we have found in self-help, spiritual, and professional development texts, identifying protection and its importance. Of course, every coach, speaker, and thought leader has called it something different, and most have fallen just short of figuring out the final piece of the puzzle. In fact, as a collective whole, we have been trying to pinpoint and identify this idea of the Science of Protection for several decades.

This is why Einstein himself said that imagination was more important than knowledge. He understood the driving force of our entire Universe, energy, and furthermore recognized our ability to both increase and decrease our energy frequency based on the lives we could imagine for ourselves.

With the application of frequency and energy, we can easily see how true it is that protection is a law of nature, written into the very code of our existence, maintaining the ebb and flow of the existence of everything you see, hear, touch, and feel. When you have the right frequency of energy you have the deserving power to have protection around yourself and your achievements and progress.

Our frequency is either coherent or incoherent

The degree to which our frequency is coherent or incoherent is the degree to which we can create or diminish our deserving power. Hence why coherence is one of the important steps of the Science of Protection. We want to optimize our coherence to utilize the new good energy we've gained access to through purification. This then activates and supports being in the leadership state which gives you good capacity of awareness and focus to make more spontaneous right actions. This then generates more deserving power to support getting the results and protected achievement and progress we want.

Two Men, a Gold Coin and Brothel and a Temple and Snake

This fable story illustrates this effect of coherent versus incoherent frequency clearly. A man goes into a brothel and comes out and finds a gold coin. Another man goes into a temple and comes out and gets bitten by a snake.

The moral of the story is the man with the gold coin was supposed to get a whole treasure chest of gold coins, but because he'd lowered his frequency he only got one gold coin. The man who went into the temple was supposed to die, because he'd taken the time to raise his frequency, he only got bitten by a snake and didn't die. The moral of the sorry is we can affect our positive or negative deserving power based on the frequency we get ourselves in.

"God Helps Those Who Helps Themselves" Is About Frequency

Many think the message of this biblical saying is I've got to take a lot of massive action for God to help me. When really all it's asking is to first get yourself in a good energy frequency aligned with God's intelligence—which is something you have direct control over—then God and life are more likely to help you when you take action.

QUICK TIP: When meeting with people, don't come to the table expecting, needing, or calculating anything. Simply come with a good energy frequency to give what you can.

Why? Because going to anything with a giving energy frequency raises your deserving power, positioning you to naturally receive what you want without having expectations or neediness.

In summary, deserving power is the icing on the cake of the Science of Protection and allows everything to come together to fulfill the goal of protected achievement and progress. We could say luck and good fortune are created through having good deserving power which comes from development of the previous of five steps of purification, coherence, leadership state, capacity and spontaneous right action.

Deserving power supports and protects you being in the zone, having good capacity and have very little, if any, worry because you feel so supported in things working out and falling into place. Leaders worry because they can't see the full story and are using their intellect too much to work things out. Functioning like this you can't be relaxed. When you're relaxed, because you have all the six steps activated, it allows timing to be on your side and you're luckier and more fortunate. For most people luck is explaining what we can't comprehend. When in reality it's having the deserving power for your vision to be supported.

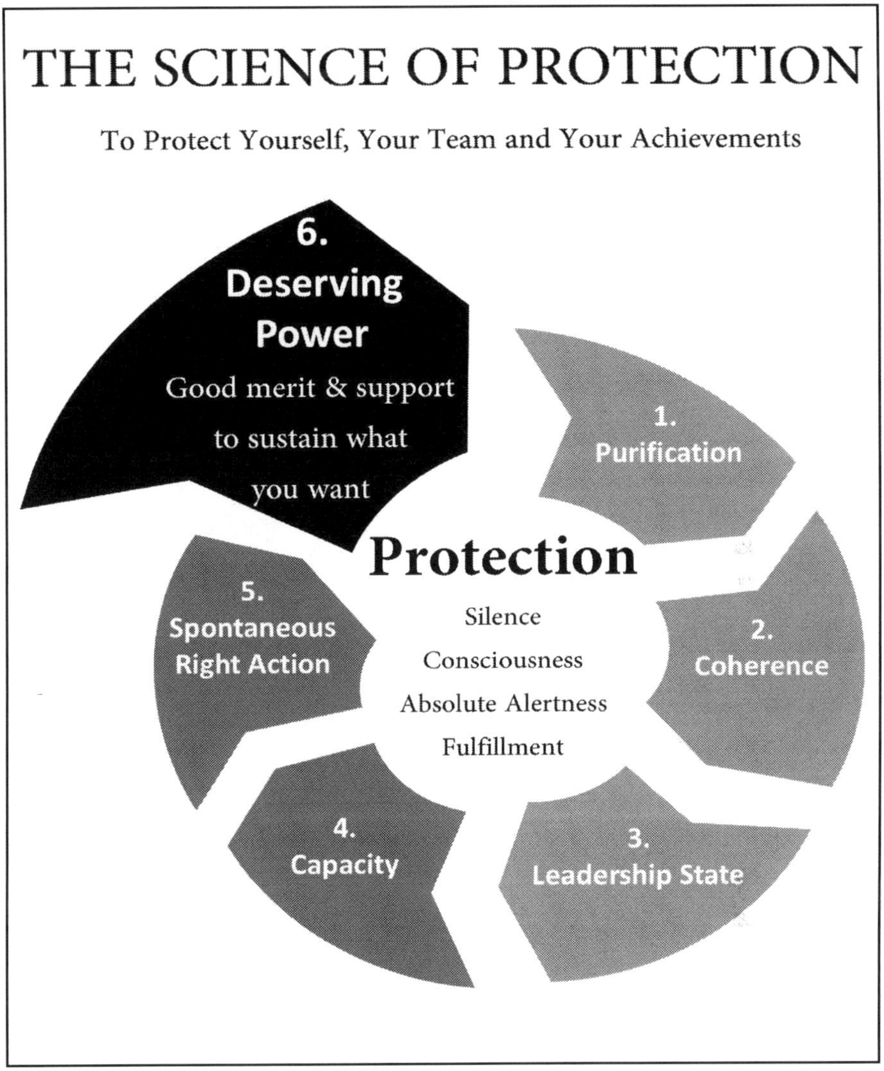
THE SCIENCE OF PROTECTION
To Protect Yourself, Your Team and Your Achievements
6.
Deserving Power
Good merit & support to sustain what you want
1.
Purification
2.
Coherence
3.
Leadership State
4.
Capacity
5.
Spontaneous Right Action
Protection
Silence
Consciousness
Absolute Alertness
Fulfillment

YOUR TURN

Revitalizing Your Deserving Power Frequency

This is an approximately 30 minute routine to change and strengthen your subconscious frequency (positive inner self-talk) to boost your feeling and believing to create more deserving power.

Ideally, go to the beach or body of water once or twice a week, half an hour before sunset or sunrise, and if you can, walk barefoot on the wet sand and in the shallow water. This reduces inflammation and tension in the body.

Then do the following:

1. For the first 5 minutes, just walk, appreciate and have gratitude for the abundance and fulfillment that already exists inside and outside you. This helps your conscious and subconscious be more aligned with the abundance that life naturally is.
2. For the next 5 minutes, walk while gently breathing in fully through your nose, for a count of 4, and then fully out through your nose or mouth for a count of 8. This will soothe stress, remove bad energy and air, and infuse new energy and oxygen into your heart and brain.
3. Then, for next 5 minutes repeat mentally and/or verbally quietly, with a feeling of sincerity, like you mean it, with your hand on your heart: "I love and believe in you." "I" being your higher self and 'you" being your inner child self. This will change your subconscious frequency about how you think and feel about yourself which then affects how others see, think, and feel about you.
4. For the next 10-20 minutes, sit comfortably, either on the sand or ground, on a bench, or in your car, and close your eyes and do either of the following:

A. Just be, by observing your silence and the thoughts coming from your silence like clouds passing in the sky.

B. What are three external things you are grateful you have? What are three qualities you have that you are grateful for? What are three life lessons you are grateful for?.

C. Pray to your higher power (which includes listening to them).

D. Meditate however you know how.

We recommend Transcendental Meditation (visit TM.org) because it's scientifically validated by over 600 studies and is the simplest, most natural, and effortless technique we know of. It allows the mind to go beyond thinking to the source of thinking rather than managing or being mindful of thoughts and feelings which keeps the mind more on the surface. Going beyond thinking allows the mind to be in its happiest natural state of being settled and alert, which activates more of the whole brain. This is the go-to mental relaxation and brain development technique practiced by many of the top leaders in the world, including Oprah, Ray Dalio, and Arianna Huffington.

5. Then for a few minutes do the following self-awareness visualization exercise:

A. Visualize, see, the highest most enlightened version of who you see yourself being and becoming.

B. See how you want people to see you, including how you want the most important people in your life to see you.

C. Then see how you want to see others, including how you want to see the most important person in your life...the best version of themselves.

D. With a smile, see yourself fully giving what you have to give to your world...simply for the joy of giving.

This will help raise your deserving power frequency, because it helps remove sub-conscious self-limiting doubts, fears and anxieties. Then your conscious thinking and actions are more supported because you're coming from a more deserving abundant state. When you more clearly see something inside yourself you're more likely to create it outside yourself. It's as if it's already happened and been accomplished at least on the level of your awareness first. Then the process of going through the necessary external steps is more of a formality because you've accepted, expected and claimed it as your reality first. Remember, doubting destroys everything, especially you.

Most of all, enjoy this process of working on yourself, because it's the quality of your subconscious frequency that has the biggest influence on your deserving power, and on protecting yourself and what you achieve, when working on your business.

This is because our subconscious mind and energy is thousands of times more powerful than our conscious mind and energy. Whatever we're experiencing outside our self reflects how we've been existing inside our self. The subconscious has a huge impact on how much deserving power you have going for you. When you have strong power of deserving you're not affected by problems and more able to protect yourself, your team and your achievements and become an enlightened leader.

PART 4

SETTING PROTECTION TO PROTECT YOU, YOUR TEAM and ACHIEVEMENT

9 Protection Setting

That Which You Protect, You Keep

When we think about goal-setting, we might think of the self-help greats such as Dale Carnegie and Stephen Covey, but the real father of self-help, setting goals, and building habits was actually Benjamin Franklin. Did you know that Mr. Franklin was the inspiration for self-help bestsellers such as *How to Win Friends and Influence People* and *The Seven Habits of Highly Successful People*?

In 2017, Tim Ferris, bestselling author of *The 4-Hour Work Week*, gave a TED Talk where he encouraged leaders to fear-set instead of goal-set. Mr. Ferris took the stance that defining your fears, instead of your goals, was much more effective. The approach for fear-setting is to develop mental toughness, and decrease the fear of loss through a simple activity of defining what your fears are, understanding what the worst case scenario could be if that fear actualized and asking yourself if you'll still be okay if that happened. While this approach of stoicism is a step ahead of goal-setting, we believe today's leaders have the capacity and awareness to go even one step further ahead, which is what we call protection setting.

Protection setting goes beyond relying on goals, habits, and positivity as a means for growth; it deals with unfolding more of your innate capacity as a means for growth. By defining why protection is important to you, what protection looks like in action for you, and how it will change your leadership state, just as Mr. Ferris does with fear-setting, you can begin to simplify your role as a leader as well as magnify your capacity. This innately helps you be more protected from the pressures of your on-demand high performance responsibility. For example, doing things to protect your health you're more likely to keep yourself in good health to perform at high levels,

This is something I, Raamon, failed to do as an athlete namely because I didn't have the know how or the right mindset or protection-set.

At the end of every day, it is about whether you can protect yourself and what you achieve as you achieve—and not burn yourself out in the process. If we don't protect our health we don't get to keep it. This is why you get up every day and do what you do. This is why you push and take risks. This is why you pour everything you have into your role.

For Example, Protecting Setting Around Your Capacity

One of the biggest lessons we've learned from our own and others experience in business is whether we and others are doing things according the capacity they have. This is especially important when it comes to giving, receiving, borrowing, lending, investing and being invested in. How we utilize money is a great real life barometer of our capacity. What we found is that even though a company can have a great product, great strategy and great people the business still may not work out because of the lack of capacity of the leaders to utilize resources, learn and adapt according to the capacity of where the company is. On average most successful startups pivot 3-4 times before they find a winning business model, this is because the leaders of those startups have the capacity and humility to do so.

The Danger of Confident Leaders with Strong Egos and Will Power

Confident leaders with strong egos and will power, who really believe and back themselves can have a blind spot of overestimating their capacity to handle a situation and properly utilize resources given to them. Their capacity is not great enough to meet the demands of the situation so whatever money is given ends up being lost.

Often a tell-tale sign someone is stretching outside their capacity is signs of desperation we're they're pleading they just need this amount to get through this and everything will be okay. The reality is that when someone is in this state their capacity is stretched, they're under pressure and stress to make it all work to not let people down, especially themselves and their own hopes and dreams. This then weakens their mindset and can also weaken their mental, emotional and physical health. This is not the state and time to be giving, receiving, lending, borrowing or investing money because the mindset, capacity and structure is not right and aligned with reality. As a result, the strategy and product will not work effectively either. This requires a lot of honesty, truth and reality checking because confident leaders with strong egos and will power can override this to the detriment of themselves and others they get involved with their project. Meaning they've created an obligation they may not be able to fulfill which then blocks and slows their and others future progress until they're they able to correct it.

It's much better to help and protect people in this situation by first helping them stop the bleeding immediately, retract expansion or even maintenance, scale back according to current capacity and the basics. Then it's about re-grouping and resetting the mindset and strategy according to what the leaders can handle and building from there. More and more investors looking at IPOs or high flying companies are looking at the capacity of the existing leader and how they have been handling things.

> **"Your leadership capacity determines your invincible tenacity"**
>
> —*Raamon Newman, co-founder/CEO of New Mavericks*

The Side Effects of Failing to Protection Set Around Capacity

Sometimes you can have the capacity and tenacity to make things better and sometimes, if you haven't continued to develop your capacity, things can fall back again, as Marvin Ellison experienced in his tenure as CEO of J.C. Penney. Marvin Ellison stepped in as CEO of J.C. Penney to revive the struggling retailer. In 2016, the company had a positive net income for the first time since 2010 with $514 million more in total earnings than in 2015.

In an effort to boost sales he reinvested in hair salons, more affordable brands and brought back some of the old department store charm. Unfortunately, this wasn't enough and Ellison left the company in 2018 after a $69 million loss in the first quarter of 2018.

This illustrates that even if you have the capacity to be a great leader you can still fall because you don't have protection which comes from developing all six steps of the Science of Protection. Ellison had the capacity to be selected to step in as the new leader and create some good initial improvements but unfortunately wasn't able to sustain and build on this because he wasn't developing more of his inner capacity to have heightened awareness to see, feel and know what was the next thing that would enable J.C. Penny's progress to be protected and stay out of the red. He didn't invest in enhancing the most important asset, the capacity of his and his team's human capital. Relying on one's current level of awareness, energy and capacity to create the next level of growth will only create stress and blocks for yourself and others. It's like trying to make a car go faster with the same level of horse power, it creates a strain on the capacity of the current system and leads to eventual breakdown if you keep forcing it, instead of a breakthrough.

In tennis, a player must have the proper stance, body language, foot placement, and so on, to be successful on the court. So the coach would say, "Fix your feet, and bend your knees, and don't even think about hitting a ball until you have a strong platform." The player might toss the ball in the air above their head 50 or 100 times before they ever actually attempt a serve. They do this because the coach knows that unless the player has a strong platform first, the player will make mistakes. Protection setting is the same. We set ourselves up to succeed or to fail, depending on how strong and expanded our capacity platform is.

The Protection Setting Steps

Hence why we're advocating you protect set around yourself and your goals. Here are three simple steps to go about this:

1. **Start with having a coherent settled alert mind** when you set a goal, so you're not deluded by your own ego and will power, and ask is it according to your current capacity, reality and resources. If not, how can you first either gain more capacity or adjust it according to your current reality and obligations.

2. **Then imagine, create and protect the outcome in your mind** by clearly seeing and deeply feeling, knowing and believing the outcome based on what you'll be experiencing beyond fulfilling the outcome. For example, if you want to win an Oscar imagine yourself presenting an Oscar to someone else which implies you've already won one because generally only Oscar winners can give Oscars to Oscar winners. Do this for 10-15 minutes before your start your day and do without attachment or expectation of the outcome or the process, knowing the process will be derived and unfold from you protecting the outcome in your mind.

   There can be a fear factor caused by growth that creates resistance. To overcome this, you have to be solid and clear on your vision personally, which you can discuss with others also. The vision is how things are going to unfold the next 5-10-20 years, being really clear imagining it. Imagining it is the start of making it happen.

Not imagining it, you'll be bound by the past. Vision comes from imagining it, saying it and writing it. Writing can be by drawing pictures and diagrams as your sub-conscious works in images. It doesn't have to be neat; scribbly is better as it's more natural and organic. Without a proper vision it can't be elaborated and manifested.

It's having the vision and then believing in it. Not believing in a vision is because we're still fighting against the invisible resistances of the past. Whatever achievements and protection we have, reflects what we believe and what we deserve. Upgrading your believing is what helps you overcome past and present resistances.

You defy old patterns most powerfully through vision and believing from silence. It's integrating the vision and believing, both together, through seeing it on the thinking level and believing on the feeling level from the level of silence. Silence is the basis of asking, believing and achieving because this is where all the energy, organizing power and intelligence comes from. Silence is the light that removes the darkness, which is the resistance.

It's important to do this regularly to protect the goal you have in your mind because the process and the stress of going through the process can cause incoherence to come into your mind and corrupt and corrode the goal. The last thing you want is the process and journey to become the goal; otherwise you'll forever be on the journey and never arrive at the goal because it wasn't protected well enough inside you, so you get lost on the never-ending journey to it. Also, by cultivating the six steps of the Science of Protection you'll find you and your goals are more naturally protected also.

3. **Know that everything is created, maintained and dissolved and adjust accordingly.** This means things are always evolving and unfolding so we should not be attached to any concept or idea as it will change. So, when in a creating phase also get ready to maintain it. When in a maintaining phase be alert to when to dissolve. When in a dissolving phase be alert to how to next move into the creating phase again, and so on and so forth you go evolving through these phases.

10 The Science of Protection Summarized

The Wholeness That Integrates All the Parts Together

"Leaders lead by virtue of who they are."
—Kevin Cashman, bestselling author, Leadership From The Inside Out, and CEO development expert

If you've stuck with us to this point in the book, then you deserve a pat on the back. The amount of ground we've covered in the preceding chapters and pages is vast, with some new deep concepts and terminology. But the hard work you've put in so far is a necessary step on your path to reaching a higher level of leadership. Your ability to protect yourself, your team and your achievements and become more of an enlightened leader has been strengthened through this knowledge of the science of protection. As we close out our final chapter, we would like to summarize the material we've presented so that you may revisit this final chapter at any time for a refresher when you are feeling out of alignment or unsure of your next steps.

THE UNIVERSAL FORCE OF PROTECTION

Protection is a law of nature, existing within you, others, and the Universe as you know it. Protection is our term for that intelligence that coherently creates, preserves or dissolves based on what is best for the whole to continue to thrive and evolve. It's like a universal immune system that protects your whole life and development as a person and a leader. Protection allows you to stay at the top of the mountain of progress, regardless of conditions, shifts in the economy, potential stressors, and avalanches of change.

THE SCIENCE OF PROTECTION

The Science of Protection is a leadership formula for having the silence, consciousness and awareness to coherently conceive, believe, and achieve so you protect yourself, your team and your achievements and become an enlightened leader. This protection is a by-product of development of consciousness and coherence, and is fundamental to the Science of Achievement we so often hear about in the self-help world. The Science of Protection enables one to achieve as much as they want, for as long as they want, with minimal chance of achievement, progress, wealth, health, happiness, relationships, and reputations being corrupted, diminished, or lost.

LEADERSHIP REALITY

As is true with the literal definition of existence, leadership is "to stand out." Your ability to lead and to stand out is inherent in your natural abilities and in your existence. Leadership is not a person, habits, or a set of qualities.

A leader cannot progress unless they first protect their people so they can flourish and achieve without their mind, heart and body being diminished or corrupted. A leader's fundamental role is to protect and develop people so they can achieve and progress in the most evolutionary way.

REFRAMING FAILURE

It has almost become cliché that to succeed you have to fail forward fast, but we think people lose sight of their focus here. Your focus shouldn't be on the failing. Your focus should be on what that failure is trying to show you. That failure is trying to show you where you are so you can focus on becoming even more coherent on the inside, allowing you to achieve better on the outside.

Failure has a cause and the source of that cause can only be within ourselves first because everything is first created on the level of thinking, and then becomes manifested through our actions.

The Science of Protection starts with connecting to the source of protection, that invincible field of consciousness, awareness and fulfillment deep within. This stimulates internal protection development through purifying what needs to be purified and turning that into progress. This unfolds more coherent thinking that enables you to be in the leadership state, a state that averts danger and enhances progress. Then it's about taking this internal protection development and integrating it externally. The Leadership State supports you in having more capacity to handle any situation and take more spontaneous right action which gives you more deserving power to achieve what you want, as much as you want, for as long as you want.

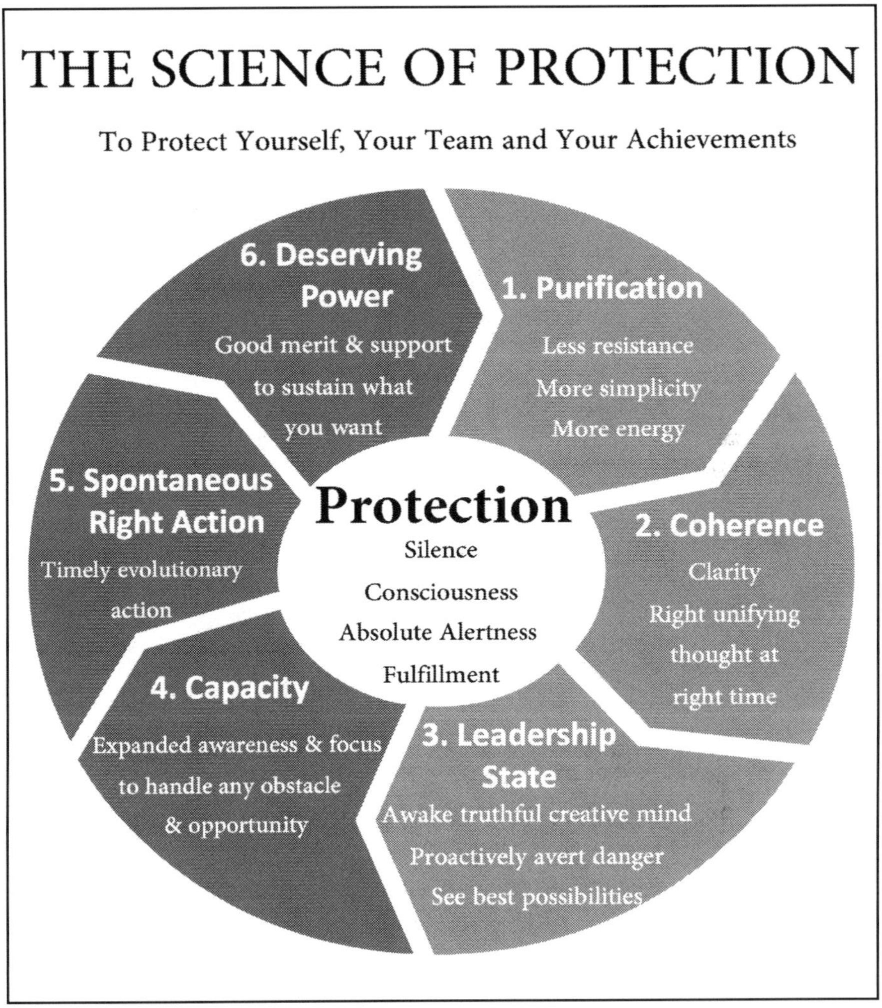

PURIFICATION

Purification is the process of removing unwanted impurities, incoherencies, and disruptions from a system. By purifying hidden fear, stresses, negativity, past bad impressions, and inner enemies (vices like greed, anger, lust, jealousy, vanity, and false attachments), progress can unfold in a more supported and protected way with less resistance, more simplicity and energy.

Purification is first and foremost to start on the road to more assured and protected achievement and progress. Purification is the process of removing, dissolving or resolving anything negative that could be blocking, corrupting, diminishing, or damaging you, your team and the environment living its full potential.

If something is not moving you forward and making you a better leader then purification is required so progress can unfold in a more evolutionary and coherent way.

When you reduce or eliminate impurities, you enjoy less stress, less friction, and fewer negative impressions. These changes make more room for increased vigilance. A more vigilant leader predicts better, therefore increasing their chances of getting what they want, protecting it, and keeping it.

MASTERING THE FEAR OF LOSS

In business, the fear of loss is that feeling of gnawing anxiety, an over-the-top form of clinginess and possessiveness, as opposed to a healthy desire to protect what you have, that if you do not stay in constant motion, you will lose. This same fear tells you that you have to hold onto everything you achieve, and causes unnecessary stress around change and growth. The fear of loss is an overwhelming lump in your throat, holding you back and then pushing you forward at the wrong times, based on the wrong reasons.

Mastering the fear of loss starts with purifying the stress, negativity and vices than cause it in the first place. This is done through knowledge, coaching and understanding, and techniques that get one back to a restfully alert peaceful state where you see and know what is unfolding.

RELEARNING PATIENCE

To be in tune with change requires patience. Sometimes you have to briefly pause and allow the best solutions to appear. If you haven't mastered the fear of loss, this will be seemingly impossible, because the fear will encourage action over patience. Patience through pausing allows you to be separate of the gripping fear of a fast-paced life.

DISSOLVING BAD IMPRESSIONS, STRESSES, and VICES

Stress is the unseen enemy in your life. Another word for stress is incoherence. When internal and or external incoherence becomes stronger than our ability to handle it we become stressed. When left unchecked, this can lead to incoherent thoughts, feelings, behaviors, actions, crime, or even violent crime. We often view stress as situational; however stress doesn't live in a little box. It touches every area of your life as you move through life with it in your mind and body.

INNER ENEMIES

Lust, anger, greed, delusion, intoxication, vanity, jealousy, false attachment and procrastination are all inner enemies that prevent you from performing at the top of your leadership game. Past experiences, failures, fears, and your ego are in the driver's seat when it comes to inner enemies, and while it is interesting to know where these inner enemies come from, the source isn't really the topic of importance here. The result of these inner enemies, once they've taken root, is what really needs to be addressed.

Protecting yourself from these inner enemies requires purification on all levels of your ego, intellect, mind, heart and body.

COHERENCE

THE CEO OF YOU

The prefrontal cortex is the CEO of you, that part of your brain that makes and executes all of your decisions, goals, motivations, and beliefs about yourself and the world around you. Your prefrontal cortex, and its integration and coherence with the whole brain, is vitally important if you want to make what we call Evolutionary Decision Making.

Coherence brings about protection. Another word for coherence is orderliness, which is what the brain really (really) wants, so it can build up its functionality to become a powerful ally. The definition of coherence is the quality of forming a unified whole. In nature, we see that coherence is how ecology protects itself to survive. In our brain, it's the integrated coherence between all parts of our brain, Global Alpha Coherence, especially through activating coherence of the pre-frontal cortex allows us to have the clarity to have the right unifying thought at the right time. This allows us to correctly interpret the impulses from the flight-flight-freeze functioning amygdala so it performs its highest function of vigilance to avert the dangers and see the opportunities before they arise.

MIND-BRAIN DEVELOPMENT

Coherence supports greater neuroplasticity and higher mind-brain development which is the ability of the mind and brain to make fundamental shifts to new realities, as well as the way we look upon ourselves, others, and the world. The high-performance researchers mentioned in this book, Dr. Fred Travis, Harald Harung and Alarik Arenander, have found this to be far more important than the accumulation of what we do, or the knowledge, skills, and relationships we have for improving and sustaining higher performance.

THE LEADERSHIP STATE

The leadership state, the ultimate zone of clarity and right-thought / right-action coherence, is the future of business. This is your opportunity to align with change by having a fully awake, truthful and creative mindset that is fine-tuned to proactively predict and avert danger and see the best possibilities to enhance progress. This will be the new definition of success for the future of business. The only other alternative is to fall victim to the increasing accelerated growth that is headed your way, which is the fate awaiting leaders who fail to develop themselves.

REACHING INVINCIBILITY

Invincibility does not exist outside in the field of change, where everything is always in flux. It does exist inside the field of non-change. Invincibility is a state of being, not doing, in which you are at your most coherent fluid and agile level of functioning to be in tune with change, not a victim of it. The effectiveness of your action reflects this. To achieve invincibility is to go within to be aligned with the field of invincibility on the level of consciousness itself. This is the ultimate leadership state where you're fully 360 degrees awake to being truthful and creative to avert danger and enhance progress. The by -product of this is you gain maximum external alignment with change and changes required.

MORAL DECISION MAKING

Coherence gives way to a more ethical and broader thought processes in which you inherently know what is right and most truthful for yourself, others and the environment. This leads to higher levels of morally sound reasoning and decision making, protecting you from negative influences.

Our high-performance researchers found top level managers do have higher levels of moral reasoning than lower performing managers, and this correlates with their higher levels of brain integration. This is a great finding because we can increase the moral decision making of all leaders through developing higher levels of brain integration. This can help reverse that 80% of Americans do not trust corporate executives and 50% of all managers do not trust their executives.

CAPACITY

This is the degree to which you have developed, expanded, and are utilizing your full intelligence, awareness, and focus- to naturally handle any situation, obstacle and opportunity.

EXPANDED FOCUSED AWARENESS

A spoonful of salt in a glass makes it barely drinkable. The same amount in a lake would go unnoticed. The point to this analogy is that you are not the salt, you are the container, and the more you expand your capacity, the less you taste the salt, which is the problems, pains, stresses, pressures and resistances you deal with as a leader. When you have the capacity of the lake, the problem/pain/salt doesn't have the same negative influence or effect on you. Your leadership state, expanded focused awareness to handle any situation, creates alignment with protection, is nothing other than being settled in a state which allows you to have more capacity. Another way to think about capacity is to understand that when your capacity is small and confined, you experience the problem. When your capacity is expanded, the problem becomes small. The key to life and business is having the capacity to give and serve with a settled mind. It isn't achievement, it isn't experience, and it isn't any of the things you are acquiring outside of yourself.

Those should always be step two, the second part of the growth process, not the first. This is why we see so many leaders lose so much. It isn't about luck or being "good" ... it's about having enough expanded capacity to be settled, coherent, and protected.

TIMING

The timing of our lives works hand-in-hand with our capacity. You can only do, be, give, and have based on the capacity you have. The reason so many leaders get their timing wrong is because they are closed off to the idea of alignment over control.

SPONTANEOUS RIGHT ACTION

To achieve victory before war, timely or spontaneous evolutionary right action in tune with the need of the time is required. If your actions are compromised because they don't match your belief system or what your environment requires your achievement and fulfillment will not be protected. This is not to demotivate you, rather to help you re-align to be in tune with the right action required.

VICTORY BEFORE WAR

In war, you have to make sacrifices to win. In war, you have to make compromises to win. If you want victory before war, evolutionary action is required. If your actions are compromised and don't match your belief system, your achievements will not be sustainable. An undeveloped leader cannot continuously take evolutionary action. You must be established in your leadership state first. This is your baseline, your foundation, your path to victory before war. Without inner development, you cannot sustain the alignment necessary for this higher level of true leadership. To gain the ultimate competitive advantage in war, you must establish yourself enough to avoid battle altogether. Conquering your mind is the only real battle you're fighting and with the right knowledge and methods you can always win this battle because you have direct control over it. It's challenging yourself not challenging others or others challenging you that makes you grow.

LEAST RESISTANCE LEADERSHIP

There are two types of Least Resistance Leadership:

1. *Taking* the path of least resistance.
2. *Creating* the path of least resistance.

» Type #1 is the action or inaction taken that skirts around issues and conflicts rather than proactively resolving them.
» Type #2 is the only Least Resistance Leadership option that has protection as a foundation.

A leader resisting change will fall eventually. A leader can create the path of least resistance by:

» Dissolving bad impressions and stresses.
» Minimizing the impact of potential failures.
» Increasing leadership capacity.
» Taking evolutionary action.
» Stabilizing and protecting their high-performance leadership state.

THE ZERO FACTOR

The time gap between having a great winning thought and taking the right action on it is near zero; effortless, spontaneous right-action.

The Zero Factor allows for more flawless execution of high-performance thoughts. The reality you see now is a vast unfolding of all of your past thoughts, feelings, conversations, goals, and beliefs. These are the seeds you plant, day in and day out, before your eyes now. They've taken root in your life, and have become very real and tangible. This is why right thought/right action protects you.

DESERVING POWER

The power of deserving, having good merit and support to get, protect and sustain what you want, is the final prerequisite to having protection to create stellar success that lasts. It means one has earned the right to deserve to achieve and you and that achievement are protected in the process. You have the power of deserving when you've done the work in developing and giving of yourself so you have a threshold of good positive energy and merit that makes breakthrough results inevitable because you're well supported by the market and people in your environment.

FREQUENCY RESONANCE

We know that when two frequencies are brought together, the lower will always rise up to meet the higher. This is something we call resonance, and also applies to biological systems. The reason we are pointing this out is simple: your frequency determines your leadership ability, and your leadership ability determines your success. That means your success, the part you can see, is only a manifestation of your frequency, the part you can't see.

PROTECTION SETTING

We advocate the process of protection setting as the basis for goal and fear setting. On the journey and process of life goals can get overshadowed and fears can overwhelm us so when we protection set around them we're more likely to avert that happening and achieve goals and overcome fears more easily and quickly. Use our three-step protection setting process to do this.

SCIENCE OF PROTECTION BASED ACHIEVEMENT

Your achievement and success in life, and degree to which you and it is protected, is the absolute manifestation of your frequency, which we can also say is your belief frequency. We get according to our frequency of believing and deserving. This is the result of your internal protection development of purification coherence and leadership state and external protection integration via your capacity, spontaneous right action and deserving power.

Success fluctuates as your frequency fluctuates, based on what seems to be a million moving pieces or elements. Without protection, those fluctuations will break down the empire you've built up, sometimes in a decade, a year, or even in a day or moment of weakness.

When it comes to creating truly protected success on all fronts, top leaders and high performers should and will always require top advisors/coaches/mentors to help them work on themselves so they have more coherence and capacity to:

- » Better work on and in their business and performance.
- » Maintain integrity, with integrity being one's ability to remain in tune with the whole of business and life. There's no good being good in one area of life while falling down in the others areas; that amounts to a zero-sum game.
- » Have the self-awareness to remain humble, because as Bill Gates said, *"Success is a lousy teacher. It seduces smart people into thinking they can't lose."* Plus, anyone who thinks they're bigger than the game of life itself is bound to fall, as many leaders in history have discovered.

Working on yourself is the profound factor in what drives and affects your business and performance, because without you being in your most optimal leadership state, your business and performance can't evolve to the next stage. Everyone—but especially those in upper leadership positions who are required to perform at a high level—require advisors, coaches, and mentors to do this. Google or Facebook "why everyone needs a coach" and you'll find three minutes of a TED Talk given by Atul Gawande, a top surgeon who believed he didn't need a coach until he experienced what having a fellow surgeon observe and coach him did for improving his performance. His book *Being Mortal* is also a must read.

The statistics show that every month you spend without some sort of advisor/coach, you lose 3 months of momentum. So, by spending 4 months with an advisor or coach, you'll gain more momentum than a year spent on your own! Plus, things compound from there. This is what we've experienced working with leaders and high performers around the world who were looking to ensure they got, protected, and kept what they wanted. You, too, can experience this with the right knowledge and approaches.

Warren Buffet summed it up beautifully in his quote below about investing in yourself (which is, really, going out of your way to find that knowledgeable advisor or coach who has the wisdom you require to develop yourself and protect your progress):

> **"Investing in yourself is the most important investment you'll make in your life. There's no financial investment that'll ever match it because if you develop more skill, more ability, more insight, more capacity, that's what's going to really prove economic freedom. It's those skills that really make that happen."**
>
> —*Warren Buffet*

So, there you have it, the sum total of all we know that helps you as a leader create an invisible invincible shield of protection around yourself and your team's achievement and progress. Protection is the hinge and leverage that allows you to actually be more vulnerable, open and supported to take on bigger responsibility, risks and higher purpose because the Science of Protection has literally got your back, your health, wealth, happiness, relationships and reputation from being corrupted, diminished or lost. And even if you have or do fall this science will help you bounce back like nothing negative even happened because negativity is incoherent and weak compared to coherence. So, in case you missed it, here's:

ONE LAST POINT TO CONSIDER

If there is one key piece of information we hope you will take from this book, it is simply that you are not the sum of your experiences. You are the result of your development, and the most important natural law you can align with, to further that development and continue evolving your leadership, is protection. Your state of consciousness is who you are, and the only clear path to getting what you want, protecting it, and keeping it.

This simple yet profound truth has a deep and lasting effect because knowledge is fundamentally structured and sourced from your and others consciousness. Therefore, we want our and everyone's consciousness to be the most developed it can be. As we become even more awake on the level of consciousness, our intellect wakes up as well. You've sub-consciously known this for your entire existence. We're just helping clarify this understanding so you fully consciously own it. A client affirmed this when he said "you're waking up the sub-conscious of the organization".

However, perhaps for the first time in your life, you are awakening to these truths, which is the step through the doorway of unleashing unending potential. Forge your new path wisely, with protection at the helm, and you will cement your place in history as a leader of leaders, a superhero among mortals, and a new maverick of the future.

We will leave you with the following, written by American author Wallace D. Wattles in the year 1910, more than a century ago:

> **"Everything you see on Earth is made from one original substance, out of which all things proceed… there is a thinking stuff from which all things are made, and which, in its original state, permeates, penetrates, and fills the interspace of the Universe… a thought, in this substance, produces the thing that is imagined by thought… man can form things in his thought, and, by impressing his thought upon formless substance, can cause the thing he thinks about to be created."**
>
> *—excerpt from The Science of Getting Rich,*
> *circa 1910, by Wallace D. Wattles*

Those who care for and protect natural law, natural law cares for and protects them.

Appendix 1

From: Mark Waller, Former Chairman and CEO, EBOS Healthcare

Hi, until now, I've kept this close to my chest as it has been so game changing for me and other leaders at EBOS that I wanted to validate its consistent efficacy over time. Now at the age of 64 my focus is more about significance than achievement, so I am writing today to help you answer one simple question:

How can I accomplish more as a CEO in less time, with less stress and more support?

What I am about to share has helped me to achieve more between 2010 and 2017 than in the previous 25 years.

Here's the question nobody is asking: According to a Hay Group Study, we have a 50-70% influence on the climate and culture of our company, which explains as much as a 28% variance in the bottom line. Yet what influences us as leaders so we can better influence those in our company?

That's what Raamon Newman and Paolo D'Angelo asked me back in 2010, after I was sent to them by my doctor to help deal with the high blood pressure I was suffering with at the time. Since then, I can hand-on-heart tell you these two non-executive advisors have made a huge impact on both myself and our company, including:

1. Playing a bigger game: For example, at one stage I had a deal fall through and felt like I should throw in the towel. They helped me "reset" and complete another deal 2 ½ times the size within 6 months.

2. Building a more cohesive team: Gone is the suspicion and manipulation you'll find in many organizations, and so has the need to look over my shoulder to check on my team. It was replaced by more trust and less friction, which allowed us to achieve our objectives faster, and with less stress.

3. Focusing on the right things: As CEOs, it's so easy to get caught up in "task-oriented" issues. They've helped me see this is actually lazy and focus on the things that generate far greater results.

Essentially, Raamon and Paolo from New Mavericks have made my thinking sharper, and helped me see more and make better decisions—unlike any coach or consultant I've ever worked with.

They have a fresh new approach and the results speak for themselves, even in a very competitive and tight-margin industry.

Warmly,

Mark Waller
Former Chairman and CEO, EBOS Group

Accomplishing 484% Growth in Less Time and More Calm

As a veteran CEO with a long track record of 25 years in the listed company environment, I've always been curious how a self- motivated person reinvigorates "thinking". Clear ideas along with the inner confidence to carry them out drive success. Sustaining and feeding this inner drive has been assisted by the clarity that personal "quiet time" provides. This, along with the sessions with Paolo and Raamon has heightened my awareness and understanding of the great practical value of this for others and myself.

This has raised new ideas, new ways of looking at things and understanding people (including myself). It provides the "glue" for a common and valuable shared experience. The calls give an opportunity to step outside the normal work routine and provide a platform to look at issues in a fresh and positive way, making the calls a very useful tool to "work on yourself" so you can better "work on the business" rather than "in" the business.

Their approach, supported by scientifically validated technologies for developing human potential, we hope will continue to assist us as we grow. Their cutting-edge approach has been around for millenniums yet it has been deeply misunderstood in terms of its highly practical value in today's fast-paced modern world. There is nothing new under the sun; we have just simply forgotten some of the most valuable timeless principles and practices that truly serve us in developing our human potential or at very least our own good health, balance, and well-being. Paolo and Raamon provide great clarity around the topic of "real knowledge" and minimize the clutter in our daily lives that dull thinking. Whether you are generation X, Y or Z just one call with these gentlemen will open up a new field of all possibilities, insights, and support for becoming the best person and leader you can be.

Organizing the biggest deal in our corporate history involved long hours, tight time frames and multiple go/no-go hurdles etc...and multiple possibilities for stress. Despite this, I personally feel like I am the eye of the storm...all is calm and relaxed! Interestingly, since our session yesterday, a few issues seem to be falling into place.

If you're leading a small, medium or large business in this age of exponential change, and want to be in tune with change rather than a victim of it, you've got to have at least one call with Paolo and Raamon to truly know the deeper value they bring in enhancing and protecting leader's achievement and progress.

Their wisdom, insights, support, and value has made a profound difference in enhancing my experience as a leader and is something I haven't found anywhere else.

—Mark Waller, Former Chairman and CEO, EBOS Group,
New Zealand, CEO of the Year 2010 and
New Zealand Business Hall of Fame 2019

Appendix 2

*From: Kelvin Hyland, Former GM, EBOS Healthcare,
Now Managing Director, OSSIS*

Hi, I want to share one of the biggest mistakes I've made over the years…

Playing referee almost crippled my team

Like most leaders, I used to struggle with the locking of horns and banging of heads. Thankfully, 10 years ago, I stumbled onto some new insights and…

- Staff turnover dropped from 22% to less than 5%
- Staff engagement jumped 55%
- Turnover accelerated and I became the leader of the best performing health care business within the EBOS group.

In the earlier stages of my career as a leader, the lack of cohesion, different personality types and fallouts meant… we wasted years trying to gain momentum and traction.

It was frustrating. I wanted to be setting the vision and taking people on a journey, not "blowing the whistle" and putting out fires. But I was at a loss…

- I used to lie in bed at night worrying.
- I used to get stopped by roadblocks I couldn't see past.
- I used to be stressed all the time.

Now I don't. It seems counterintuitive, but the less I've struggled the more successful my team has become. And I owe much of this to a couple of guys, Raamon Newman and Paolo D'Angelo, from New Mavericks. I've worked with dozens of coaches. Most of them only work on a surface level and never get to the fundamentals, leaving people to revert back to their original conditioning.

These guys go to a much deeper place, and the results speak for themselves. Having worked with them for over 8 years, they have my highest endorsement.

Warmly,

Kelvin Hyland
Managing Director, Ossis

Heighted Awareness for Lasting Change and Development

The calls I have with Paolo and Raamon are highly insightful, providing the link between self-development and the practical application to business, which I have not found elsewhere. I find the time spent invaluable for stopping to reflect deeply and meaningfully, helping challenge long held views and conventional practices and see things for what they really are, which is necessary in our fast paced and rapidly changing world.

This has resulted in greater clarity of thought and heightened awareness which I believe has made me more effective as a GM. Having regular calls provides me with timely practical supportive input, giving a more comprehensive perspective of matters which in turn enables me to act with more clarity and confidence, keeping me on track and ensuring that lasting change and development can be effected.

—Kelvin Hyland, GM of EBOS Healthcare

(Kelvin has now evolved to being a leader in three different privately held companies.)

Appendix 3

From: Stefan Crooks, Managing Director, Westie Food Group

Hi, I want to emphasize the fact...If a dog feels your fear, they're more likely to fear you.

Negotiation is no different. Yet even though there is perhaps no more important skill which has an impact on our bottom line… over the past 12 months, I've discovered I've been getting it all wrong for decades. I've got no doubt its cost me millions. Yet it's not from a lack of effort. Like you, I've focused on the words, the techniques, the way you dress, the strategies. And yet, it was like polishing my car—instead of fixing the engine.

But recently I've found an approach which has allowed me to get deals to go through faster, while wasting less time on things that don't matter.

For instance, I used to walk into a big client meeting with a 30-page presentation. Today I walk in with a single page. And since I've been doing this…

My close rate on major deals has jumped by 100%.
I refer to it as my "x-factor."

And it doesn't just apply to negotiating deals—it spreads across daily negotiations with my personal assistant, the store man, the end users and all the company's stakeholders.

Are you interested in getting the same unfair advantage? Then I urge you to reach out to Raamon and Paolo from New Mavericks to start a conversation.

Warmly,

Stefan Crooks,
Managing Director, Westie Food Group

Additional Resources

Affirmations

Affirmations are a powerful tool to help leaders reprogram their thought process or even change your mood or state of existence, depending on how powerful those affirmations are and how well you metabolize and believe them.

Affirmations work because they have the ability to program your mind into believing the concept you are stating. Your mind doesn't know the difference between what is stated and what is real, much like when you watch a movie, the emotions, mood, and state you are in are very real even though you're only observing it and not directly involved in it.

We put together the following powerful protection affirmations to strengthen your protection alignment, leadership state, coherence, and abundance. Ideally, you should set aside 5-10 minutes, after settling your mind, to read your chosen affirmation.

You can find the audio versions, a free gift, as part of your Leadership Protection Toolkit at ScienceOfProtection.org

Protection Affirmation

I am deeply happy and grateful that the best thoughts, feelings, and actions are revealed to me at the right time. These thoughts, feelings, and actions serve my, others, and the world's protected progress. I create this by allowing my mind, heart, and senses to experience the most settled, silent, alert and awake level of myself. Through this I'm aligned with the invincible protective field of coherence and orderliness that has always been there, is always there, and will always be there for me and everyone. Beyond the ever-changing levels of myself is the non-changing level of myself where protection exists. This invincible field of protection cannot be overcome or conquered by any internal or external stresses, vices, or incoherence. Through continually expanding capacity and coherence I gain even more vigilance and tenacity to protect and enhance myself, my team and what we achieve and become an enlightened leader who protects the world.

Leadership State Affirmation

Being in my leadership state gives me an awake truthful creative mind to proactively avert danger and see the best possibilities. I'm able to feel more, see more, know more what is best for everyone. This absolute alertness gives me unshakable authentic presence to clearly conceive and interpret, fully believe and trust, and precisely achieve and progress based on love, without fear or doubt. I love and respect myself and others, my and their abilities, what I and they want and do what is required to protect and uplift everyone. Through cultivating a more silent settled alert mind, a warm, content and fulfilled heart I evolve to being permanently established in my leadership state and become an enlightened leader.

Coherence Affirmation

I am a fully coherent leader inside and out. Being coherent I have the clarity to have the right unify life supporting thought and feeling at the right time. Through coherence my heart and mind are one, coordinated in supporting each other. Through coherence my higher moral brain and lower instinctive brain work together harmoniously to protect myself and others. Coherence enhances my ability to be both creative and rational. It creates a wholeness between me and my team, strategic partners, clients, vendors, the marketplace, my environment, and the world at large, that is greater than the sum of their parts. Developing and deepening the coherence between the who I am, my vision, goals and actions I fulfill my purpose. Coherence connects the bigger long-term picture with the short-term details required to fulfill that bigger picture. Cultivating more and more all-encompassing coherence brings even greater clarity, stability, focus and alignment to every area of my leadership and life.

Abundance Affirmation

I am infinitely abundant because I am created from abundance. My thoughts, feelings, speech, and actions, are the expression of abundance. An abundance of possibilities, opportunities, relationships, ideas, money, and love exists when I am awake to all the abundance in and around me. I wholeheartedly give, serve, and receive abundance with grace, gratitude, and reverence. Abundance flows through me, giving me abundant energy, clarity and creativity to fulfill life-supporting intentions. I am full, this is full, everything is full with abundance. I am infinite invincible abundance that has always been there, is always there, and will always be there for me and everyone.

Get In Touch

Ready to more fully align with the awesome Universal force that is protection to more quickly and easily protect yourself, your team and your achievements and become an enlightened leader who creates sustainable stellar success.

Meet us here: ScienceOfProtection.org

Get in touch via support@newmavericks.com with any questions, comments and feedback.

The breakfast, lunch, and dinner of champions is high quality feedback, so we'd love to hear from you.

Download your free Leadership Protection toolkit at ScienceOfProtection.org/toolkit which includes:

1. Protection Quotient (PQ) Worksheet
2. 7 Protection-Based Leadership Behaviors
3. Protection Affirmation Audios

For more information and research about world-class global alpha brain coherence, check out ***World Class Brain*** by Dr. Harald Harung and Dr. Fred Travis on Amazon.com.

Ready and keen to work with us?

Great!

We'd love to be of service to you with our two-decade time-and-field-tested proven winning formula that guarantees CEOs and investors protected progress for themselves and those they lead in any market.

Our joy is boosting and bulletproofing your and your team's leadership performance through our Leadership Breakthrough Protection program or Enlightened Leader Mastermind.

Feel free to reach out at support@newmavericks.com and tell us a bit about yourself, what you're working on and how we can help.

Acknowledgments

This book would not exist were it not for the collaborative effort and generosity of a handful of key individuals.

The scientific nature of this book and our ability to add coherence to these complex sciences is thanks to the following great neuroscientists:

When we set out to understand and simplify the processes of the brain, and the importance of understanding these processes for leaders in business, we relied heavily on knowledge from Dr. Alarik Arenander, PhD, Director of Iowa's Brain Research Institute and President of The Leader's Brain, who dedicated hours of overseas phone conversations, notes, and suggestions for this text. Alarik, you are a gem in the world of brain and life wisdom. The time spent hearing you expound the virtues and potentials of the brain and how to optimize it for success shall remain deeply imprinted on us for the rest of our lives.

Big thanks also go to Dr. Fred Travis, co-author *Excellence through Mind-Brain Development: The Secrets of World-Class Performers and World Class Brain*, who kindly offered great assistance and answered every one of our rigorous questions, something we are very grateful for. Fred, spending time interacting with you is priceless because the very fine nuances of understanding you have about the brain is so enlightening. We shall forever remember you as the one who coined Global Alpha Coherence. Be sure to get and read Fred's book, *Your Brain Is a River, Not a Rock*, about the incredible neuroplasticity of the brain, so you will develop an even greater appreciation of this most precious organ and be able to take care of it for the rest of your life.

Also, on matters of the brain, quantum theory, and mind-brain development, we relied heavily on Dr. Harald Harung, PhD, Associate Professor of Management and Performance at Oslo and Akershus University College of Applied Sciences, in Norway, and also co-author of *Excellence through Mind-Brain Development: The Secrets of World-Class Performers*. Harald, you're a true expert on the topic of brain cognition and how it relates to the world of business, performance, and leadership. We have a deep appreciation for you and your deep appreciation for the full potential of all humans. It is truly inspiring, thank you! We revere your contribution to invincible success through your own book, *Invincible Leadership: Building Peak Performance Organizations by Harnessing the Unlimited Power of Consciousness,* which we highly recommend every leader read and also your latest book with Fred, *World-Class Brain.*

Raamon would like to acknowledge and deeply thank his wife, Emily Rose Shaw, whose unconditional nourishment; love, cheerleading, and enthusiasm—not to mention her patience in waiting for me to get to the dinner table—have been an invaluable, comforting and supportive influence in completing this book.

Our current and past clients were paramount in helping us to understand why we needed to bring this text and knowledge to leaders everywhere, and we would not be where we are without them. Thank you so much for allowing us to contribute to your leadership journey and giving us the opportunity to field-test our knowledge and technologies. Special thank you to those clients who made time to be interviewed and contributed their experiences to this book. You're our co-co-authors too!

There were two key individuals who contributed their time, expertise, and energy to this book. We would like to extend a sincere and heartfelt thank you to Paul Haft and Nicholle Gulcur for various contributions made to the content and completion of this book. One of the greatest gifts we can offer others is our knowledge. Both Paul and Nicholle bring this philosophy to life, and we are incredibly grateful.

Big thank you to our editor Kent Sorsky at Linden Publishing whose brilliance and refined intellect not only honed and sharpened the flow of the book but went the extra mile to give us tremendous structural and connectivity input that took this book to the next level. Much thanks to Adam Barr at RTB Financial Group for recommending Kent.

A BIG warm thank you to our parents and families. Thank you for bringing us into this world, protecting and encouraging us the best you knew how and passing on your life experience and wisdom. Without you we would not have this opportunity to share this new leadership intelligence of protection with the world.

Sincere gratitude goes to all our teachers, coaches, trainers, and advisors who have paved the way by giving their valuable input into our lives, the leaders of leaders of human and leadership development like Tony Robbins, Zig Ziglar, Napoleon Hill, Dale Carnegie, Stephen Covey, Dr. Wayne Dyer, and John C. Maxwell. A special thank you goes to my running coach Arch Jelley (coach of Olympic gold medal winner and former mile world record holder, John Walker), whose wise, astute temperament has always been an example to me and for your invaluable guidance in pursuing my athletic potential. Another big thank you to Martin Jelley, Arch's son, and his wife Judy, for their guidance and wisdom, and for being my Transcendental Meditation teacher. Thanks also for introducing us to a number of our clients over the years.

Our deep appreciation and gratitude go to Maharishi Mahesh Yogi for creating the opportunity in this modern era to experience what it's like to be a full-time meditating monk, and for all the profound, timeless wisdom of peace, silence, consciousness, and coherence you gave the world through the scientifically validated benefits of transcending (TM.org) in today's fast paced world. A heartfelt thank you also goes to Dr. Raju, Krishna Raju, and Raju Family (DrRaju.com) for their profound understanding of Ayurveda and helping our clients maintain their innate perfect health.

Sincere special thanks to Dr. David Lovell-Smith, author of *Perfect Blood Pressure Naturally*, who kindly introduced us to our top longest-standing client.

To Carla Green at Clarity Designworks, this book would not look and feel the way it does without your meticulous attention to detail and formatting. Thank you very much for all your diligence and flexibility!

To all the leaders and thought leaders of the world, past and present, who toil away every day, endeavoring to lead things forward in a better way with the coherence and capacity they have, we take our hats off to you with deep respect, appreciation, and gratitude for stepping up and moving the needle in your industry and in your way. Your experiences have also helped shape our thinking and knowledge of how to create more assured and protected success for the leaders of today and the future.

Finally, to all of you who felt the inspiration and calling to pick up, purchase, and read this book, we thank you and appreciate your intentions to create a more protected progress in your life and in the lives of those you lead. Through you the Science of Protection can go on for generations to come!

As my late Granny, a role model of leadership and protection in her own right, being one of the first women allowed on a club rugby board in New Zealand, who passed away 3 months shy of her 100th birthday, would say…

May peace be with you! (Which includes protection)

—Raamon, Paolo & Sara

About the Authors

Raamon Newman is Co-founder and CEO of New Mavericks, a 25 year leadership development consultancy that develops CEOs' and executives' capacity and skill to make decisions that maximize all stakeholders' value. He's been a top three nationally ranked track athlete, 2-time National schools cross-country team winner, 4-time state championship winning rugby player, 10-year full-time meditating monk, Meisner trained actor and philanthropist. While engaged in acting training in NYC during the 2007-8 global financial crisis, he realized a calling, based on his life experience, to help protect leaders' achievement and progress. Raamon is a graduate from the University of Auckland, New Zealand, with a Bachelor's of Commerce in Marketing.

Paolo D'Angelo is Co-founder and Chief Development Officer of New Mavericks, a 25 year leadership development consultancy that develops CEOs' and executives' capacity and skill to make decisions that maximize all stakeholders' value. Paolo came from a background of not graduating high school to being a competitive bodybuilder and personal trainer owning his own gym, security company, and sport and entertainment ticket selling business. He's been a philanthropist for the last 25 years. At the age of 25 he realized that true fulfillment really started on the inside. Paolo devoted himself to 15 years meditating full-time (8 hours per day, 7 days per week, with six of those years 7,000 feet up in the Himalayas) for his own personal development, enlightenment, and contribution to world peace.

Sara Burke is an International High Level Content Creation Expert, Founder of Empire Coaching and Podcast Host. She's also a mother, loving partner, writer, and self-proclaimed truth seeker. Sara has dedicated herself to achieving expertise in the areas of behavioral analysis, psychology, and applied behavioral psychology, with degrees, certifications, and professional experience in those categories. Operating out of Columbus, Ohio, she has offered her professional expertise for almost a decade through her development firm, Empire Coaching. Dedicated to education, Sara homeschools her children and is a fierce advocate for meditation, personal growth, and children's rights within education. She has been writing development content and contributing to high-level development books for her clients over the past decade.

Two Decades of Experience

For the last two decades, Raamon and Paolo have been globally trusted leadership breakthrough protection partners to CEOs and executives of multi-million and billion-dollar companies.

They've worked with top CEOs and executives in New Zealand, Australia, US, and Europe, providing breakthrough leadership development and protection support to leaders of "forward thinking" companies such as EBOS Group, Oliver's Real Food's, Feedback ASAP, Hawthorne Direct, Retail Holdings Ltd, The O'Halloran Group, Novartis, Woodmart, Reef Shipping, Warner Group, Natel, Buttoned-Up, Westie Foods, Franklin Wiz Ltd, Investigroup, Advanced Braking Technologies, Arafura Resources Ltd., Karara Capital, Turner Manufacturing-Kleenrite, Sports Hero Ltd, Technical Investing Ltd, Novus Capital, as well as top property developers and realtors.

For more information, go to
NewMavericks.com / ScienceOfProtection.org

To you and your team living
The Science of Protection
24 / 7 / 365!

Thank you for reading and learning about
The Science of Protection.

To help inspire more leaders about
protection-based leadership,
please write a review about how the
science of protection inspired you at
goodreads.com and **amazon.com**

Thank you!

Made in the USA
Columbia, SC
01 December 2025

b0d15a04-746a-49a5-83a0-cc27feb20485R01